COCKTAILS
MADE EASY

COCKTAILS MADE EASY

WRITTEN BY
SIMON DIFFORD

FIREFLY BOOKS

INTRODUCTION

Over the past seven years, my annual publication, 'diffordsguide Cocktails', has developed to feature thousands of recipes using a great number of specialist and often obscure ingredients.

These titles are perfect for professional bartenders and keen amateurs, but we thought possibly a little overwhelming for those of you that just wanted to make delicious cocktails in your own home.

This book uses the 14 most frequently occurring 'Key Ingredients' in the 2,600 recipes featured in *Difford's Encyclopedia of Cocktails* and the 500 plus cocktails which can be made using them. I have omitted harder to make cocktails such as the Ramos Gin Fizz to ensure this book is indeed easy. So all you need are these 14 Key Ingredients, a shaker, some other everyday kitchen tools and some common items from the supermarket and you can make all 500 cocktails in this guide.

I'd be the first to admit that some of the recipes are better than others (most definitely including my own) and so I've graded cocktails on a scale of one to five and discreetly indicated this score by dots above each drink's name. The more dots, the more I like it.

Cocktail recipes are a very personal thing, and I would love to hear what you think of the recipes in this book. Is one of your own creations worth inclusion in future editions? Drop me a line at simon@diffordsguide.com

I also write email newsletters with drinks, bar reviews and new cocktail recipes from all around the world. If you'd like to receive these, please email me direct, or sign up at our website, www.diffordsguide.com.

Lastly, I'd like to thank all of my friends, in particular Dan Malpass, Hannah Sharman-Cox, John Coe, Bob Nolet, Rob Lawson, Andrew Fell, Sharon Reid and Mike Birch.

Cheers!
Simon Difford
simon@diffordsguide.com

A FIREFLY BOOK

Published by Firefly Books Ltd. 2016
Copyright © Sauce Guides Limited 2016
Text and image copyright © 2016 Simon Difford

First printing

Publisher Cataloging-in-Publication Data (U.S.)
Names: Difford, Simon, author.
Title: Cocktails made easy : 500 recipes, 14 key ingredients / Simon Difford.
Description: Richmond Hill, Ontario, Canada : Firefly Books, 2016. | Previous published 2010. |
   Summary: "This book is the perfect guide to making cocktails more easily and includes all
   the ingredients necessary to create them. Photographs of each drink, along with ingredient
   measurements, garnish, variations and information on the cocktail's origin are all included to
   help any home mixologist along" — Provided by publisher.
Identifiers: ISBN 978-1-77085-775-9 (paperback)
Subjects: LCSH: Cocktails.
Classification: LCC TX951.D544 |DDC 641.874 – dc23

Library and Archives Canada Cataloguing in Publication
Difford, Simon, author
   Cocktails made easy : 500 recipes, 14 key ingredients / Simon Difford.
Previously published: 2010.
ISBN 978-1-77085-775-9 (paperback)
   1. Cocktails. I. Title.
 TX951.D51 2016   641.87'4   C2016-903837-8

Published in the United States by
Firefly Books (U.S.) Inc.
P.O. Box 1338, Ellicott Station
Buffalo, New York 14205

Published in Canada by
Firefly Books Ltd.
50 Staples Avenue, Unit 1
Richmond Hill, Ontario L4B 0A7

Printed in China

diffordsguide° are

Publisher & Author Simon Difford
Design & Art Direction Dan Malpass
PR & Marketing Hannah Sharman-Cox
Cocktail Photography Rob Lawson

Originally published by Sauce Guides Limited
1 Futura House, 169 Grange Road, London, SE1 3BN, England.
diffordsguide.com

Please drink responsibly.

ALL YOU NEED

TO MAKE ALL THE COCKTAILS IN THIS GUIDE

THE 14 KEY INGREDIENTS
1. Ketel One vodka
2. Tanqueray London dry gin
3. Bacardi Superior rum
4. Don Julio tequila
5. Johnnie Walker Scotch whisky
6. Courvoisier V.S.O.P. Cognac
7. Bulleit Bourbon whiskey
8. Cointreau triple sec liqueur
9. Grand Marnier liqueur
10. Bols apricot brandy liqueur
11. Crème de Cassis or Chambord liqueur
12. Noilly Prat Blanc dry vermouth
13. Martini Rosso sweet vermouth
14. Brut Champagne

ICE
Buy copious amounts of ice bags from the supermarket. A standard domestic ice-cube tray will barely hold enough ice to make two cocktails. To make crushed ice, simply wrap your cubed ice in a tea-towel and bash with your muddler or rolling pin on a stout surface.

BASIC EQUIPMENT
Cocktail shaker (see page 32)
Tea strainer or fine strainer (see page 34)
Measure (alternatively a medicine measure or small shot glass)
Long handled spoon
Knife & cutting board
Citrus juicer
Muddler or Rolling pin
Tea towels
Electric blender

FRIDGE & PANTRY ESSENTIALS
You will need a few mixers, some fresh fruit and a handful of kitchen basics listed on page 29.

Ketel One is the creation of one of Holland's oldest distilling dynasties, the Nolet family of Schiedam, who have been making spirits since Johannes Nolet started his business in 1691.

Johannes Nolet opened his distillery near the mouth of the great river Mass on the North Sea, attracted to the area due to its accessibility to shipping and its close proximity to one of Holland's largest grain auctions. By 1882 the Nolet Distillery was one of 394 distilleries operating in Schiedam. Today there are only four. Ten generations after Johannes, Carolus Nolet now runs the company with the help of his two sons, Carl and Bob.

Like the families of great wineries, the Nolets have dedicated themselves to the traditional craft of distilling premium spirits. Also like many of the great names in wine, Ketel One is a descriptive name with its own heritage, not merely a contrived marketing device. The name heralds from the original 'Distilleerketel #1', the centuries-old alembic copper pot still that is still used to produce Ketel One Vodka at the Nolet Distillery today.

KETEL ONE VODKA

It is from this traditional copper pot still method of distillation that the living legacy of the Nolet family originates. Recipes found in Johannes Nolet's journals dating back to when he first established the business in 1691 are all based around small-batch pot still distillation. These journals have been passed down the generations through to the company's current chairman, who with the help of these secret family formulas continues to build upon the family's commitment to maintaining and strengthening the distillery's reputation for excellence.

The family's pride in their distilling traditions and reputation is obvious when they talk about their heritage and use of traditional methods today. They insist upon the best raw materials, always ensuring that the focus is on quality rather than quantity. These are used in small batch distillations requiring the painstaking attention of a master distiller to hand-stoke the fire, oversee the distillation process and regulate the temperature. The first 100 gallons (known as the head) of every distillation is discarded due to being too harsh. The last 100 gallons (the tail) are also discarded because they are too weak. Only the heart of the distillate has the purity, clarity and smoothness required to make Ketel One Vodka. Multiple distillations and charcoal filtration are used to produce a superbly smooth, ultra premium wheat grain vodka. As a final check, each batch of Ketel One must be tasted by a member of the Nolet family before it is approved for release and deemed worthy of the family name.

www.KetelOne.com

The Tanqueray family were originally silversmiths and left France for England early in the 18th century, where three successive Tanquerays became rectors in Bedfordshire. In 1830 Charles Tanqueray, then aged just twenty, broke with family tradition and rather than become a clergyman, established a distillery in London's Finsbury, then noted for its spa water.

Until 1947, Tanqueray was sold in many different shaped bottles. The design we recognise today was inspired by a 1920s range of Tanqueray pre-mixed cocktails that were sold in bottles designed to resemble a cocktail shaker - not a fire hydrant as some mistakenly believe. The name 'Special Dry' was introduced in 1950 and today is still applied to Tanqueray 47.3% abv. The same iconic bottle is used for the more recent Tanqueray Export Strength, which is made to the same recipe but with a lower 43.1% abv strength that is perfect for cocktail use.

TANQUERAY
LONDON DRY GIN

Both Special Dry and Export strength Tanqueray gins are distilled by the traditional one-shot process in a 200 year old copper pot still nicknamed 'Old Tom'. The recipe which has remained unchanged since 1830 has three dominant botanicals: Tuscan juniper, angelica and coriander, giving both these gins the same crisp, dry style with a rich juniper flavour.

Tanqueray No. Ten is an ultra premium gin based on the traditional Tanqueray botanical recipe but with unusual extras such as camomile and fresh grapefruit. It takes its name from the distillery's number 10 still, known as Tiny Ten. Dating back to the 30s, this small pot still was originally used as an experimental, or trial-run, still and is a scale replica of the Old Tom still.

Tiny Ten is used for the first distillation, which produces the citrus spirit known as the 'citrus heart' of No. Ten. Wheat grain neutral spirit is distilled with chopped Florida oranges, Mexican limes and grapefruits to produce this essence.

The second and final distillation takes place in the larger Old Tom still. This is charged with the citrus heart previously distilled in Tiny Ten and wheat grain neutral spirit. Traditional botanicals such as juniper, coriander, angelica and liquorice are added, along with camomile flowers and slices of fresh limes.

While the juniper, coriander, angelica and liquorice come from the same sources as those used in standard Tanqueray production, their proportions differ: in particular, substantially less juniper is used, so as not to dominate No. Ten's fresh citrus character.

www.tanqueray.com

The story of Bacardi starts with Don Facundo Bacardi Massó, an emigrant from Spanish Catalonia, who established a wine merchants in Santiago, Cuba, and started to experiment with ways of producing a lighter style of rum.

Don Facundo bought a small tin roofed distillery overlooking the Caribbean Sea and formed Bacardi y Compañía in February 1862 - and the Ron Bacardi brand name was created. The now famous 'bat' trademark was chosen because fruit bats lived in the rafters of the old distillery and were considered a sign of good fortune. A bat trademark has appeared on every Bacardi bottle since 1862.

The rums Don Facundo distilled were the first ever to be charcoal filtered, which removed impurities and gave his rums a smooth premium style. Years of experimentation also led Don Facundo to a series of other crucial innovations: selecting only the finest ingredients, isolating a specific yeast strain, the creation of a 'parallel' production process and the purposeful ageing of rum.
It is no exaggeration to say that he set the standard for all future rum production

BACARDI SUPERIOR RUM

The art of creating Bacardi Superior Rum has been handed down through seven generations of Maestros de Ron Bacardi. They are the custodians of Don Facundo's legacy and the keepers of his proprietary process and ingredients. Their skill and expertise ensures that each bottle of Bacardi Superior Rum consistently matches the flavour profile of the first blending in 1862.

Bacardi Rum is still made using Cuba's oldest cultured yeast strain, La Levadura Bacardi, which gives Bacardi Rum its unique flavour profile. The Maestros de Ron Bacardi refine this flavour profile and blend it to match a historical reference standard that can be traced back to Don Facundo's first batch in 1862.

With its light, subtle flavours and sublime balance of character and smoothness it is the perfect mixing spirit. Bacardi Superior Rum was so extraordinary that it revolutionised the spirits world and inspired cocktail pioneers from the late 1800's to create a whole new genre of light, refreshing cocktails such as the Daiquirí, Mojito, and the Bacardi Cocktail. These cocktails have become famous classics and these and many more feature in this book.

Bacardi y Compania is still a family run company. To discover more about Bacardi's history and heritage and cocktail legacy go to:

www.bacardi.com

Pronounced 'Don Hoo-Lio', this Tequila is named after Don Julio González, who started working in his uncle's Tequila distillery as a child and established his own distillery, La Primavera in Atotonilco el Alto, Jalisco in 1942, when he was only seventeen.

Tequila is made from Blue Agave – a plant with long, spiny leaves, which can take from 8 to 12 years to mature. The plants, of which there are more than 400 species, are native to North America and predominately Mexico. The decision concerning when a plant is ready to be harvested is crucial as it's the core of the plant, or piña, which is roasted to make tequila. If a plant is harvested too early there won't be enough sugars produced, too late and the plant will have used these sugars.

DON JULIO TEQUILA

The Don Julio distillery do not prune their Agave plants to maximise the liquid and volume from each plant - instead, plants are given room to develop naturally and whilst some producers harvest an entire field when it reaches a specific age, Don Julio only harvest the plants once they have reached maturity, regardless of how young or old they are.

The piñas are then cooked for 24 hours and then allowed to cool for 48 hours, which allows the complexities of flavours to develop. Don Julio also develop their own specific strain of yeast to use in the fermentation process, a sample of which is sent each year and cultivated on-site for fresh use each week.

During the distillation process, Tequila Don Julio uses nine stills of different sizes, all producing slightly different spirits. The fermented liquid is distilled twice, with only the heart of each distillation taken. The final spirit comes off the stills at a relatively low strength of around 58%abv to maximise its flavour and softness. The products of the various stills are then blended together to create the different Don Julio variants, thus ensuring consistency and complexity.

Don Julio Blanco
The Blanco is un-aged, merely being rested for a short period in inert containers before being bottled. It has light aromas of citrus, with a clean, dry palate, delicately savoury malty undertones. It is an ideal base for classic tequila cocktails such as the Margarita.

Don Julio Reposado
At least three months aging produces a lightly-coloured spirit with a complex and intriguing hints of pear, apple, and lemon fruit, with vanilla from the oak and rich satisfying notes of dark chocolate, nuts and spice.

Don Julio Añejo
Don Julio Añejo is aged from 18 months to 2 years to produce a refined tequila with notes of marzipan, dried tropical fruits, aromatic teas, and perfumed wood.

www.donjulio.com

In 1820, John Walker, the son of an Ayrshire farmer, established the family grocer's business at the age of fifteen in Kilmarnock and began selling Scotch whisky. His son, Alexander, joined the business a year before his father died in 1857, and by the time his sons joined the business, it was no longer a grocers, but a firm of whisky merchants.

John Walker's grandsons patented the name Johnnie Walker in 1908 and launched a White Label, Special Red Label and Extra Special Black label whisky. The white was dropped, but the red and black in their easily recognisable square bottles with the 'striding dandy' became internationally successful blends - the red became the world's best-selling Scotch.

JOHNNIE WALKER
BLENDED SCOTCH WHISKY

Johnnie Walker Black

Johnnie Walker Black Label contains around forty single malt whiskies including Talisker, Cardhu, and Lagavulin. It has a high proportion of Islay malts and is matured for twelve years in oak casks. The brand was originally called 'Extra Special Old Highland Whisky' – the name was changed to 'Black Label' because customers always ordered by the colour of the label. Johnnie Walker was Sir Winston Churchill's favourite Scotch - his 1932 oil painting 'Bottlescape' features a bottle of JWBL.

Johnnie Walker Gold

This 'Centenary Blend' was created by Sir Alexander Walker in 1920 to celebrate the founding of the company by John Walker 100 years before. The blend consists of whiskies from both the Highlands and Islay, each matured in oak for at least eighteen years.

Johnnie Walker Blue

An even more premium version of the already deluxe Johnnie Walker Black Label, with a proportion of malts as old as 60 years in the blend. There is however no age actually listed on the bottle as it is a blend of Walker's most exceptional and rare whiskies and so not restricted by age. The blue-green flint glass, square sided bottle which tapers to the base is a replica of the original Johnnie Walker bottle. The cork stopper has cord seal with a dangling medallion commemorating the brands establishment in 1820.

www.johnniewalker.com

Cognac is named after the small town in South West France, which has given its name to the surrounding area where the product must be made. Within the region of Cognac there are six sub-regions reflecting the variations in climate and soil – in order of importance these are: Grande Champagne, Petite Champagne, Borderies, Fine Bois, Bons Bois and Bois Ordinaires.

To qualify as a cognac the spirit must be a blend of at least two different aged eaux-de-vie (brandies), distilled twice in copper pot stills and aged in French oak barrels.

The story of the Cognac house of Courvoisier starts early in the 19th century when Emmanuel Courvoisier established his Cognac business in Jarnac and Louis Gallois separately established his wine and spirit wholesale business. The Gallois family sold the Cognacs produced by the Courvoisier family until in 1835 the sons of the original founders merged the two businesses.

COURVOISIER COGNAC

The visit of Napoléon I to the Gallois warehouse in 1811 heralded the beginning of a close relationship between the imperial courts of Napoléon I, II and III and Courvoisier, a relationship which led to Courvoisier establishing the Napoléon standard. In 1909 the House of Courvoisier, adopted the slogan 'The Brandy of Napoleon' and introduced the silhouette of the emperor.

Courvoisier VSOP
A Fine Champagne Cognac blended from an average of 55% Grande and 45% Petite Champagne, this Cognac is aged between 6 and 10 years. This easy drinking smooth, vanillered cognac has hints of stewed fruit with grilled almonds, vanilla, chocolate and dried apricots.

Courvoisier VSOP Exclusif
This blend of Grande Champagne, Petite Champagne (6 to 10 years old), Fine Bois (min 5 years old) and around 20% Borderies (10 to 15 years old), has an average age of 5 to 12 years. Exclusif was developed for the Japanese market where cognac is drunk mixed with water, and so is richer, spicier and more concentrated than Courvoisier's other VSOP (above).

Unusually this blend containing Cognacs from four of Cognac's regions is more expensive than Courvoisier's Fine Champagne VSOP, containing only Grande and Petite Champagne but here at diffords-guide we consider that little extra well worth paying. Initially mellow, this flavoursome cognac balances spiciness with orange zest, cinnamon, gingerbread, hints of dark chocolate and vanilla.

www.courvoisier.com

Augustus Bulleit first created Bulleit Bourbon in Louisville, Kentucky around 1830. He came from a family of brandy makers who had emigrated from France to New Orleans in the 1700s and when Augustus moved from New Orleans to Louisville to open a tavern, he used his knowledge of French brandy making to experiment with his own small batch distilling of Kentucky bourbon.

Bulleit's popularity grew and the bourbon was sold throughout Kentucky and Indiana but in 1860 Augustus disappeared whilst transporting liquor to New Orleans. Some say he was murdered by his business partner, while others believe he was seduced by the sumptuous life in the city's French Quarter. The recipe for Bulleit Bourbon seemed to disappear with him and it was not until 1987 when Augustus' great-great grandson Tom Bulleit finally recreated Bulleit Bourbon.

BULLEIT BOURBON

For bourbon to be classified as such, it needs to meet certain criteria, introduced by the American Government in May 1964. It must be a mix of corn, rye, wheat and barley but the major component (at least 51%) must be corn. It must be distilled to no more than 80% abv. It must be 100% natural – with only water added, and it must be aged in new, charred oak barrels. If all criteria are met, it is then recognised as "a distinctive product of the United States"

Today Bulleit Bourbon is distilled and aged in small batches and stored in a single-story warehouse to reduce inconsistencies in the maturation process. It is aged in American White Oak barrels that are flame charred for at least six years, which creates maturity and smoothness. In true bourbon fashion, only limestone-filtered water is used plus unlike most other producers, Bulleit Bourbon has its own Grain Division, which acquires distiller's grade grains, grown to their own specification.

It is made up of 30% Rye – the highest rye content of any other bourbon – and initially has a sweet and buttery taste, which becomes spicier with buttery corn notes and hints of dark chocolate and coffee.

www.bulleitbourbon.com

In 1827 Jean-Baptiste Lapostolle founded a modest distillery in Neauphle-le-Château, a small village near Paris. His company, which would become Marnier-Lapostolle, soon acquired a reputation for fine fruit liqueurs but it was Eugéne, Jean-Baptiste's son, who transformed the company's fortunes. In 1870, fleeing the Franco-Prussian war, he travelled to Cognac. There he met with distillers, visited cellars and returned home laden with fine cognac and impressed by the distillers' expertise.

GRAND MARNIER
CORDON ROUGE

At home, Eugéne invited friends and family to appraise his samples, among them his son-in-law, Louis-Alexandre Marnier-Lapostolle. Louis-Alexandre was so inspired by his father-in-law's enthusiasm and the quality of the cognacs that he immediately set about experimenting in the distillery's laboratory. His great idea was to blend cognac with orange, which was then an exotic fruit and hard to obtain. In 1880, after ten years of blending, experimenting and ageing, and sampling different test batches, he finally created a liqueur with perfectly balanced flavours.

César Ritz was one of many influential people impressed by the new liqueur and he immediately introduced it to the Savoy Hotel in London. He also advised Louis-Alexandre to go against the prevailing trend of dubbing every product 'petit'. The distiller duly called his creation 'Grand' Marnier.

Today the Grand Marnier bottle, designed by Louis-Alexandre in homage to the cognac pot still, is a familiar sight in bars around the world. Marnier-Lapostolle is still owned by Louis-Alexandre's descendants, the distillery is still based in Neauphle-le-Château and the red ribbon on every bottle is still tied by hand.

Grand Marnier has rich hints of orange zest and orange blossom and the aged cognacs within the blend add richness and depth with vanilla, caramel and subtle toffee notes.

www.grand-marnier.com

The distilling firm of Cointreau was founded in 1849 by two brothers Adolphe and Edouard-Jean Cointreau, who were confectioners in Angers, France. The liqueur we know today was created by Edouard Cointreau, the son of Edouard-Jean, and first marketed in 1871. Cointreau is made with the peel of bitter oranges from the Carribbean, sweet orange peel from Spain, neutral alcohol, sugar and water.

COINTREAU
TRIPLE SEC LIQUEUR

The popularity of Cointreau was originally driven in Britain by an English wine shipper, George Glendenning, who discovered the liqueur when visiting Bordeaux in 1902. He was so impressed that he travelled to Angers to meet Edouard and subsequently started importing Cointreau. However, in 1923 Glendenning informed the Cointreau family that their product was too sweet for the British palate and an extra dry version for the British market was created. It is this 'triple sec' (triple dry) version that has since been marketed around the world.

In the period between the two World Wars, Cointreau removed the term 'triple sec' from the label to differentiate it from any similar liqueur produced by other liqueur houses. However, if you are following a cocktail recipe that calls for 'triple sec' then Cointreau is almost certainly the liqueur the author intended to be used.

www.cointreau.com

In 1575, the Bols family arrived in Amsterdam to open 'het Lootsje' (which translates as 'The Little Shed') to distil liqueurs. Despite 'het Lootsje' being a wooden shed, fire risks dictated that the distillery had to be built outside Amsterdam's city walls. As the distillery grew, new stone buildings replaced the original wooden structure, but the name 'Lootsje' stuck.

BOLS APRICOT
BRANDY LIQUER

Lucas Bols was born in 1652 and is the man credited with first taking Bols into the international market. He was also a major shareholder of The Dutch East India Company who, during the prolific time of the Dutch Golden Age, brought exotic herbs, spices and fruits back to Amsterdam. These unusual new flavours were used to create new liqueurs – the hand written recipes of many of which still remain today.

After years of prosperity the last male member of the Bols family died in 1816 and the company was offered for conditional sale - requesting that the name Lucas Bols should always be retained. The Latin words "Semper Idem" inscribed in the Bols family coat of arms mean "always the same", which to the distiller means "Always the same end product of the same high quality".

Apricot Brandy is sometimes also known as 'apry'. It is a liqueur produced by infusing apricots in selected cognacs and flavouring the infusion with various herbs to bring out the best flavour and aroma of the apricots. Enriched with a hint of almond, this amber coloured liqueur is one of Bols most popular.

With an aroma of juicy apricots, this distinctively flavoured liqueur is suited to use in a variety of different cocktails. The light clean taste features apricot with a hint of brandy and almond.

www.bols.com

Like other 'crème de' liqueurs, this term comes from de French phrase "crème de la crème" meaning 'best of the best' and does not mean the liqueur contains any cream.

Crème de cassis is a blackcurrant liqueur that originated in France and is made by both infusion and maceration. The original recipe for a crème de cassis is thought to have been formulated by Denis Lagoute in 1841 in the French Dijon region, where many of the best examples are still produced today.

EEC law states that crème de cassis must have a minimum of 400g of sugar per litre and a minimum alcoholic strength of 15%. Unfortunately no minimum is set for the fruit content although the best brands will contain as much as 600g of blackcurrants per litre. Brands with a high fruit content will have a more fruity taste and a deeper colour than low-fruit brands.

CRÈME DE CASSIS & CHAMBORD LIQUEURS

Crème de mûre liqueur is similar in style to crème de cassis but usually contains less sugar. 'Mûre' means blackberry, so French blackberry liqueurs are often termed crème de mûre.

Both 'crème de cassis' and 'crème de mûre' are generic terms and numerous brands are available. In contrast we also recommend 'Chambord' for use in place of crème de cassis. This proprietary brand is described as being a "black raspberry liqueur". It is a suitable alternative to crème de cassis and many of the recipes featured in this guide were originally created using Chambord rather than cassis. We suggest you experiment with these and other rich berry liqueurs to find one that best suits your taste.

www.chambordonline.com

At the turn of the 18th century, Lyonnais Joseph Noilly was a herbalist making both perfumes and drinks. After some experiment he came up with the recipe for a new, wine based apéritif, the first dry vermouth to compete with the sweet vermouth styles already being produced in Turin. Vermouths were fashionable at the time due to their perceived health benefits and Lyonnais sought to capitalise on this.

In 1811 Lyonnais' son Louis took over the now very successful business and years later when his daughter ran off with an English coachman called Claudius Prat, Louis forgivingly brought him into the business making Claudius a partner in 1855, when the business became known as Noilly Prat. After the deaths of both Louis and Claudius the business was passed to Anne (daughter and wife respectively) in 1865 and she continued to run the business very successfully until 1902. At a time when women still faced unnecessary challenges in the work place – this was an extraordinary achievement.

NOILLY PRAT BLANC
DRY VERMOUTH

Noilly Prat is made in the picturesque fishing port of Marseillan in the French Languedoc region. Fortified local Picpoul and Clairette wine is aged in Canadian oak casks for eight months before being transferred into smaller casks. These casks are then left in the open air for a further year where the combined affect of the oak and sea air give the wine an amber hue and distinctive taste. Locally, this aged wine is known as 'vin cuit' or 'cooked wine'. The wine is then transferred to large vats where it is blended with raspberry and lemon essence, mistelle, camomile, coriander and other herbs which create both the aromatic nose and fresh herbaceous palate.

The blend is left to marry for a year before bottling meaning the whole process takes three years to complete.

www.noillyprat.com

In the mid 1800s, Turin's Distilleria Nazionale di Spirito di Vino was formed, specialising in the production and sale of wine, vermouth and liqueurs. Out of this Distilleria, three key figures emerged - Alessandro Martini – an apprentice maître licorist who had trained alongside Gaspare Campari in Turin, Luigi Rossi - a wine expert and Teofilo Sola – the business man in the group.

MARTINI ROSSO
SWEET VERMOUTH

Together, they took the company forward, changing its name in 1863 to Martini, Sola & Cia. Rossi went on to create Martini Rosso and the company prospered. In 1879, Teofila Sola died and his sons chose sell their shares. The company was renamed Martini & Rossi after the two remaining directors. In 1922 the company officially became known as Martini, except in the United States where they were forced to keep 'Martini & Rossi' because the word Martini was already associated with the infamous cocktail.

Martini & Rossi vermouth is 75% wine blended with a mix of herbs, spices, and fruits, including ginger, cinnamon, mint, raspberry, coriander, cardamom and at least twenty other ingredients – the exact recipe is, of course, kept secret by the company and although now a global brand, this secret botanical mix is still prepared in Turin.

Martini Rosso, the first vermouth created by the company is deep red in colour due to the addition of caramel to the mix.

The same imagery is used on the labels throughout the range of Martini vermouths. This depicts Vittoria, the mythological Roman goddess of victory, blowing her trumpet over the flags of conquered nations, and signifies the many countries where Martini is sold. Also shown is the bull of Turin, the city's coat of arms and the Italian royal coat of arms.

www.martini.com

The production of champagne only became possible at the end of the 17th century. Before this time, the glass available was not strong enough to withstand the high pressures (equivalent to the pressure of a double-decker bus tyre). Suitable bottles and corks first became available in London where sparkling wine was first produced around 1665. French sparkling wine production did not commence until the very end of the 17th century.

Although production of sparkling wines in champagne is comparatively recent, still wines have been made there since the 15th century, when the Pinot Noir grape was first introduced to the region and made into light red wines.

The vineyards of the Champagne region are the most northerly in France, lying north-east of Paris, on either side of the River Marne. Most of the champagne houses are based in one of the two towns synonymous with champagne: Epernay and Reims.

CHAMPAGNE

Champagne, surprisingly, is made predominantly from black grapes. The three grape varieties used are Pinot Noir (the red grape of Burgundy), Pinot Maunier (a fruitier relative of Pinot Noir) and lastly Chardonnay.

Difford's Tips on Champagne

Non-vintage: A blend of several years wines to produce a 'house style'. Must spend a minimum of 15 months on its lees.
Vintage: A blend of a single vintage. Must spend a minimum of three years on its lees. Only 80% of a year's crop may be sold as vintage. Vintage champagnes are fuller in body and have a greater intensity of fruit than non-vintage champagnes.
Prestige Cuvée: A superior champagne, usually produced from a single vintage.
Rosé: Champagne produced by blending red and white wines together.
Blanc de Blancs: A champagne only produced from Chardonnay grapes.
Blanc de Noirs: A white champagne only made from black grapes.

Non-vintage champagne (those without a production year featured on the bottle) should be consumed within five years of purchase. Vintage wines usually take ageing better and can be kept for eight to ten years. But remember that champagne is released when it's ready to drink and even if you keep your bottle laying down in perfect conditions, it will still change over the years, likely as not for the worse. The colour will darken, it will loose effervescence and freshness. However, some with high acidity and good fruit may actually be more interesting with a couple of years extra age.

FRIDGE & PANTRY ESSENTIALS

CRANBERRY JUICE	ORANGE JUICE	PRESSED APPLE JUICE	GRAPEFRUIT JUICE (PINK)	PINEAPPLE JUICE	TOMATO JUICE	COLA
SODA WATER	GINGER ALE & GINGER BEER	TONIC WATER	LEMONADE	LIME CORDIAL	ANGOSTURA BITTERS	MILK
FRESH LEMONS	FRESH LIMES	FRESH MINT	STRAWBERRIES	RASPBERRIES	MARASCHINO CHERRIES	EGGS
BLUEBERRIES	BANANAS	WHITE GRAPES	RED GRAPES	RUNNY HONEY	EARL GREY TEA	DOUBLE CREAM

SUGAR SYRUP

Many cocktails benefit from sweetening but granulated sugar does not dissolve easily in cold drinks. Hence pre-dissolved sugar syrup (also known as 'simple syrup') is used.

Make your own sugar syrup by gradually pouring and stirring two cups of granulated sugar into a saucepan containing one cup of hot water and simmer until the sugar is dissolved. Do not let the water even come close to boiling and only simmer for as long as it takes to dissolve the sugar. Allow syrup to cool and pour into an empty bottle. Ideally, you should finely strain your syrup into the bottle to remove any undissolved crystals which could otherwise encourage crystallisation. If kept in a refrigerator this mixture will last for a couple of months.

POMEGRANATE (GRENADINE) SYRUP

To make your own pomegranate syrup simply follow the instructions for sugar syrup above but use one cup of pomegranate juice (Pom Wonderful) in place of the water.

BARTENDING BASICS

By definition any drink which is described as a cocktail contains more than one ingredient. So if you are going to make cocktails you have to know how to combine these various liquids. Firstly, as in cooking, there is a correct order in which to prepare things and with few exceptions, that runs as follows:

1. Select glass and chill or pre-heat (if required).
2. Prepare garnish (if required).
3. Pour ingredients.
4. Add ice (if required - add last to minimise melt).
5. Combine ingredients (shake, stir, blend or build).
6. Add garnish (if required). 7. Consume or serve to guest.

Essentially, there are four different ways to mix a cocktail: shake, stir, blend and build. (Building a drink means combining the ingredients in the glass in which the cocktail will be served.)

A fifth construction method, 'layering', isn't strictly mixing. The idea here is to float each ingredient on its predecessor without the ingredients merging at all. At the heart of every cocktail lies at least one of these five methods. So understanding these terms is fundamental.

Shake

When you see the phrase "shake with ice and strain" or similar in a method, you should place all the necessary ingredients with cubed ice in a cocktail shaker and shake briskly for fifteen seconds. Then you should strain the liquid into the glass, leaving the ice behind in the shaker.

Shaking not only mixes a drink, it also chills and dilutes it. This dilution is just as important to the resulting cocktail as using the right proportions of each ingredient. If you use too little ice it will quickly melt in the shaker, producing an over-diluted drink - so always fill your shaker at least two-thirds full with fresh ice.

Losing your grip while shaking is likely to make a mess and could result in injury, so always hold the shaker firmly with two hands and never shake fizzy ingredients (unless in a minute proportion to rest of drink). Although shakers come in many shapes and sizes there are two basic types.

Standard Shaker

A standard shaker consists of three parts and hence is sometimes referred to as a three-piece shaker. The three pieces are 1/ a flat-bottomed, conical base or 'can', 2/ a top with a built-in strainer and 3/ a cap.

I recommend this style of shaker for amateurs due to its ease of use. Be sure to purchase a shaker with a capacity of at least one pint as this will allow the ice room to travel and so mix more effectively.

To use:

1/ Combine all ingredients in the base of the shaker and fill two-thirds full with ice. 2/ Place the top and cap firmly on the base. 3/ Pick up the closed shaker with one hand on the top and the other gripping the bottom and shake vigorously. The cap should always be on the top when shaking and should point away from guests. 4/ After shaking briskly for a count of around 15 seconds, lift off the cap, hold the shaker by its base with one finger securing the top and pour the drink through the built-in strainer.

Boston Shaker

A Boston shaker comprises two flat-bottomed cones, one larger than the other. The large cone, or 'tin', is made of stainless steel while the smaller cone can be either glass or stainless steel. I prefer glass as this allows both mixer and guest to see the drink being made.

Avoid Boston shakers that rely on a rubber ring to seal. I use Alessi Boston tins as I find these seal without a thump and open with the lightest tap. However good your Boston shaker, these devices demand an element of skill and practice is usually required for a new user to become proficient.

To use:

1/ Combine ingredients in the glass, or smaller of the two tins.

2/ Fill the large tin with ice and stand on work surface.

3/ Whilst steadying the large tin with one hand, pick up the glass/small tin and pour it's contents into the ice-filled shaker.

4// In the same motion rest the now empty smaller can or glass on top of the larger tin. The glass/small tin will naturally want to sit on the large tin at a slight angle. This is ok and it is actually beneficial not to try and straighten.

5/ Lightly tap the top of the upturned glass/small tin with the heel of your hand to help ensure a seal is made between the two parts of the shaker.

6/ Lift shaker with one hand on the top and the other gripping the base and shake vigorously. The glass/small tin should always be on the top when shaking and should point safely away from guests.

7/ After shaking for around 15 seconds, hold the larger (base) tin in one hand and break the seal between the two halves of the shaker by tapping the base tin with the heel of your other hand at the point where it meets the upper tin (or glass). 5/ Before pouring place a strainer with a coiled rim (also known as a Hawthorne strainer) over the top of the tin and strain the mixture into the glass, leaving the ice cubes behind.

Fine Strain

Most cocktails that are served 'straight up' without ice benefit from an additional finer strain, over and above the standard strain which keeps ice cubes out of the drink. This 'fine strain' removes small fragments of fruit and fine flecks of ice which can spoil the appearance of a drink. Fine straining is achieved by simply holding a fine sieve, like a tea strainer, between the shaker and the glass. Another popular term for this method is 'double strain'.

Stir

If a cocktail recipe calls for you to 'stir with ice and strain', stir in a mixing glass using a bar spoon with a long, spiralling stem. If a lipped mixing glass is not available, one half of a Boston shaker, or the base of a standard shaker, will suffice.
Combine the ingredients in the mixing glass, adding the ice last. Slide the back of the spoon down the inside of the mixing glass and stir the drink. You should stir a drink for at least 20 seconds, then strain into a glass using a strainer (or the top of a standard shaker if you are using a standard shaker base in place of a mixing glass).

Blend

When a cocktail recipe calls for you to 'blend with ice', place ingredients and ice into a blender and blend until a smooth, even consistency is achieved. Ideally you should use crushed ice, as this lessens wear on the blender's blades. Place liquid ingredients in the blender first, adding the ice last, as always. If you have a variable speed blender, always start slowly and build up speed.

Layer

As the name would suggest, layered drinks include layers of different ingredients, often with contrasting colours. This effect is achieved by carefully pouring each ingredient into the glass so that it floats on its predecessor.

The success of this technique is dependent on the density (specific gravity) of the liquids used. As a rule of thumb, the less alcohol and the more sugar an ingredient contains, the heavier it is. The heaviest ingredients should be poured first and the lightest last. Syrups are non-alcoholic and contain a lot of sugar so are usually the heaviest ingredient. Liqueurs, which are high in sugar and lower in alcohol than spirits, are generally the next heaviest ingredient. The exception to this rule is cream and cream liqueurs, which can float.

One brand of a particular liqueur may be heavier or lighter than another. The relative temperatures of ingredients may also affect their ability to float or sink. Hence a degree of experimentation is inevitable when creating layered drinks.

Layering can be achieved by holding the bowl end of a bar spoon (or a soup spoon) in contact with the side of the glass and over the surface of the drink and pour slowly over it.

The term 'float' refers to layering the final ingredient on top of a cocktail.

Muddle

Muddling means pummelling fruits, herbs and/or spices with a muddler (a blunt tool similar to a pestle) so as to crush them and release their flavour. (You can also use a rolling pin.) As when using a pestle and mortar, push down on the muddler with a twisting action.

Only attempt to muddle in the base of a shaker or a suitably sturdy glass. Never attempt to muddle hard, unripe fruits in a glass as the pressure required could break the glass. I've witnessed a bartender slash his hand open on a broken glass while muddling and can't over-emphasize how careful you should be.

Measuring (Shots & Spoons)

Balancing each ingredient within a cocktail is key to making a great drink. Therefore the accuracy with which ingredients are measured is critical to the finished cocktail.

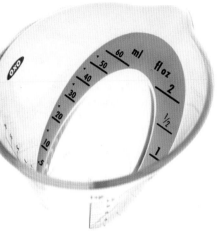

In this guide I've expressed the measures of each ingredient in 'shots'. Ideally a shot is 25ml or one US fluid ounce (29.6ml), measured in a standard jigger. (You can also use a clean medicine measure or even a small shot glass.) Whatever your chosen measure, it should have straight sides to enable you to accurately judge fractions of a shot. Look out for measures which are graduated in ounces and marked with quarter and half ounces.

The measure 'spoon' refers to a bar spoon, which is slightly larger than a standard teaspoon. Personally, I measure in ounces and count a flat bar spoon as an eighth of an ounce.

Some bartenders attempt to measure shots by counting time and estimating the amount of liquid flowing through a bottle's spout. This is known as 'free-pouring' and in unskilled hands can be terribly inaccurate. I strongly recommend the use of a physical measure and a great deal of care.

Ice

A plentiful supply of fresh ice is essential to making good cocktails. When buying bagged ice avoid the hollow, tubular kind and the thin wafers. Instead look for large, solid cubes of ice.

When filling ice cube trays, use bottled or filtered water to avoid the taste of chlorine often apparent in municipal water supplies. Your ice should be dry, almost sticky to the touch. Avoid 'wet' ice that has started to thaw.

Whenever serving a drink over ice, always fill the glass with ice, rather than just adding a few cubes. This not only makes the drink much colder, but the ice lasts longer and so does not dilute into the drink.

Never use ice in a cocktail shaker twice, even if it's to mix the same drink as last time. You should always throw away ice after straining the drink and use fresh ice to fill the glass if so required. Not straining shaken ice and pouring it straight into the glass with the liquid is one of the worst crimes a bartender can commit.

Unless otherwise stated, all references to ice in this guide mean cubed ice. If crushed ice is required for a particular recipe, the recipe will state 'crushed ice'. This is available commercially. Alternatively you can crush cubed ice in an ice-crusher or simply bash a bag or tea towel of cubed ice with a rolling pin.

Flame

The term ignite, flame or flambé means that the drink should be set alight. Please exercise extreme care when setting fire to drinks. Be particularly careful not to knock over a lit drink and never attempt to carry a drink which is still alight. Before drinking, cover the glass so as to suffocate the flame and be aware that the rim of the glass may be hot.

How to make sugar syrup

To make your own sugar syrup, gradually pour TWO cups of granulated sugar into a saucepan containing ONE cup of hot water. Stir as you pour and carry on stirring and simmering until the sugar is dissolved. Do not let the water even come close to boiling and only simmer for as long as it takes to dissolve the sugar. Allow syrup to cool and pour into an empty bottle. Ideally, you should finely strain your syrup into the bottle to remove any undissolved crystals which could otherwise encourage crystallisation. If kept in a refrigerator this mixture will last for a couple of months.

Garnishes

Garnishes are used to decorate cocktails and are often anchored to the rim of the glass. Strictly speaking, garnishes should be edible, so please forget about paper parasols. Anything from banana chunks, strawberries or redcurrants to coffee beans, confectionery, basil leaves and slices of fresh ginger can be used as a garnish. The correct garnish will often enhance the aroma and flavour as well as the look of a drink.

Fruit should be unblemished and washed prior to use. Olives, in particular, should be washed thoroughly to prevent oil from spoiling the appearance of a drink. Cut citrus fruits have a maximum shelf life of 24 hours when refrigerated. Cherries and olives should be stored refrigerated and left in their own juices.

Olives, cherries, pickled onions and fresh berries are sometimes served on cocktail sticks. A whole slice of citrus fruit served on a cocktail stick 'mast' is known as a 'sail': this is often accompanied by a cherry.

Celery sticks may be placed in drinks as stirring rods while cinnamon sticks are often placed in hot drinks and toddies.

To sprinkle chocolate on the surface of a drink you can either shave chocolate using a vegetable peeler or crumble a Cadbury's Flake bar. The instruction 'dust with chocolate' refers to a fine coating of cocoa powder on the surface of a drink. (When dusting with nutmeg it is always best to grate fresh nutmeg as the powdered kind lacks flavour.)

Citrus peels are often used as a garnish. Besides the variations listed under 'zest twist', thin, narrow lengths of citrus peel may be tied in a 'knot'. A 'Horse's Neck' is the entire peel of either an orange, a lemon or a lime, cut in a continuous spiral and placed so as to overhang the rim of the glass.

Wedges of lemons and limes are often squeezed into drinks or fixed to the glass as a garnish. A wedge is an eighth segment of the fruit. Cut the 'knobs' from the top and bottom of the fruit, slice the fruit in half lengthwise, then cut each half into four equal wedges lengthwise.

Mint sprigs are often used to garnish cups and juleps.

Zest Twist

This term refers to flavouring a drink by releasing the aromatic oils from a strip of citrus zest. Using a knife or peeler, cut a half inch (12mm) wide length of zest from an unwaxed, cleaned fruit so as to leave just a little of the white pith. Hold it over the glass with the thumb and forefinger of each hand, coloured side down. Turn one end clockwise and the other anti-clockwise so as to twist the peel and force some of its oils over the surface of the drink. Deposit any flavoursome oils left on the surface of the peel by wiping the coloured side around the rim of the glass. Finally, drop the peel onto the surface of the drink. (Some prefer to dispose of the spent twist.)

A flamed zest twist is a dramatic variation on this theme which involves burning the aromatic oils emitted from citrus fruit zest over the surface of a drink. Lemons and limes are sometimes treated in this way but oranges are most popular. Firm, thick-skinned navel oranges, like Washington Navels, are best.

You will need to cut as wide a strip of zest as you can, wider than you would for a standard twist. Hold the cut zest, peel side down, between the thumb and forefinger about four inches above the drink and gently warm it with a lighter flame. Then pinch the peel by its edges so that its oils squirt through the flame towards the surface of the drink - there should be a flash as the oils ignite. Finally, wipe the zest around the rim of the glass.

Salt/Sugar Rim

Some recipes call for the rim of the glass to be coated with salt, sugar or other ingredients such as desiccated coconut or chocolate: you will need to moisten the rim first before the ingredient will hold. When using salt, wipe a cut wedge of lime around the outside edge of the rim, then roll the outside edge through a saucer of salt. (Use sea salt rather than iodised salt as the flavour is less biting.) For sweet ingredients like sugar and chocolate, either use an orange slice as you would a lime wedge or moisten a sponge or paper towel with a suitable liqueur and run it around the outside edge of the glass.

Whatever you are using to rim the glass should cling to the outside edge only. Remember, garnishes are not a cocktail ingredient but an optional extra to be consumed by choice. They should not contaminate your cocktail. If some of your garnish should become stuck to the inside edge of the glass, remove it using a fresh fruit wedge or a paper towel.

It is good practice to salt or sugar only two-thirds of the rim of a glass. This allows the drinker the option of avoiding the salt or sugar. If you rim glasses some hours prior to use, the lime juice or liqueur will dry, leaving a crust of salt or sugar crystals around the rim. The glasses can then be placed in a refrigerator to chill ready for use.

A professional piece of equipment with the unfortunate title of a 'rimmer' has three sections, one with a sponge for water or lime juice, one containing sugar and another containing salt. Beware, as this encourages dipping the glass onto a moist sponge and then into the garnish, and so contaminating the inside of the glass.

GLASSWARE

Cocktails are something of a luxury. You don't just ping a cap and pour. These drinks take time and skill to mix so deserve a decent glass.

Before you start, check your glassware is clean and free from chips and marks such as lipstick. Always handle glasses by the base or the stem to avoid leaving finger marks and never put your fingers inside a glass.

Ideally glassware should be chilled in a freezer prior to use. This is particularly important for martini and flute glasses, in which drinks are usually served without ice. It takes about half an hour to sufficiently chill a glass in the freezer.

If time is short, you can chill a glass by filling it with ice (ideally crushed, not cubed) and topping it up with water. Leave the glass to cool while you prepare the drink, then discard the ice and water once you are ready to pour. This method is quicker than chilling in the freezer but not nearly so effective.

To warm a glass ready for a hot cocktail, place a bar spoon in the glass and fill it with hot water. Then discard the water and pour in the drink. Only then should you remove the spoon, which is there to help disperse the shock of the heat.

There are thousands of differently shaped glasses, but if you own those mentioned here you have a glass to suit practically every drink and occasion. Failing that, a set of Collins, Martini and Old-fashioned or Rocks glasses, and possibly flutes if you fancy champagne cocktails, will allow you to serve the majority of drinks in this guide. Use a Martini in place of a Coupette and a Collins as a substitute for Hurricane and Sling glasses.

1. Martini/Coupette

Those in the old guard of bartending insist on calling this a 'cocktail glass'. It may once have been, but to most of us today a V-shaped glass is a Martini glass. The recent resurgence in vintage cocktails has also led to a vogue for using a champagne saucer or Coupette, to serve straight-up drinks. Whatever your glassware preference, when choosing either a Martini or a Coupette it should be no bigger than 7oz, as a Martini-style drink warms up too much without the benefit of ice to keep it cool. I'd suggest keeping your glasses in the refrigerator or even the freezer so they are chilled before use.

Capacity to brim: 7oz / 20cl

2. Sling

This elegant glass has recently become fashionable again – partly due to the popularity of long drinks such as the Russian Spring Punch.

Capacity to brim: 11oz / 32cl

3. Shot

Shot glasses come in all shapes and sizes. You'll need small ones if you're sensible and big ones if you're not!

Capacity to brim (pictured glass): 2oz / 6cl

4. Flute

Flutes are perfect for serving champagne cocktails as their tall, slim design helps maintain the wine's fizz. Chill before use.

Capacity to brim: 6oz / 17cl

5. Collins

In this guide I refer to a tall glass as a 'Collins'. A hi-ball is slightly squatter than a Collins but has the same capacity. A 12oz Collins glass will suffice for cocktails and is ideal for a standard 330ml bottle of beer. However, I favour 14oz glasses with the occasional 8oz for drinks such as Fizzes which are served tall but not very long.

Capacity to brim: 14oz / 40cl or 8oz / 24cl

6. Margarita

Named after the cocktail with the same name, this glass is still used predominately for the Mexican cocktail – the rim is crying out for salt.
Capacity to brim: 8oz / 24cl

7. Goblet

Not often used for cocktails, but worth having, if for no other reason than to enjoy your wine. An 11oz glass is big enough to be luxurious.
Capacity to brim: 11oz / 32cl

8. Boston

A tall, heavy conical glass with a thick rim, designed to be combined with a Boston tin to form a shaker. It can also be used as a mixing glass for stirred drinks.
Capacity to brim: 17oz / 48cl

9. Hurricane

Sometimes referred to as a 'poco grande' or 'Piña Colada' glass, this big-bowled glass is commonly used for frozen drinks. It screams out for a pineapple wedge, a cherry and possibly a paper parasol as well. Very Del Boy.
Capacity to brim: 15oz / 43cl

10. Old-fashioned

Another glass whose name refers to the best-known drink served in it. It is also great for enjoying spirits such as whiskey. Choose a luxuriously large glass with a thick, heavy base. Alternatively, the similarly shaped 'Rocks' glass has a thick rim and is usually made from toughened glass so better suited to drinks that require muddling in the glass.
Capacity to brim: 11oz / 32cl

11. Snifter

Sometimes referred to as a 'brandy balloon'. The bigger the bowl, the more extravagant the glass appears. Use to enjoy cocktails and deluxe aged spirits such as Cognac.
Capacity to brim: 12oz / 35cl

12. Toddy

Frequently referred to as a 'liqueur coffee glass', which is indeed its main use, this glass was popularised by the Irish Coffee. Toddy glasses have a handle on the side, allowing you to comfortably hold hot drinks.
Capacity to brim: 8.5oz / 25cl

13. Sour

This small glass is narrow at the stem and tapers out to a wider lip. As the name would suggest, it is used for serving Sours straight-up. I favour serving Sours over ice in an Old-fashioned but any of the recipes in this guide can be strained and served 'up' in this glass.
Capacity to brim: 4oz / 12cl

14. Rocks

Like an Old-fashioned with a thick rim, this is usually made from toughened glass - perfect for drinks that require muddling in the glass. A hardy glass, if there is such a thing.
Capacity to brim: 9oz / 27cl

COCKTAILS
A-Z

A

A1

Glass: Martini
Garnish: Orange zest twist
Method: SHAKE all ingredients with ice and fine strain into chilled glass.

1¾	shot(s)	**Tanqueray London dry gin**
1	shot(s)	**Grand Marnier liqueur**
¼	shot(s)	**Freshly squeezed lemon juice**
⅛	shot(s)	**Pomegranate (grenadine) syrup**

Comment: Nothing subtle about this full-on orange, gin based short drink.

ABBEY MARTINI

Glass: Martini
Garnish: Orange zest twist
Method: SHAKE all ingredients with ice and fine strain into chilled glass.

2	shot(s)	**Tanqueray London dry gin**
1	shot(s)	**Martini Rosso sweet vermouth**
1	shot(s)	**Freshly squeezed orange juice**
3	dashes	**Angostura aromatic bitters**

Origin: This 1930s classic cocktail is closely related to the better known Bronx.
Comment: A dry, orangey, herbal, gin laced concoction.

ABSOLUTELY FABULOUS

Glass: Flute
Garnish: Strawberry on rim
Method: SHAKE first two ingredients with ice and strain into glass. **TOP** with champagne.

1	shot(s)	**Ketel One vodka**
2	shot(s)	**Ocean Spray cranberry juice**
Top up with		**Brut champagne**

Origin: Created in 1999 at Monte's Club, London, England, and named after the Absolutely Fabulous television series where Patsy consumed copious quantities of Stoli and Bolly – darlings.
Comment: Easy to quaff – Patsy would love it.

ACE

Glass: Martini
Garnish: Maraschino cherry on rim
Method: SHAKE all ingredients with ice and fine strain into chilled glass.

2	shot(s)	**Tanqueray London dry gin**
½	shot(s)	**Pomegranate (grenadine) syrup**
½	shot(s)	**Double (heavy) cream**
½	shot(s)	**Milk**
½	fresh	**Egg white**

Comment: Pleasant, creamy, sweetened gin. Add more pomegranate syrup to taste.

ADAM & EVE

Glass: Martini
Garnish: Raspberries on stick plus lemon zest twist
Method: SHAKE all ingredients with ice and fine strain into chilled glass.

1	shot(s)	**Tanqueray London dry gin**
1	shot(s)	**Courvoisier V.S.O.P. cognac**
1	shot(s)	**Crème de cassis or Chambord**
⅛	shot(s)	**Freshly squeezed lemon juice**

Comment: Fruity but not too sweet.

ADDINGTON

Glass: Martini
Garnish: Orange zest twist
Method: SHAKE first two ingredients with ice and fine strain into chilled glass. **TOP** with just the merest squirt of soda from chilled siphon.

2	shot(s)	**Martini Rosso sweet vermouth**
1	shot(s)	**Noilly Prat Noilly Prat dry vermouth**
Top up with		**Soda from chilled siphon**

Origin: Vintage cocktail of unknown origin.
Comment: Substitute vermouths such as Antica Formula by Giuseppe B. Carpano dramatically alter the character of this cocktail.

ADDISON

Glass: Martini
Garnish: Maraschino cherry
Method: STIR all ingredients with ice and fine strain into chilled glass.

1½	shot(s)	**Tanqueray London dry gin**
1½	shot(s)	**Martini Rosso sweet vermouth**

Comment: Basically a very wet, sweet Martini.

ADIOS AMIGOS COCKTAIL

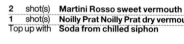

Glass: Martini
Garnish: Lemon zest twist
Method: SHAKE all ingredients with ice and fine strain into chilled glass.

1	shot(s)	**Bacardi Superior rum**
½	shot(s)	**Noilly Prat dry vermouth**
½	shot(s)	**Courvoisier V.S.O.P. cognac**
½	shot(s)	**Tanqueray London dry gin**
¼	shot(s)	**Freshly squeezed lime juice**
¼	shot(s)	**Sugar syrup** (2 sugar to 1 water)
½	shot(s)	**Chilled mineral water** (omit if wet ice)

Origin: Adapted from Victor Bergeron's 'Trader Vic's Bartender's Guide' (1972 revised edition).

ADIOS AMIGOS #2

Glass: Martini
Garnish: Lemon zest twist
Method: SHAKE all ingredients with ice and fine strain into chilled glass.

1	shot(s)	Tanqueray London dry gin
½	shot(s)	Courvoisier V.S.O.P. cognac
½	shot(s)	Bacardi Superior rum
½	shot(s)	Martini Rosso sweet vermouth
½	shot(s)	Freshly squeezed lemon juice
⅛	shot(s)	Sugar syrup (2 sugar to 1 water)

Comment: I have added a dash of sugar to what was originally a bone dry recipe.

AFFINITY

Glass: Martini
Garnish: Lemon zest twist
Method: STIR all ingredients with ice and strain into chilled glass.

1	shot(s)	Johnnie Walker Scotch whisky
1	shot(s)	Martini Rosso sweet vermouth
1	shot(s)	Noilly Prat dry vermouth
1	dashes	Angostura aromatic bitters

AKA: Scotch Manhattan
Comment: Aperitif style cocktail which when shaken has an almost creamy, soft, mouth feel. Stir, as the recipe originally intended and the Scotch notes are more pronounced. I prefer mine shaken.

AGENT ORANGE

Glass: Old-fashioned
Garnish: Orange zest twist
Method: SHAKE all ingredients with ice and strain into ice-filled glass.

1	shot(s)	Ketel One vodka
½	shot(s)	Grand Marnier liqueur
½	shot(s)	Cointreau triple sec
2	shot(s)	Freshly squeezed orange juice

Comment: Fresh orange is good for you. This has all of the flavour but few of the health benefits.

ALABAZAM

Glass: Collins
Garnish: Lemon slice
Method: SHAKE first five ingredients with ice and strain into ice-filled glass. **TOP** with soda.

2	shot(s)	Courvoisier V.S.O.P. cognac
1	shot(s)	Grand Marnier liqueur
1	shot(s)	Freshly squeezed lemon juice
½	shot(s)	Sugar syrup (2 sugar to 1 water)
1	dash	Fee Brother orange bitters (optional)
Top up with		Soda water (club soda)

Origin: Recipe adapted from William Schmidt's 1892 'The Flowing Bowl'.
Comment: Beware – this long fruity number packs a cognac charged punch.

ALAN'S APPLE BREEZE

Glass: Collins
Garnish: Apple wedge on rim
Method: SHAKE all ingredients with ice and strain into ice-filled glass.

2	shot(s)	Bacardi Superior rum
½	shot(s)	Bols apricot brandy liqueur
1½	shot(s)	Pressed apple juice
1½	shot(s)	Ocean Spray cranberry juice
½	shot(s)	Freshly squeezed lime juice
¼	shot(s)	Sugar syrup (2 sugar to 1 water)

Origin: Created in 2002 by Alan Johnston at Metropolitan, Glasgow, Scotland.
Comment: A sweet, tangy version of the Apple Breeze.

ALASKA

Glass: Martini
Garnish: Maraschino cherry on stick
Method: SHAKE all ingredients with ice and fine strain into chilled glass.

2	shot(s)	Tanqueray London dry gin
1½	shot(s)	Freshly squeezed lemon juice
½	shot(s)	Sugar syrup (2 sugar to 1 water)
¼	shot(s)	Crème de cassis or Chambord

Comment: The original recipe suggests adding the cassis separately after the drink is strained into the glass so it sinks. Looks great but the resulting drink is very sour until the cassis is stirred in.

ALICE MINE

Glass: Martini
Garnish: Orange zest twist
Method: STIR all ingredients with ice and strain into chilled glass.

1	shot(s)	Grand Marnier liqueur
½	shot(s)	Tanqueray London dry gin
½	shot(s)	Noilly Prat dry vermouth
¼	shot(s)	Martini Rosso sweet vermouth
1	dash	Angostura aromatic bitters

Origin: Vintage cocktail of unknown origin.
Comment: A Medium Dry Martini with luscious orange notes.

ALFONSO MARTINI

Glass: Martini
Garnish: Orange zest twist
Method: SHAKE all ingredients with ice and fine strain into chilled glass.

½	shot(s)	Tanqueray London dry gin
1	shot(s)	Grand Marnier liqueur
½	shot(s)	Noilly Prat dry vermouth
¼	shot(s)	Martini Rosso sweet vermouth
2	dashes	Angostura aromatic bitters
½	shot(s)	Chilled mineral water (omit if wet ice)

Origin: Adapted from Victor Bergeron's 'Trader Vic's Bartender's Guide' (1972 revised edition).
Comment: Dry yet slightly sweet with hints of orange, gin and warm spice.

A

ALICE IN WONDERLAND

Glass: Shot
Garnish: Lime wedge
Method: Refrigerate ingredients then **LAYER** in chilled glass by carefully pouring in the following order.

| 1 | shot(s) | **Grand Marnier liqueur** |
| ½ | shot(s) | **Don Julio 100% agave tequila** |

Comment: Brings a whole new dimension to tequila and orange.

ANITA'S ATTITUDE ADJUSTER

Glass: Sling
Garnish: Lemon slice & cherry on stick (sail)
Method: **SHAKE** first seven ingredients with ice and strain into ice-filled glass. **TOP** with champagne and gently stir.

½	shot(s)	**Cointreau triple sec**
½	shot(s)	**Don Julio 100% agave tequila**
½	shot(s)	**Bacardi Superior rum**
½	shot(s)	**Tanqueray London dry gin**
½	shot(s)	**Ketel One vodka**
½	shot(s)	**Freshly squeezed lime juice**
½	shot(s)	**Sugar syrup** (2 sugar to 1 water)
Top up with		**Brut champagne**

Comment: Anita has a problem – she's indecisive when it comes to choosing base spirits.

APPLE & BLACKBERRY PIE

Glass: Martini
Garnish: Cinnamon dust & blackberry
Method: **MUDDLE** blackberries in base of shaker. Add vodka and apple juice, **SHAKE** with ice and fine strain into chilled glass. **FLOAT** cream on the surface of the drink by pouring over the back of a spoon and swirl to form a thin layer. Depending on the sweetness of your blackberries, you may need to add a touch of sugar syrup.

7	fresh	**Blackberries**
2	shot(s)	**Ketel One vodka**
1	shot(s)	**Pressed apple juice**
Float		**Double (heavy) cream**

Origin: Created in 2005 by yours truly.
Comment: A dessert in a glass, but not too sweet.

APPLE DAIQUIRI

Glass: Martini
Garnish: Apple wedge on rim
Method: **SHAKE** all ingredients with ice and fine strain into chilled glass.

2	shot(s)	**Bacardi Superior rum**
1½	shot(s)	**Pressed apple juice**
½	shot(s)	**Freshly squeezed lime juice**
¼	shot(s)	**Sugar syrup** (2 sugar to 1 water)

Origin: Formula by yours truly in 2004.
Comment: A classic Daiquiri with a very subtle hint of apple.

APPLE MARTINI

Glass: Martini
Garnish: Cherry in base of glass
Method: **SHAKE** all ingredients with ice and fine strain into chilled glass.

2½	shot(s)	**Ketel One vodka**
2	shot(s)	**Pressed apple juice**
¼	shot(s)	**Sugar syrup** (2 sugar to 1 water)

Variant: Sour Apple Martini, Caramelised Apple Martini
Origin: Formula by yours truly in 2004.
Comment: If freshly pressed juice is used, it's as good if not better than other Apple Martini recipes.

APPLE VIRGIN MOJITO (MOCKTAIL)

Glass: Collins
Garnish: Mint sprig
Method: **MUDDLE** mint in base of glass. Add apple juice, sugar and lime juice. Half fill glass with crushed ice and **CHURN** (stir) with bar spoon. Fill glass to brim with more crushed ice and churn some more. Continue adding crushed ice and churning until glass is filled. Serve with straws.

12	fresh	**Mint leaves**
3	shot(s)	**Pressed apple juice**
1	shot(s)	**Freshly squeezed lime juice**
¾	shot(s)	**Sugar syrup** (2 sugar to 1 water)

Variant: Add three dashes of Angostura aromatic bitters.
Comment: As non-alcoholic cocktails go this is one of the best.

APPILY MARRIED

Glass: Martini
Garnish: Coat half rim with cinnamon and sugar
Method: **STIR** honey with vodka in base of shaker until honey dissolves. Add apple juice, **SHAKE** with ice and fine strain into chilled glass.

2	spoons	**Runny honey**
2½	shot(s)	**Ketel One vodka**
½	shot(s)	**Pressed apple juice**

Origin: Created in 2005 by yours truly.
Comment: Apple and honey are indeed a marriage made in heaven, especially when laced with grainy vodka notes.

APRICOT FIZZ

Glass: Collins (8oz max)
Garnish: Lemon wedge
Method: **SHAKE** first three ingredients with ice and strain into ice-filled glass. **TOP** with soda water.

2	shot(s)	**Bols apricot brandy liqueur**
1	shot(s)	**Freshly squeezed orange juice**
½	shot(s)	**Freshly squeezed lime juice**
Top up with		**Soda water** (from siphon)

Comment: This low-alcohol, refreshing cocktail is perfect for a summer afternoon.

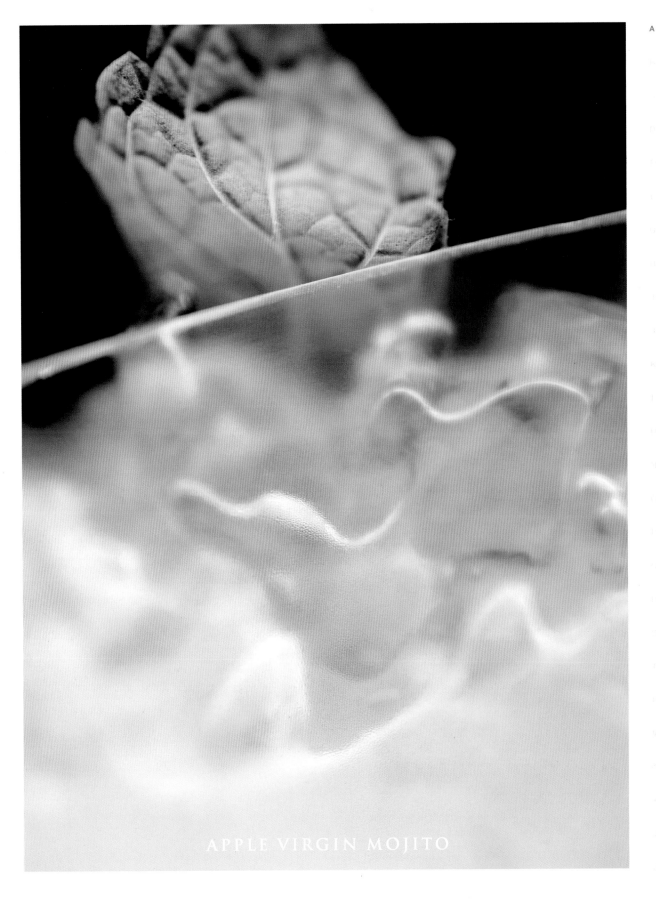

APPLE VIRGIN MOJITO

APRICOT LADY SOUR

Glass: Old-fashioned
Garnish: Lemon slice & cherry on stick (sail).
Method: SHAKE all ingredients with ice and strain into ice-filled glass.

1½	shot(s)	**Bacardi Superior rum**
1	shot(s)	**Bols apricot brandy liqueur**
1	shot(s)	**Freshly squeezed lemon juice**
¼	shot(s)	**Sugar syrup** (2 sugar to 1 water)
½	fresh	**Egg white**

Comment: This seemingly soft and fluffy, apricot flavoured drink hides a most unladylike rum bite.

DRINKS ARE GRADED AS FOLLOWS:

- ● DISGUSTING
- ●● PRETTY AWFUL
- ●● BEST AVOIDED
- ●●● DISAPPOINTING
- ●●● ACCEPTABLE
- ●●● GOOD
- ●●● RECOMMENDED
- ●●●● HIGHLY RECOMMENDED
- ●●●●● OUTSTANDING / EXCEPTIONAL

APRICOT MARTINI

Glass: Martini
Garnish: Lemon zest twist
Method: SHAKE all ingredients with ice and fine strain into chilled glass.

1½	shot(s)	**Tanqueray London dry gin**
1	shot(s)	**Bols apricot brandy liqueur**
¼	shot(s)	**Freshly squeezed lemon juice**
⅛	shot(s)	**Pomegranate (grenadine) syrup**
3	dashes	**Angostura aromatic bitters**
¾	shot(s)	**Chilled mineral water** (omit if wet ice)

Comment: This scarlet cocktail combines gin, apricot and lemon juice.

APRICOT RICKEY

Glass: Collins (small 8oz)
Garnish: Immerse length of lime peel in drink.
Method: SHAKE first three ingredients with ice and strain into ice-filled glass. **TOP** with soda.

1	shot(s)	**Tanqueray London dry gin**
1	shot(s)	**Bols apricot brandy liqueur**
½	shot(s)	**Freshly squeezed lime juice**
Top up with		**Soda water**

Comment: Light, fruity and refreshing, if a little on the sweet side.

APRICOT SOUR

Glass: Old-fashioned
Garnish: Lemon zest twist
Method: STIR apricot jam (preserve) with bourbon until it dissolves. Add other ingredients, **SHAKE** with ice and fine strain into ice-filled glass.

2	spoons	**Apricot jam (preserve)**
1½	shot(s)	**Bulleit bourbon whiskey**
½	shot(s)	**Bols apricot brandy liqueur**
1	shot(s)	**Pressed apple juice**
½	shot(s)	**Freshly squeezed lemon juice**

Origin: Created in 2005 by Wayne Collins for Maxxium UK.
Comment: Short and fruity.

ARIZONA BREEZE

Glass: Collins
Garnish: Grapefruit wedge on rim
Method: SHAKE all ingredients with ice and strain into ice-filled glass.

2½	shot(s)	**Tanqueray London dry gin**
3	shot(s)	**Ocean Spray cranberry juice**
2	shot(s)	**Freshly squeezed grapefruit juice**

Comment: A tart variation on the Sea Breeze – just as dry as Arizona.

ARNAUD MARTINI

Glass: Martini
Garnish: Blackberry on rim
Method: STIR all ingredients with ice and strain into chilled glass.

1	shot(s)	**Tanqueray London dry gin**
1	shot(s)	**Noilly Prat dry vermouth**
1	shot(s)	**Crème de cassis or Chambord**

Origin: A classic cocktail named after the pre-war stage actress Yvonne Arnaud.
Comment: An interesting balance of blackcurrant, vermouth and gin. Sweet palate and dry finish.

ARNOLD PALMER (MOCKTAIL)

Glass: Collins
Garnish: Lemon slice
Method: SHAKE all ingredients with ice and strain into ice-filled glass.

2	shot(s)	**Freshly squeezed lemon juice**
1	shot(s)	**Sugar syrup** (2 sugar to 1 water)
3	shot(s)	**Cold breakfast tea**

Variants: Tom Arnold, John Daly
Origin: A popular drink throughout the United States. Named after and said to be a favourite of the legendary golfer.
Comment: Real lemon iced tea. Balanced and wonderfully refreshing.

APRICOT RICKEY

B

BACARDI COCKTAIL

Glass: Martini
Garnish: Maraschino cherry
Method: SHAKE all ingredients with ice and fine strain into chilled glass.

2	shot(s)	**Bacardi Superior rum**
½	shot(s)	**Freshly squeezed lime juice**
¼	shot(s)	**Pomegranate (grenadine) syrup**
½	shot(s)	**Chilled mineral water** (omit if wet ice)
⅛	shot(s)	**Sugar syrup** (2 sugar to 1 water)

Origin: The BACARDI COCKTAIL™, known in many parts simply as 'the BACARDI', was born in Cuba in 1917. With the growth of the cocktail culture in the USA after prohibition, it became extremely popular.

The BACARDI COCKTAIL first started as a version of the world-renowned Daiquirí, with grenadine added to the traditional Daiquirí mix of BACARDI Superior Rum, lime and sugar.

However, as time passed it was not always made using Bacardi rum. In 1936 the Bacardi Company sought to protect their consumers, their cocktail and the brand name by issuing a lawsuit against two establishments in New York City (The Barbizon-Plaza Hotel and The Wivel Restaurant in West Fifty-Fourth Street). The charge? -substituting Bacardi Superior rum with other rum in the BACARDI COCKTAIL.

The case was built on the premise that the rum was unique and uncopyable and when a customer asks for 'Bacardi' by name they should be given Bacardi rum. Although the president of the company refused to reveal any details of production process of the rum, the New York Supreme Court found that it was indeed unique and uncopyable and ruled that a Bacardi Cocktail must be made with Bacardi – 'if it lacks Bacardi rum, no bartender's concoction can be called a BACARDI COCKTAIL'.

Now seventy years old, the ruling still stands. When someone asks for the BACARDI COCKTAIL, or any other 'BACARDI' drink, by name, they are entitled to be served Bacardi Rum.

Comment: This classic salmon-pinky drink perfectly combines the subtle notes of apricot and almond in Bacardi with the rich sourness of lime juice and the sweetness of pomegranate syrup.

BACARDI COCKTAIL

BACARDI SPECIAL

Glass: Martini
Garnish: Maraschino cherry
Method: SHAKE all ingredients with ice and fine strain into chilled glass.

1½	shot(s)	**Bacardi Superior rum**
¾	shot(s)	**Tanqueray London dry gin**
½	shot(s)	**Freshly squeezed lime juice**
¼	shot(s)	**Pomegranate (grenadine) syrup**
⅛	shot(s)	**Sugar syrup** (2 sugar to 1 water)
½	shot(s)	**Chilled mineral water** (omit if wet ice)

Origin: This vintage adaptation of the 'Bacardi Cocktail' is thought to have originated in the mid 1930s in New York City.
Comment: Hit the perfect proportions and you will strike a wondrous balance of flavoursome rum, gin botanicals, limey sourness and fruity sweetness.

BALALAIKA

Glass: Martini
Garnish: Orange zest twist
Method: SHAKE all ingredients with ice and fine strain into chilled glass.

1¼	shot(s)	**Ketel One vodka**
1¼	shot(s)	**Cointreau triple sec**
1¼	shot(s)	**Freshly squeezed lemon juice**

Comment: Richly flavoured with orange and lemon.

BALD EAGLE

Glass: Martini
Garnish: Salt rim
Method: SHAKE all ingredients with ice and fine strain into chilled glass.

2	shot(s)	**Don Julio 100% agave tequila**
¾	shot(s)	**Freshly squeezed grapefruit juice**
½	shot(s)	**Ocean Spray cranberry juice**
¼	shot(s)	**Freshly squeezed lime juice**
¼	shot(s)	**Freshly squeezed lemon juice**
¼	shot(s)	**Sugar syrup** (2 sugar to 1 water)

Origin: Created for me in 2001 by Salvatore Calabrese at The Lanesborough Library Bar, London, England.
Comment: If you like Tequila and you like your drinks on the sour side, this is for you.

BALLET RUSSE

Glass: Martini
Garnish: Lime wedge on rim
Method: SHAKE all ingredients with ice and fine strain into chilled glass.

2	shot(s)	**Ketel One vodka**
¾	shot(s)	**Crème de cassis or Chambord**
1	shot(s)	**Freshly squeezed lime juice**
¼	shot(s)	**Sugar syrup** (2 sugar to 1 water)

Comment: Intense sweet blackcurrant balanced by lime sourness.

BANANA SMOOTHIE (MOCKTAIL)

Glass: Hurricane
Garnish: Banana chunk on rim
Method: BLEND ingredients with 12oz scoop of crushed ice. Pour into glass and serve immediately with straws.

3	shot(s)	**Pressed apple juice**
7	spoons	**Natural yoghurt**
3	spoons	**Runny honey**
1	fresh	**Banana**

Origin: Created in 2005 by Lisa Ball, London, England.
Comment: Serve with breakfast cereal and you'll be set up for the day. The high fresh banana content means this drink will quickly turn brown if left. This can be countered by adding fresh lemon juice and balancing with more honey but this detracts from the fresh banana flavour.

BARNUM (WAS RIGHT)

Glass: Martini
Garnish: Lemon zest twist
Method: SHAKE all ingredients with ice and fine strain into chilled glass.

2	shot(s)	**Tanqueray London dry gin**
1	shot(s)	**Bols apricot brandy liqueur**
½	shot(s)	**Freshly squeezed lemon juice**
2	dashes	**Angostura aromatic bitters**
½	shot(s)	**Chilled mineral water** (omit if wet ice)

Origin: 1930s classic resurrected by Ted Haigh in his 2004 book 'Vintage Spirits & Forgotten Cocktails'.
Comment: A classic cocktail flavour combination that still pleases.

BATANGA

Glass: Collins
Garnish: Salt rim
Method: POUR ingredients into ice-filled glass, stir and serve with straws.

2	shot(s)	**Don Julio 100% agave tequila**
½	shot(s)	**Freshly squeezed lime juice**
Top up with		**Cola**

Origin: The signature drink of the now legendary Don Javier Delgado Corona, the owner/bartender of La Capilla (The Chapel) in Tequila, Mexico. Still mixing, even in his eighties, Corona is noted for ritualistically stirring this drink with a huge knife.
Comment: Basically a Cuba Libre made with tequila in place of rum – an improvement.

BAY BREEZE

Glass: Collins
Garnish: Pineapple wedge on rim
Method: SHAKE all ingredients with ice and strain into ice-filled glass.

2	shot(s)	**Ketel One vodka**
1½	shot(s)	**Ocean Spray cranberry juice**
2½	shot(s)	**Pressed pineapple juice**

Comment: Pink, fluffy, sweet and easy to drink.

BEACH ICED TEA

Glass: Sling
Garnish: Lemon slice
Method: SHAKE all ingredients with ice and strain into ice-filled glass.

½	shot(s)	**Bacardi Superior rum**
½	shot(s)	**Tanqueray London dry gin**
½	shot(s)	**Ketel One vodka**
½	shot(s)	**Don Julio 100% agave tequila**
½	shot(s)	**Cointreau triple sec**
1	shot(s)	**Freshly squeezed lemon juice**
½	shot(s)	**Sugar syrup** (2 sugar to 1 water)
3	shot(s)	**Ocean Spray cranberry juice**

Comment: A Long Island Iced Tea with cranberry juice instead of cola.

> 'A MAN SHOULDN'T FOOL WITH BOOZE UNTIL HE'S FIFTY; THEN HE'S A DAMN FOOL IF HE DOESN'T.'
> WILLIAM FAULKNER

BEBBO

Glass: Martini
Garnish: Lemon zest twist
Method: STIR honey with gin in base of shaker until honey dissolves. Add other ingredients, **SHAKE** with ice and fine strain into chilled glass.

2	spoons	**Runny honey**
1½	shot(s)	**Tanqueray London dry gin**
1	shot(s)	**Freshly squeezed lemon juice**
½	shot(s)	**Freshly squeezed orange juice**
¼	shot(s)	**Chilled mineral water** (omit if wet ice)

Origin: A long lost relation of the Bee's Knees. This recipe is based on one from Ted Haigh's 2004 book 'Vintage Spirits & Forgotten Cocktails'.
Comment: Fresh, clean and citrusy with honeyed notes. Choose your honey wisely.

BEE STING

Glass: Collins
Garnish: Apple slice
Method: STIR honey with whiskey in base of shaker until honey dissolves. Add tequila and apple juice, **SHAKE** with ice and strain into ice-filled glass. **TOP** with a splash of ginger ale.

1	spoon	**Runny honey**
1	shot(s)	**Bulleit bourbon whiskey**
1	shot(s)	**Don Julio 100% agave tequila**
2	shot(s)	**Pressed apple juice**
Top up with		**Ginger ale**

Origin: Discovered in 2005 at The Royal Exchange Grand Café & Bar, London, England.
Comment: A delicately spiced, long, refreshing drink.

BEE'S KNEES #2

Glass: Martini
Garnish: Orange zest twist
Method: In base of shaker **STIR** honey with gin until honey dissolves. Add lemon and orange juice, **SHAKE** with ice and fine strain into chilled glass.

2	shot(s)	**Tanqueray London dry gin**
3	spoons	**Runny honey**
1	shot(s)	**Freshly squeezed lemon juice**
1	shot(s)	**Freshly squeezed orange juice**

Variant: Made with light rum in place of gin this drink becomes a Honeysuckle Martini.
Origin: Adapted from David A. Embury's 1948 'The Fine Art of Mixing Drinks'.
Comment: This concoction really is the bee's knees.

BEE'S KNEES #3

Glass: Martini
Garnish: Lemon zest twist
Method: In base of shaker **STIR** honey with gin until honey dissolves. Add lemon juice, **SHAKE** with ice and fine strain into chilled glass.

2	shot(s)	**Tanqueray London dry gin**
3	spoons	**Runny honey**
¾	shot(s)	**Freshly squeezed lemon juice**

Comment: The combination of honey and lemon suggests flu relief but don't wait for an ailment before trying this soothing concoction.

BERMUDA ROSE COCKTAIL

Glass: Martini
Garnish: Apricot slice (dried or fresh) on rim
Method: SHAKE all ingredients with ice and fine strain into chilled glass.

2	shot(s)	**Tanqueray London dry gin**
½	shot(s)	**Bols apricot brandy liqueur**
¼	shot(s)	**Pomegranate (grenadine) syrup**
½	shot(s)	**Chilled mineral water** (omit if wet ice)

Origin: Adapted from Victor Bergeron's 'Trader Vic's Bartender's Guide' (1972 revised edition).
Comment: Delicate, floral and aromatic. A hint of sweetness but not so as to offend.

BETWEEN DECKS

Glass: Collins
Garnish: Pineapple wedge, mint & cherry
Method: SHAKE all ingredients with ice and strain into ice-filled glass.

2½	shot(s)	**Tanqueray London dry gin**
1	shot(s)	**Freshly squeezed orange juice**
1	shot(s)	**Ocean Spray cranberry juice**
½	shot(s)	**Freshly squeezed lime juice**
¼	shot(s)	**Sugar syrup** (2 sugar to 1 water)
½	shot(s)	**Chilled mineral water** (omit if wet ice)

Origin: Adapted from Victor Bergeron's 'Trader Vic's Bartender's Guide' (1972 revised edition).
Comment: I've upped the ante on this drink with more gin and less fruit than the original - so beware.

BETWEEN THE SHEETS #1 (CLASSIC FORMULA)

Glass: Martini
Garnish: Lemon zest twist
Method: SHAKE all ingredients with ice and fine strain into chilled glass.

1	shot(s)	**Bacardi Superior rum**
1	shot(s)	**Courvoisier V.S.O.P. cognac**
1	shot(s)	**Cointreau triple sec**
¼	shot(s)	**Freshly squeezed lemon juice**

Origin: Created in the 1930s by Harry MacElhone, of Harry's New York Bar in Paris, and derived from the Sidecar.
Comment: Three shots of 40% alcohol and a splash of lemon juice make for a tart drink which should not be undertaken lightly.

'TO ALCOHOL! THE CAUSE OF, AND SOLUTION TO, ALL OF LIFE'S PROBLEMS!'
HOMER SIMPSON

BETWEEN THE SHEETS #2 (DIFFORD'S FORMULA)

Glass: Martini
Garnish: Lemon zest twist
Method: SHAKE all ingredients with ice and fine strain into chilled glass.

¾	shot(s)	**Bacardi Superior rum**
¾	shot(s)	**Courvoisier V.S.O.P. cognac**
¾	shot(s)	**Cointreau triple sec**
¼	shot(s)	**Freshly squeezed lemon juice**
⅛	shot(s)	**Sugar syrup** (2 sugar to 1 water)
½	shot(s)	**Chilled mineral water** (omit if wet ice)

Comment: Maintains the essential flavour and ingredients of the classic formula but is a little more approachable.

BEVERLY HILLS ICED TEA

Glass: Sling
Garnish: Lime zest spiral
Method: SHAKE first five ingredients with ice and strain into ice-filled glass. TOP with champagne and gently stir.

¾	shot(s)	**Tanqueray London dry gin**
¾	shot(s)	**Ketel One vodka**
1	shot(s)	**Cointreau triple sec**
½	shot(s)	**Freshly squeezed lime juice**
½	shot(s)	**Sugar syrup** (2 sugar to 1 water)
Top up with		**Brut champagne**

Comment: Very strong and refreshing.

BIARRITZ

Glass: Old-fashioned
Garnish: Orange slice & cherry on stick (sail)
Method: SHAKE all ingredients with ice and strain into ice-filled glass.

2	shot(s)	**Courvoisier V.S.O.P. cognac**
1	shot(s)	**Grand Marnier liqueur**
¾	shot(s)	**Freshly squeezed lemon juice**
½	fresh	**Egg white**
3	dashes	**Angostura aromatic bitters**

Comment: Basically a brandy sour with a little something extra from the orange liqueur.

BINGO

Glass: Collins
Garnish: Lemon slice
Method: SHAKE first four ingredients with ice and strain into ice filled glass. TOP with soda water.

1	shot(s)	**Ketel One vodka**
1	shot(s)	**Grand Marnier liqueur**
1	shot(s)	**Bols apricot brandy liqueur**
½	shot(s)	**Freshly squeezed lemon juice**
Top up with		**Soda water** (club soda)

Comment: Refreshing, fruity long drink.

BITTER SWEET SYMPHONY

Glass: Martini
Garnish: Apricot slice
Method: SHAKE all ingredients with ice and fine strain into chilled glass.

½	shot(s)	**Ketel One vodka**
1	shot(s)	**Cointreau triple sec**
1	shot(s)	**Bols apricot brandy liqueur**
½	shot(s)	**Freshly squeezed lime juice**
1½	shot(s)	**Freshly squeezed grapefruit juice**

Origin: Adapted from a drink created in 2003 by Wayne Collins for Maxxium UK.
Comment: This roller coaster ride of bitter and sweet mainly features apricot and grapefruit.

BLACK CHERRY MARTINI

Glass: Martini
Garnish: Fresh or maraschino cherry
Method: SHAKE all ingredients with ice and fine strain into chilled glass.

2½	shot(s)	**Ketel One vodka**
1	shot(s)	**Crème de cassis or Chambord**

Comment: Subtle berry fruit tames vodka's sting.

BLACK FEATHER

Glass: Martini
Garnish: Lemon zest twist
Method: STIR all ingredients with ice and strain into chilled glass.

2	shot(s)	**Courvoisier V.S.O.P. cognac**
1	shot(s)	**Noilly Prat dry vermouth**
½	shot(s)	**Cointreau triple sec**
1	dash	**Angostura aromatic bitters**

Origin: Adapted from a drink created in 2000 by Robert Hess and published on drinkboy.com.
Comment: Rounded cognac notes with a hint of orange. For dry, adult palates.

BLACK MAGIC

Glass: Flute
Garnish: Black grape on rim
Method: MUDDLE grapes in base of shaker. Add liqueur, **SHAKE** with ice and fine strain into chilled glass. **TOP** with champagne.

12	fresh	**Red grapes**
½	shot(s)	**Grand Marnier liqueur**
Top up with		**Brut champagne**

Comment: More peachy in colour than black but balanced and tasty. Not sweet.

BLACK 'N' BLUE CAIPIROVSKA

Glass: Old-fashioned
Method: MUDDLE berries in base of glass. Add other ingredients. Fill glass with crushed ice, **CHURN** (stir) with bar spoon and serve with straws.

6	fresh	**Blackberries**
10	fresh	**Blueberries**
2	shot(s)	**Ketel One vodka**
½	shot(s)	**Freshly squeezed lime juice**
¾	shot(s)	**Sugar syrup** (2 sugar to 1 water)

Comment: A great fruity twist on the regular Caipirovska.

BLIMEY

Glass: Old-fashioned
Garnish: Lime wedge
Method: MUDDLE blackberries in base of shaker. Add other ingredients, **SHAKE** with ice and fine strain into glass filled with crushed ice. Serve with straws.

7	fresh	**Blackberries**
2	shot(s)	**Ketel One vodka**
¾	shot(s)	**Crème de cassis or Chambord**
1	shot(s)	**Freshly squeezed lime juice**
⅛	shot(s)	**Sugar syrup** (2 sugar to 1 water)

Origin: Created in 2002 by yours truly.
Comment: This blackberry and lime blend is both fruity and aptly named.

BLING! BLING!

Glass: Shot
Method: MUDDLE raspberries in base of shaker. Add vodka, lime and sugar, **SHAKE** with ice and fine strain into glass. **TOP** with champagne.

7	fresh	**Raspberries**
½	shot(s)	**Ketel One vodka**
½	shot(s)	**Freshly squeezed lime juice**
¼	shot(s)	**Sugar syrup** (2 sugar to 1 water)
Top up with		**Brut champagne**

Origin: Created in 2001 by Phillip Jeffrey at the GE Club, London, England.
Comment: An ostentatious little number.

BLINKER

Glass: Martini
Garnish: Lemon twist
Method: SHAKE all ingredients with ice and fine strain into chilled glass.

2	shot(s)	**Bulleit bourbon whiskey**
1	shot(s)	**Freshly squeezed grapefruit juice**
¼	shot(s)	**Pomegranate (grenadine) syrup**

Origin: A 1930s classic revisited.
Comment: Back in the 1930s David Embury wrote of this drink, "One of a few cocktails using grapefruit juice. Not particularly good but not too bad." How times have changed!

BLOODY JOSEPH

Glass: Collins
Garnish: Stick of celery
Method: SHAKE all ingredients with ice and strain into ice-filled glass.

2	shot(s)	**Johnnie Walker Scotch whisky**
4	shot(s)	**Pressed tomato juice**
½	shot(s)	**Freshly squeezed lemon juice**
7	drops	**Tabasco pepper sauce**
4	dashes	**Lea & Perrins Worcestershire sauce**
½	spoon	**Horseradish sauce**
2	pinches	**Celery salt**
2	pinches	**Black pepper**

Comment: A Bloody Mary with whisky.

BLOODY MARIA

Glass: Collins
Garnish: Salt & pepper rim plus celery stick
Method: SHAKE all ingredients with ice and strain into ice-filled glass.

2	shot(s)	**Don Julio 100% agave tequila**
4	shot(s)	**Pressed tomato juice**
½	shot(s)	**Freshly squeezed lemon juice**
7	drops	**Tabasco pepper sauce**
4	dashes	**Lea & Perrins Worcestershire sauce**
½	spoon	**Horseradish sauce**
2	pinches	**Celery salt**
2	pinches	**Black pepper**

Comment: Tequila adds a very interesting kick to the classic Bloody Mary.

B

BLOODY MARY

(MODERN RECIPE)

Glass: Collins
Garnish: Salt & pepper rim plus celery stick
Method: SHAKE all ingredients with ice and strain into ice-filled glass.

2	shot(s)	**Ketel One vodka**
4	shot(s)	**Pressed tomato juice**
½	shot(s)	**Freshly squeezed lemon juice**
7	drops	**Tabasco pepper sauce**
4	dashes	**Lea & Perrins Worcestershire sauce**
2	pinches	**Celery salt**
2	pinches	**Black pepper**

Origin: The creation of The Bloody Mary is a matter of some dispute, but is generally credited to Fernand Petiot. Whether this was in 1920 (or 1921), when Petiot was a young bartender at Harry's New York Bar in Paris, or in America, during the 1940s, after the comedian George Jessel had first popularised the unspiced combination of vodka and tomato juice, is not clear.

If you believe that Petiot first created it around 1920, then you will believe that the name is borrowed not from the English Queen Mary I, whose persecution of Protestants gave her that name, or for the silent movie actress Mary Pickford, but from one of Petiot's customers, apparently the entertainer Roy Barton. He had worked at a nightclub (or knew a bar) called the Bucket of Blood in Chicago, where there was a waitress known as 'Bloody Mary', and he said the drink reminded him of her.

If you believe Petiot invented it in New York, where he worked at the St. Regis Hotel certainly from the end of Prohibition, then he may have had assistance in its creation from Serge Obolansky, the manager of the hotel, who asked him to spice up his 50-50 blend of vodka and tomato juice. According to this version, he attempted to rename the drink Red Snapper, after Vincent Astor, who owned the hotel, found the name too crude for his clientele. (nowadays a Red Snapper is a Bloody Mary made with gin.)

The celery stick garnish apparently dates back to 1960 when a bartender at the Ambassador Hotel in Chicago noticed a lady stirring her drink with a celery stick.

Whatever the precise story behind this fantastic drink, Bloody Mary recipes are as personal as Martinis. Purists will only use Tabasco, Worcestershire sauce, salt and lemon to spice up tomato and vodka but everything from oysters to V8 can be added. Variations include:

Asian Mary (with wasabi, ginger & soy sauce)
Bloody Bull (with beef consommé)
Bloody Caesar (with clam juice)
Bloody Joseph (with Scotch whisky)
Bloody Maria (with tequila)
Bloody Maru (with sake)
Bloody Shame (without alcohol)
Bullshot (with beef bouillon)
Cubanita (with rum)
Red Snapper (with gin)
Comment: The classic brunch cocktail.

BLOODY MARY

BRAMBLE

BLOODY SHAME (MOCKTAIL)

Glass: Collins
Garnish: Celery stick
Method: SHAKE all ingredients with ice and strain into ice-filled glass.

5	shot(s)	**Pressed tomato juice**
½	shot(s)	**Freshly squeezed lemon juice**
8	drops	**Tabasco pepper sauce**
4	dashes	**Lea & Perrins Worcestershire sauce**
½	spoon	**Horseradish sauce**
2	pinches	**Celery salt**
2	pinches	**Black pepper**

AKA: Virgin Mary
Comment: Somehow missing something.

BLUE BLAZER

Glass: Two old-fashioned glasses
Method: STIR honey with boiling water until honey dissolves. Add Scotch and peel. **FLAME** the mixture and stir with a long handled bar spoon. If still alight, extinguish flame and strain into second glass.

2	spoons	**Runny honey**
¾	shot(s)	**Boiling water**
3	shot(s)	**Johnnie Walker Scotch whisky**
6	twists	**Lemon peel**

Variant: This drink was originally mixed by pouring the ingredients from one metal mug to another while ignited.
Origin: Created by 'Professor' Jerry Thomas, inventor of many famous cocktails in the 19th century. Thomas toured the world like a travelling showman, displaying this and other drinks.
Comment: Only attempt to make this the original way if you're very experienced or very stupid.

BORA BORA BREW (MOCKTAIL)

Glass: Collins
Garnish: Pineapple wedge
Method: SHAKE first two ingredients with ice and strain into ice-filled glass. **TOP** with ginger ale.

3	shot(s)	**Pressed pineapple juice**
⅛	shot(s)	**Pomegranate (grenadine) syrup**
Top up with		**Ginger ale**

Comment: Fruity and frothy ginger beer.

BOSTON

Glass: Martini
Garnish: Apricot slice on rim
Method: SHAKE all ingredients with ice and fine strain into chilled glass.

1¾	shot(s)	**Tanqueray London dry gin**
1	shot(s)	**Bols apricot brandy liqueur**
1	shot(s)	**Freshly squeezed lemon juice**
¼	shot(s)	**Sugar syrup** (2 sugar to 1 water)
⅛	shot(s)	**Pomegranate (grenadine) syrup**

Comment: Gin laced tangy fruit.

BOURBON SMASH

Glass: Collins
Garnish: Lime slice
Method: MUDDLE raspberries in base of shaker. Add other ingredients, **SHAKE** with ice and fine strain into ice-filled glass.

12	fresh	**Raspberries**
4	fresh	**Torn mint leaves**
2½	shot(s)	**Bulleit bourbon whiskey**
3	shot(s)	**Ocean Spray cranberry juice**
1	shot(s)	**Freshly squeezed lime juice**
½	shot(s)	**Sugar syrup** (2 sugar to 1 water)
2	dashes	**Angostura aromatic bitters**

Comment: This refreshing long drink has a sharp edge that adds to its appeal.

BOXCAR

Glass: Martini
Garnish: Sugar rim
Method: SHAKE all ingredients with ice and fine strain into chilled glass.

2	shot(s)	**Tanqueray London dry gin**
½	shot(s)	**Cointreau triple sec**
¾	shot(s)	**Freshly squeezed lime juice**
⅛	shot(s)	**Pomegranate (grenadine) syrup**
½	fresh	**Egg white**

Comment: A White Lady in a sugar-rimmed glass with the addition of a dash of grenadine and substituting lemon juice for lime.

> **'ALWAYS DO SOBER WHAT YOU SAID YOU'D DO WHEN YOU WERE DRUNK. THAT WILL TEACH YOU TO KEEP YOUR MOUTH SHUT!'**
> CHARLES SCRIBNER, JR.

BRAMBLE

Glass: Old-fashioned
Garnish: Blackberries & lemon slice
Method: SHAKE first three ingredients with ice and strain into glass filled with crushed ice. **DRIZZLE** liqueur over drink to create a 'bleeding' effect in the glass. Serve with short straws.

2	shot(s)	**Tanqueray London dry gin**
1	shot(s)	**Freshly squeezed lemon juice**
½	shot(s)	**Sugar syrup** (2 sugar to 1 water)
½	shot(s)	**Crème de cassis or Chambord**

Origin: Created in the mid-80s by Dick Bradsell at Fred's Club, Soho, London, England.
Comment: One of the most enduring and endearing drinks to come out of the 1980s.

B

BRANDY BLAZER

Glass: Snifter & old-fashioned
Garnish: Lemon & orange zest twists
Method: POUR cognac into a warmed glass and rest the bowl of the glass on an old-fashioned glass so it lies on its side supported by the rim. **FLAME** the cognac and carefully move the glass back to an upright position sitting normally on your work surface. **POUR** in hot water (this will extinguish any remaining flame) and sugar. Stir, garnish and serve.

2	shot(s)	**Courvoisier V.S.O.P. cognac**
2	shot(s)	**Hot water**
¼	shot(s)	**Sugar syrup** (2 sugar to 1 water)

Origin: A variation on 'Professor' Jerry Thomas' Blue Blazer which involved theatrically pouring ignited brandy between two mugs. Please don't try this at home, kids.
Comment: One way to warm your winter nights.

'THE RELATIONSHIP BETWEEN A RUSSIAN AND A BOTTLE OF VODKA IS ALMOST MYSTICAL.'
RICHARD OWEN

BRANDY BUCK

Glass: Collins
Garnish: Lemon wedge
Method: SHAKE first three ingredients with ice and strain into ice-filled glass. **TOP** with ginger ale and serve with straws.

2½	shot(s)	**Courvoisier V.S.O.P. cognac**
¼	shot(s)	**Grand Marnier liqueur**
¼	shot(s)	**Freshly squeezed lemon juice**
Top up with		**Ginger ale**

Comment: Lemon juice adds balance to the sweet ginger ale. Cognac provides the backbone.

BRANDY COCKTAIL

Glass: Martini
Garnish: Lemon zest twist
Method: SHAKE all ingredients with ice and fine strain into chilled glass.

5	fresh	**Mint leaves**
2	shot(s)	**Courvoisier V.S.O.P. cognac**
¼	shot(s)	**Grand Marnier liqueur**
¼	shot(s)	**Sugar syrup** (2 sugar to 1 water)
1	dash	**Angostura aromatic bitters**

Origin: Vintage cocktail of unknown origin.
Comment: Subtle mint and citrus lightly flavour the cognac.

BRANDY FIZZ

Glass: Collins (8oz max)
Garnish: Lemon slice
Method: SHAKE first three ingredients with ice and fine strain into chilled glass (without ice). **TOP** with soda.

2	shot(s)	**Courvoisier V.S.O.P. cognac**
½	shot(s)	**Freshly squeezed lemon juice**
¼	shot(s)	**Sugar syrup** (2 sugar to 1 water)
Top up with		**Soda water** (from siphon)

Comment: A refreshing and tasty dry drink: cognac and lemon balanced with a little sugar and lengthened with soda.

BRANDY FLIP

Glass: Wine goblet or Martini
Garnish: Dust with freshly ground nutmeg
Method: SHAKE all ingredients with ice and fine strain into chilled glass.

1½	shots	**Courvoisier V.S.O.P. cognac**
¼	shot(s)	**Sugar syrup** (2 sugar to 1 water)
¼	shot(s)	**Double (heavy) cream**
1	fresh	**Egg**

Origin: A forgotten classic.
Comment: A serious alternative to advocaat for those without raw egg inhibitions.

BRANDY SMASH

Glass: Old-fashioned
Garnish: Mint sprig
Method: Lightly **MUDDLE** mint in base of shaker just enough to bruise. Add other ingredients, **SHAKE** with ice and fine strain into ice-filled glass.

7	fresh	**Mint leaves**
2	shot(s)	**Courvoisier V.S.O.P. cognac**
¼	shot(s)	**Sugar syrup** (2 sugar to 1 water)

Origin: A classic from the 1850s.
Comment: Sweetened cognac flavoured with mint. Simple but beautiful.

BRANDY SOUR

Glass: Old-fashioned
Garnish: Lemon slice & cherry on stick (sail)
Method: SHAKE all ingredients with ice and strain into ice-filled glass.

2	shot(s)	**Courvoisier V.S.O.P. cognac**
1	shot(s)	**Freshly squeezed lemon juice**
½	shot(s)	**Sugar syrup** (2 sugar to 1 water)
½	fresh	**Egg white**
3	dashes	**Angostura aromatic bitters**

Comment: After the Whiskey Sour, this is the most requested sour. Try it and you'll see why – but don't omit the egg white.

BRANDY FLIP

THE BUCK

BREAKFAST MARTINI

Glass: Martini
Garnish: Orange zest twist, slice of toast on rim
Method: STIR marmalade with gin in base of shaker until it dissolves. Add other ingredients, **SHAKE** with ice and fine strain into chilled glass.

1	spoon	**Orange marmalade**
2	shot(s)	**Tanqueray London dry gin**
¾	shot(s)	**Cointreau triple sec**
¾	shot(s)	**Freshly squeezed lemon juice**

Origin: Created in the late 1990s by Salvatore Calabrese at the Library Bar, London, England. It is very similar to the 'Marmalade Cocktail' created in the 1920s by Harry Craddock and published in his 1930 'The Savoy Cocktail Book'.
Comment: The success or failure of this tangy drink is partly reliant on the quality of marmalade used. Basically a White Lady with Marmalade.

BRONX (ORIGINAL)

Glass: Martini
Garnish: Maraschino cherry
Method: SHAKE all ingredients with ice and fine strain into chilled glass.

2	shot(s)	**Tanqueray London dry gin**
¼	shot(s)	**Noilly Prat dry vermouth**
¼	shot(s)	**Martini Rosso sweet vermouth**
1	shot(s)	**Freshly squeezed orange juice**

Variants: 1/ Bloody Bronx – made with the juice of a blood orange. 2/ Golden Bronx – with the addition of an egg yolk. 3/ Silver Bronx - with the addition of egg white. 4/ Income Tax Cocktail – with two dashes Angostura bitters.
Origin: Created in 1906 by Johnny Solon, a bartender at New York's Waldorf-Astoria Hotel (the Empire State Building occupies the site today), and named after the newly opened Bronx Zoo. Reputedly the first cocktail to use fruit juice.
Comment: A serious, dry, complex cocktail – less bitter than many of its era, but still quite challenging to modern palates.

THE BUCK

Glass: Collins
Garnish: Lemon wedge
Method: POUR first two ingredients into ice-filled glass and **TOP** with ginger ale. Stir and serve with straws.

2½	shot(s)	**Tanqueray London dry gin** (or other liqour)
½	shot(s)	**Freshly squeezed lemon juice**
Top up with		**Ginger ale**

Variant: The recipe above is for a Gin Buck, but this drink can also be based on brandy, calvados, rum, whiskey, vodka etc.
Comment: The Buck can be improved by adding a dash of liqueur appropriate to the spirit base. E.g. add a dash of Grand Marnier to a Brandy Buck, or Apricot Brandy to a Gin Buck.

BUCK'S FIZZ

Glass: Flute
Method: POUR ingredients into chilled glass and gently stir.

2	shot(s)	**Freshly squeezed orange juice**
Top up with		**Brut champagne**

AKA: Mimosa
Origin: Created in 1921 by Mr McGarry, first bartender at the Buck's Club, London.
Comment: Not really a cocktail and not that challenging, but great for brunch.

BULLDOG HIGHBALL

Glass: Collins
Garnish: Orange slice
Method: SHAKE first two ingredients with ice and strain into ice-filled glass. **TOP** with ginger ale and lightly stir. Serve with straws.

2	shot(s)	**Tanqueray London dry gin**
1½	shot(s)	**Freshly squeezed orange juice**
Top up with		**Ginger ale**

Comment: Light and easy drinking. Gin and orange lightly spiced with ginger.

BULLFROG

Glass: Collins
Garnish: Lime wedge
Method: POUR vodka and lime into ice-filled glass and **TOP** with lemonade.

2	shot(s)	**Ketel One vodka**
½	shot(s)	**Freshly squeezed lime juice**
Top up with		**Lemonade/Sprite/7-Up**

Comment: Long, dry and fresh.

BULL'S BLOOD

Glass: Martini
Garnish: Orange zest twist
Method: SHAKE all ingredients with ice and fine strain into chilled glass.

½	shot(s)	**Bacardi Superior rum**
1	shot(s)	**Courvoisier V.S.O.P. cognac**
1	shot(s)	**Grand Marnier liqueur**
1½	shot(s)	**Freshly squeezed orange juice**

Comment: This beautifully balanced fruity cocktail has a dry finish.

CACTUS BANGER

Glass: Martini
Garnish: Lime wedge on rim
Method: SHAKE all ingredients with ice and fine strain into chilled glass.

1	shot(s)	**Don Julio 100% agave tequila**
1	shot(s)	**Grand Marnier liqueur**
2	shot(s)	**Freshly squeezed orange juice**
½	shot(s)	**Freshly squeezed lime juice**

Comment: A golden, sunny looking and sunny tasting drink.

CAIPIRISSIMA

Glass: Old-fashioned
Method: MUDDLE lime in base of glass. Add other ingredients and fill glass with crushed ice. **CHURN** (stir) drink with bar spoon and serve with straws.

¾	fresh	**Lime cut into wedges**
2	shot(s)	**Bacardi Superior rum**
¾	shot(s)	**Sugar syrup** (2 sugar to 1 water)

Comment: A Daiquiri style drink made like a Caipirinha to give that rustic edge.

CAIPIROVSKA

Glass: Old-fashioned
Method: MUDDLE lime in base of glass. Add other ingredients and fill glass with crushed ice. **CHURN** (stir) drink with bar spoon and serve with straws.

¾	fresh	**Lime cut into wedges**
2	shot(s)	**Ketel One vodka**
¾	shot(s)	**Sugar syrup** (2 sugar to 1 water)

Comment: Lacks the character of a cachaça-based Caipirinha.

CALL ME OLD-FASHIONED

Glass: Old-fashioned
Garnish: Orange peel twist
Method: STIR sugar syrup and bitters with two ice cubes in a glass. Add one shot of cognac and two more ice cubes. Stir some more and add another two ice cubes and another shot of cognac. Stir lots more and add more ice.

2	shot(s)	**Courvoisier V.S.O.P. cognac**
¼	shot(s)	**Sugar syrup** (2 sugar to 1 water)
2	dashes	**Angostura aromatic bitters**

Origin: Created in 2001 by yours truly.
Comment: An Old-Fashioned made with cognac instead of whiskey – works well.

CANADIAN APPLE (MOCKTAIL)

Glass: Collins
Garnish: Apple slice
Method: SHAKE all ingredients with ice and fine strain into ice-filled glass.

3½	shot(s)	**Pressed apple juice**
1½	shot(s)	**Freshly squeezed lemon juice**
¾	shot(s)	**Maple syrup**

Origin: Adapted from a drink discovered in 2005 at the Four Seasons Hotel, Prague, Czech Republic.
Comment: Refreshing and balanced with just the right amount of citrus acidity.

CANCHANCHARA

Glass: Old-fashioned
Garnish: Lemon slice
Method: STIR honey with rum in the glass drink is to be served in. Add lemon juice and ice. **STIR** and serve.

3	spoons	**Runny honey**
2	shot(s)	**Bacardi Superior rum**
1½	shot(s)	**Freshly squeezed lemon juice**

Origin: The Cuban forerunner of the Daiquiri, as drunk by Cuban revolutionaries fighting off the Spanish at the end of the nineteenth century. To be really authentic omit the ice. Origin and this recipe from Christine Sismondo's 2005 'Mondo Cocktail'.
Comment: Achieve the perfect balance between sweet honey and sour lemon and this is a great drink.

CAPE CODDER

Glass: Old-fashioned
Garnish: Lime wedge
Method: SHAKE all ingredients with ice and strain into ice-filled glass.

2	shot(s)	**Ketel One vodka**
3	shot(s)	**Ocean Spray cranberry juice**
¼	shot(s)	**Freshly squeezed lime juice**

Variant: Without lime juice this is a Cape Cod. Lengthened with soda becomes the Cape Cod Cooler.
Origin: Named after the resort on the Massachusetts coast. This fish shaped piece of land is where some of the first Europeans settled in the US. Here they found cranberries, the indigenous North American berry on which this drink is based.
Comment: Dry and refreshing but not particularly interesting.

CAPPERCAILLE

Glass: Martini
Garnish: Pineapple wedge on rim
Method: STIR honey with whisky until honey dissolves. Add other ingredients, **SHAKE** with ice and fine strain into chilled glass.

2	spoons	**Runny honey**
2	shot(s)	**Johnnie Walker Scotch whisky**
½	shot(s)	**Cointreau triple sec**
½	shot(s)	**Bols apricot brandy liqueur**
1	shot(s)	**Pressed pineapple juice**
½	shot(s)	**Freshly squeezed lemon juice**

Origin: Created by Wayne Collins for Maxxium UK.
Comment: Wonderfully tangy, fruity Scotch.

CAIPIROVSKA

A

B

C

D

E

F

G

H

I

J

K

L

M

N

O

P

Q

R

S

T

U

V

W

X

Y

Z

CHAMPAGNE COCKTAIL

CARROL COCKTAIL

Glass: Martini
Garnish: Pickled walnut or onion
Method: STIR all ingredients with ice and strain into chilled glass.

2	shot(s)	**Courvoisier V.S.O.P. cognac**
1	shot(s)	**Martini Rosso sweet vermouth**

Origin: Adapted from Victor Bergeron's 'Trader Vic's Bartender's Guide' (1972 revised edition).
Comment: Aromatic wine and cognac – dry yet easy.

CASSINI

Glass: Martini
Garnish: Three blackberries
Method: SHAKE all ingredients with ice and fine strain into chilled glass.

2	shot(s)	**Ketel One vodka**
1½	shot(s)	**Ocean Spray cranberry juice**
¼	shot(s)	**Crème de cassis or Chambord**

Origin: Created in 1998 by yours truly.
Comment: A simple but pleasant berry drink.

CELTIC MARGARITA

Glass: Coupette
Garnish: Salt rim & lemon wedge
Method: SHAKE all ingredients with ice and fine strain into chilled glass.

2	shot(s)	**Johnnie Walker Scotch whisky**
1	shot(s)	**Cointreau triple sec**
1	shot(s)	**Freshly squeezed lemon juice**

Origin: Discovered in 2004 at Milk & Honey, London, England.
Comment: A Scotch Margarita – try it, it works.

CHAM CHAM

Glass: Flute
Garnish: Berries
Method: POUR liqueur into chilled glass and top with champagne.

½	shot(s)	**Crème de cassis or Chambord**
Top up with		**Brut champagne**

Comment: A pleasing blend of fruit and champagne to rival the Kir Royale.

CHAMPAGNE COCKTAIL

Glass: Flute
Garnish: Orange zest twist (spray & discard)
Method: COAT sugar cube with bitters and drop into glass. POUR cognac over soaked cube, then TOP with champagne.

1	cube	**Brown sugar**
3	dashes	**Angostura aromatic bitters**
1	shot(s)	**Courvoisier V.S.O.P. cognac**
Top up with		**Brut champagne**

Origin: First recorded in Jerry Thomas's 1862 book 'How To Mix Drinks', or 'The Bon Vivant's Companion', where he almost certainly mistakenly specifies this as a shaken drink. That would be explosive. Another early reference to Champagne cocktails is in Mark Twain's 1869 novel, Innocents Abroad. It is thought the drink found popularity after a bartender named John Dougherty won an 1899 New York cocktail competition with a similar drink named Business Brace.
Comment: This over hyped classic cocktail gets sweeter as you reach the dissolving cube at the bottom.

> **'I'VE BEEN DRUNK FOR ABOUT A WEEK NOW, AND I THOUGHT IT MIGHT SOBER ME UP TO SIT IN A LIBRARY.'**
> F. SCOTT FITZGERALD

CHAMPAGNE CUP

Glass: Flute
Garnish: Maraschino cherry
Method: STIR first three ingredients with ice and strain into chilled glass. TOP with champagne and gently stir.

¾	shot(s)	**Courvoisier V.S.O.P. cognac**
½	shot(s)	**Grand Marnier liqueur**
¼	shot(s)	**Maraschino syrup** (from cherry jar)
Top up with		**Brut champagne**

Comment: Sweet maraschino helps balance this dry drink.

CHELSEA SIDECAR

Glass: Martini
Garnish: Lemon zest twist
Method: SHAKE all ingredients with ice and fine strain into chilled glass.

1½	shot(s)	**Tanqueray London dry gin**
1	shot(s)	**Cointreau triple sec**
1	shot(s)	**Freshly squeezed lemon juice**
¼	shot(s)	**Sugar syrup** (2 sugar to 1 water)

Comment: Gin replaces cognac in this variation on the classic Sidecar.

C

CHEZ REVOLUTION

Glass: Martini
Garnish: Pineapple wedge on rim
Method: **MUDDLE** mint with rum in base of shaker. Add other ingredients, **SHAKE** with ice and fine strain into chilled glass.

4	fresh	**Mint leaves**
2	shot(s)	**Bacardi Superior rum**
¼	shot(s)	**Maple syrup**
2	shot(s)	**Pressed pineapple juice**

Origin: Created in 2003 by Ben Reed for the launch party of MJU Bar @ Millennium Hotel, London, England.
Comment: Complex and smooth with hints of maple syrup and mint amongst the pineapple and rum.

DRINKS ARE GRADED AS FOLLOWS:

● DISGUSTING	●● PRETTY AWFUL ●● BEST AVOIDED
●●● DISAPPOINTING	●●● ACCEPTABLE ●●●● GOOD
●●●● RECOMMENDED	●●●●○ HIGHLY RECOMMENDED
	●●●●● OUTSTANDING / EXCEPTIONAL

CHIMAYO

Glass: Martini
Garnish: Float apple slice
Method: **SHAKE** all ingredients with ice and fine strain into chilled glass.

2	shot(s)	**Don Julio 100% agave tequila**
½	shot(s)	**Crème de cassis or Chambord**
¾	shot(s)	**Pressed apple juice**
¼	shot(s)	**Freshly squeezed lemon juice**

Origin: Named after El Potrero de Chimayó in northern New Mexico, USA.
Comment: Apple juice and cassis take the sting off tequila.

CHIN CHIN

Glass: Flute
Method: **STIR** honey with Scotch in base of shaker until honey dissolves. Add apple juice, **SHAKE** with ice and strain into chilled glass. **TOP** with champagne.

½	spoon	**Runny honey**
1	shot(s)	**Johnnie Walker Scotch whisky**
½	shot(s)	**Pressed apple juice**
Top up with		**Brut champagne**

Origin: Created in 2002 by Tony Conigliaro at Isola, Knightsbridge, London, England.
Comment: Golden honey in colour and also in flavour. An unusual and great tasting

CINDERELLA

Glass: Collins
Garnish: Lemon slice
Method: **SHAKE** first five ingredients with ice and strain into ice-filled glass. **TOP** with soda water.

2	shot(s)	**Freshly squeezed orange juice**
1½	shot(s)	**Pressed pineapple juice**
¾	shot(s)	**Freshly squeezed lemon juice**
⅛	shot(s)	**Pomegranate (grenadine) syrup**
3	dashes	**Angostura aromatic bitters**
Top up with		**Soda water** (club soda)

Comment: Long, fresh and fruity.

CITRUS RUM COOLER

Glass: Collins
Garnish: Orange slice
Method: **SHAKE** first three ingredients with ice and strain into ice-filled glass. **TOP** with lemonade. Lightly stir and serve with straws.

1	shot(s)	**Bacardi Superior rum**
½	shot(s)	**Grand Marnier liqueur**
2	shot(s)	**Freshly squeezed orange juice**
Top up with		**Sprite/lemonade/7-Up**

Origin: Light, fruity, easy and very refreshing.

CLARIDGE COCKTAIL

Glass: Martini
Garnish: Lemon zest twist
Method: **SHAKE** all ingredients with ice and fine strain into chilled glass.

1½	shot(s)	**Tanqueray London dry gin**
1½	shot(s)	**Noilly Prat dry vermouth**
½	shot(s)	**Cointreau triple sec**
½	shot(s)	**Bols apricot brandy liqueur**

Origin: Adapted from Harry Craddock's 1930 'The Savoy Cocktail Book'.
Comment: Gin for strength, vermouth for dryness and liqueur to sweeten – an interesting combination.

CLIPPER COCKTAIL

Glass: Martini
Garnish: Lemon peel knot
Method: **SHAKE** all ingredients and fine strain into glass filled with crushed ice.

2	shot(s)	**Bacardi Superior rum**
2	shot(s)	**Noilly Prat dry vermouth**
½	shot(s)	**Pomegranate (grenadine) syrup**

Origin: Peggy Guggenheim's biography mentions that this cocktail was served during the 1940s on the Boeing flying boats known as Clippers.
Comment: Light, easy drinking and very refreshing.

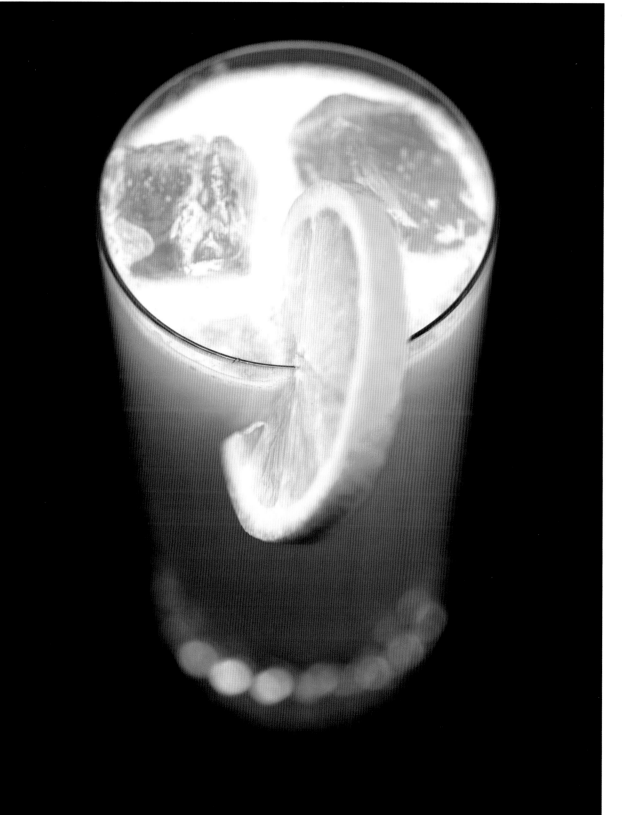

CITRUS RUM COOLER

COLONEL COLLINS

CLOCKWORK ORANGE

Glass: Collins
Garnish: Orange slice in glass
Method: SHAKE all ingredients with ice and strain into ice-filled glass.

1½	shot(s)	Courvoisier V.S.O.P. cognac
1½	shot(s)	Grand Marnier liqueur
3	shot(s)	Freshly squeezed orange juice

Comment: Neither as memorable nor as controversial as the film but a pleasant orange drink all the same.

> 'IF YOU DRINK, DON'T DRIVE.
> DON'T EVEN PUTT.'
> DEAN MARTIN

CLOVER CLUB COCKTAIL

Glass: Coupette/Martini
Garnish: None
Method: SHAKE all ingredients with ice and fine strain into chilled glass.

1½	shot(s)	Tanqueray London dry gin
½	shot(s)	Noilly Prat dry vermouth
¼	shot(s)	Freshly squeezed lemon juice
¼	shot(s)	Pomegranate (grenadine) syrup
½	fresh	Egg white

AKA: With a mint leaf garnish this drink called a 'Clover Leaf'.
Origin: The earliest known written recipe for a Clover Club lies in Paul E. Lowe's 1909 book 'Drinks - How to Mix and Serve'. Lowe's recipe omits the lemon juice but this is thought to be a mistake. Albert Stevens Crockett credits the creation of this cocktail to the Bellevue-Stratford Hotel, Philadelphia in his 1931 book Old Waldorf Bar Days.
Comment: This recipe Clover Club recipe is interesting due to its inclusion of vermouth.

CLOVER LEAF COCKTAIL #1 (CLASSIC)

Glass: Martini
Garnish: Float mint leaf
Method: SHAKE all ingredients with ice and fine strain into chilled glass.

2	shot(s)	Tanqueray London dry gin
¾	shot(s)	Freshly squeezed lemon juice
¾	shot(s)	Pomegranate (grenadine) syrup
½	fresh	Egg white

Variant: With raspberry syrup in place of pomegranate syrup.
AKA: Called a 'Clover Club' without the mint garnish.
Origin: This classic cocktail is thought to have been created at the Bellevue-Stratford Hotel in Philadelphia.
Comment: Smooth, aromatic, fruity & medium sweet.

CLOVER LEAF COCKTAIL #2 (MODERN)

Glass: Martini
Garnish: Clover/mint leaf
Method: MUDDLE raspberries in base of shaker. Add other ingredients, SHAKE with ice and fine strain into chilled glass.

7	fresh	Raspberries
3	fresh	Mint leaves (torn)
2	shot(s)	Tanqueray London dry gin
¾	shot(s)	Freshly squeezed lemon juice
½	shot(s)	Pomegranate (grenadine) syrup
½	fresh	Egg white

Comment: Carpet scaring red, this fruity adaptation perhaps has a wider appeal than the original Clover Leaf.

COLONEL COLLINS

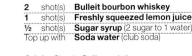

Glass: Collins
Garnish: Orange slice & cherry on stick (sail)
Method: SHAKE first three ingredients with ice and strain into ice-filled glass. TOP with soda, stir and serve with straws.

2	shot(s)	Bulleit bourbon whiskey
1	shot(s)	Freshly squeezed lemon juice
½	shot(s)	Sugar syrup (2 sugar to 1 water)
Top up with		Soda water (club soda)

Origin: Classic Collins variation.
Comment: Sweetened, soured and diluted bourbon.

COLONEL T

Glass: Sling
Garnish: Pineapple wedge
Method: SHAKE all ingredients with ice and strain into ice-filled glass.

2	shot(s)	Bulleit bourbon whiskey
1	shot(s)	Bols apricot brandy liqueur
2½	shot(s)	Pressed pineapple juice

Comment: Mellow pineapple, apricot and bourbon.

THE COMET

Glass: Martini
Garnish: Lemon zest twist
Method: MUDDLE grapes in base of shaker. Add other ingredients, SHAKE with ice and fine strain into chilled glass.

7	fresh	White grapes
2	shot(s)	Courvoisier V.S.O.P. cognac
¾	shot(s)	Grand Marnier liqueur
1	dash	Angostura aromatic bitters

Origin: Created by Eddie Clark at the Albany Club, Albemarle Street, London, to celebrate the launch of the Comet jetliner in 1952.
Comment: Cognac with freshly extracted grape juice and a splash of orange liqueur.

COSMOPOLITAN

COSMOPOLITAN
(DIFFORD'S FORMULA)

Glass: Martini
Garnish: Flamed orange zest twist
Method: SHAKE all ingredients with ice and fine strain into chilled glass.

1	shot(s)	**Ketel One vodka**
1	shot(s)	**Cointreau triple sec**
1½	shot(s)	**Ocean Spray cranberry juice**
½	shot(s)	**Freshly squeezed lime juice**
1	dash	**Fee Brother orange bitters** (optional)

Origin: The Cosmopolitan is one of those drinks that has had various incarnations through the ages – some of them, quite probably, independent of one another. And during the 1990s, the familiar blend of cranberry, citrus and vodka was one of the most popular cocktails in London and New York.

Most people agree a Cosmopolitan appeared on the West Coast of America at some point during the 1980s, and travelled from there to New York and beyond. Cheryl Cook has a claim to have invented the drink during the later half of the 1980s while head bartender at The Strand on Washington Avenue, South Beach, Miami. She apparently based her drink on the newly available Absolut Citron vodka and added a splash of triple sec, a dash of Rose's lime and, in her own words, "just enough cranberry to make it oh so pretty in pink". Her version is believed to have travelled by way of San Francisco to Manhattan where Toby Cecchini is credited with first using fresh lime juice in place of Rose's at his Passerby bar.

A likely early ancestor of the Cosmopolitan is the Harpoon, a drink promoted by Ocean Spray during the 1960s which consisted of vodka, cranberry juice and a squeeze of fresh lime. And a long-forgotten 1934 book of gin recipes, 'Pioneers of Mixing Gin at Elite Bars', contains a recipe for a Cosmopolitan that is very similar to today's drink, only with lemon in place of lime, gin in place of vodka, and raspberry in place of cranberry.

Whatever the origin, however, it was Sex And The City's Carrie Bradshaw who popularised the drink when she swapped Martinis for Cosmos. And New York's Dale DeGroff played a large part in refining today's popular recipe.

Comment: An authentic Cosmopolitan should be made with citrus vodka and this formula also works well if flavoured vodka is substituted. However, I prefer the simplicity of this recipe which when quality juice with at least 24% cranberry is used, the balance of vodka, citrus, berry fruit and sweetness is perfect.

COSMOPOLITAN (1934 RECIPE)

Glass: Martini
Garnish: Orange zest twist
Method: SHAKE all ingredients with ice and fine strain into chilled glass.

2	shot(s)	**Tanqueray London dry gin**
½	shot(s)	**Cointreau triple sec**
¾	shot(s)	**Freshly squeezed lemon juice**
¼	shot(s)	**Pomegranate (grenadine) syrup**

Origin: Recipe adapted from 1934 'Pioneers of Mixing Gin at Elite Bars'.
Comment: Reminiscent of a Sidecar and, dependent on your syrup, well balanced. Thanks to drinkboy.com forum for first bringing this drink to my attention.

COUNTRY BREEZE

Glass: Collins
Garnish: Berries
Method: SHAKE all ingredients with ice and strain into ice-filled glass.

2	shot(s)	**Tanqueray London dry gin**
½	shot(s)	**Crème de cassis or Chambord**
3½	shot(s)	**Pressed apple juice**

Comment: Not too sweet. The gin character shines through the fruit.

COWBOY HOOF MARTINI

Glass: Martini
Garnish: Orange zest twist
Method: SHAKE all ingredients (including mint) with ice and fine strain into chilled glass.

7	fresh	**Mint leaves**
3	shot(s)	**Tanqueray London dry gin**
½	shot(s)	**Sugar syrup** (2 sugar to 1 water)
3	dashes	**Fee Brother orange bitters** (optional)

AKA: The Cooperstown Cocktail
Variant: Detroit Martini
Origin: Created in the early 90s by Dick Bradsell at Detroit, London, England.
Comment: Sweetened gin shaken with fresh mint.

CRANBERRY DELICIOUS (MOCKTAIL)

Glass: Collins
Garnish: Mint sprig
Method: MUDDLE mint in base of shaker. Add other ingredients, **SHAKE** with ice and strain into ice-filled glass.

12	fresh	**Mint leaves**
1	shot(s)	**Freshly squeezed lime juice**
½	shot(s)	**Sugar syrup** (2 sugar to 1 water)
4	shot(s)	**Ocean Spray cranberry juice**
3	dashes	**Angostura aromatic bitters**

Origin: Adapted from a drink created in 2006 by Damian Windsor at Bin 8945 Wine Bar & Bistro, West Hollywood, USA.
Comment: Cranberry juice given more interest with mint, lime and bitters. This drink contains trace amounts of alcohol but remains an effective driver's option.

CRANBERRY & MINT MARTINI

Glass: Martini
Garnish: Dried cranberries in base of glass & float mint leaf.
Method: Lightly **MUDDLE** mint in base of shaker, just enough to bruise. Add other ingredients, **SHAKE** with ice and fine strain into chilled glass.

9	fresh	**Mint leaves**
2	shot(s)	**Ketel One vodka**
1½	shot(s)	**Ocean Spray cranberry juice**
¼	shot(s)	**Pomegranate (grenadine) syrup**

Origin: Created in 2003 by yours truly.
Comment: This little red number combines the dryness of cranberry, the sweetness of grenadine and the fragrance of mint.

THE CROW COCKTAIL

Glass: Martini
Garnish: Lemon zest twist
Method: SHAKE all ingredients with ice and fine strain into chilled glass.

2	shot(s)	**Johnnie Walker Scotch whisky**
1	shot(s)	**Freshly squeezed lemon juice**
½	shot(s)	**Pomegranate (grenadine) syrup**

Origin: Adapted from Harry Craddock's 1930 'The Savoy Cocktail Book'.
Comment: If you use great syrup and have a penchant for Scotch then you could be pleasantly surprised by this drink.

HOW TO MAKE SUGAR SYRUP

To make your own sugar syrup, gradually pour TWO cups of granulated sugar into a saucepan containing ONE cup of hot water. Stir as you pour and carry on stirring and simmering until the sugar is dissolved. Do not let the water even come close to boiling and only simmer for as long as it takes to dissolve the sugar. Allow syrup to cool and pour into an empty bottle. Ideally, you should finely strain your syrup into the bottle to remove any undissolved crystals which could otherwise encourage crystallisation. If kept in a refrigerator this mixture will last for a couple of months.

THE CROW COCKTAIL

CRUSTA

C

CRUSTA
(GENERIC NAME)

Glass: Small wine goblet or flute

Garnish: The trick is to find a lemon or a small orange. I favour lemon, which fits into a small wineglass tightly enough to act as a watertight extension to the glass. Cut off both ends of the fruit and carefully remove the pulp to leave a barrel-shaped shell of skin. Place in the top of the glass - wineglasses tend to curve in on themselves and this helps retain the fruit. Wet the edge of the glass and exposed fruit shell with sugar syrup and dip in caster sugar to frost the edge of both peel and glass. Leave for a couple of hours to form hard crust.

Method: SHAKE all ingredients with ice and fine strain into pre-prepared glass.

2	shot(s)	**Liquor** (of your choice)
		Bacardi Superior rum
		Courvoisier V.S.O.P cognac
		Tanqueray London dry gin
		Bulleit bourbon whiskey
		Johnnie Walker Scotch whisky
½	shot(s)	**Freshly squeezed lemon juice**
¼	shot(s)	**Sugar syrup** (2 sugar to 1 water)
1	dash	**Angostura aromatic bitters**

Origin: The invention of the Crusta is credited to a Joseph Santina at the Jewel of the South or a Joseph Santini at the City Exchange in New Orleans sometime during the 1840s or 1850s. It first appeared in print as 'The Brandy Crusta' in Jerry Thomas' 1862 bartender's guide.

Crustas always contain a spirit, lemon juice and sugar – sometimes in the form of a liqueur or liqueurs. They are so named due to their sugar rim, which should be applied hours before the drink is made so that it is dried hard, or indeed crusty, when the drink is served. Crustas are also distinguished by being garnished with a band of orange or lemon zest, and are drunk from the rim of the fruit, rather than the rim of the glass.

As David A. Embury writes in his 1948 'The Fine Art of Mixing Drinks', "The distinguishing feature of the Crusta is that the entire inside of the glass is lined with lemon or orange peel. The drink may be served in either a wineglass or an Old-Fashioned glass, although it is much harder to make the peel fit in the Old-Fashioned glass."

Embury goes on to say, "While the 'Brandy Crusta' is the most common form of this drink, it is, after all, merely a Sour-type drink served in fancy style. Substitution of a different liquor as a base will give a Gin Crusta, a Rum Crusta, an Applejack Crusta, A Whisky Crusta, and so on."

Comment: Some cocktail historians, Ted Haigh included, consider the Crusta the forerunner of the Sidecar and in turn the Margarita. It's a very logical argument.

CUBA LIBRE

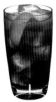

Glass: Collins
Garnish: Lime wedge
Method: **POUR** ingredients into ice-filled glass, stir and serve with straws.

2	shot(s)	Bacardi Superior rum
½	shot(s)	Freshly squeezed lime juice
Top up with		Coca-Cola

Variants: Cuba Pintada & Cuba Campechana
Origin: The Cuba Libre cocktail was born out of Cuba's War of independence with the Spanish in Cuba in 1900. Whilst drinking Bacardi Rum and Coca-Cola America Soldiers decided to make a toast to Cuba's freedom 'Por Cuba Libre!' and that's how the drink was christened.
Comment: The Cuba Libre – which originally started life as Bacardi Rum and Coca-Cola with a squeeze of fresh lime is now the world's most requested cocktail.

CUBA PINTADA

Glass: Collins
Garnish: Lime wedge
Method: **POUR** ingredients into ice-filled glass, stir and serve with straws.

2	shot(s)	Bacardi Superior rum
1	shot(s)	Cola
Top up with		Soda water

Variant: Cuba Campechana – rum with half soda and half cola; Cuba Libre – rum, cola and a dash of lime juice.
Origin: The name of this popular Cuban drink literally means 'stained Cuba' and there is just enough cola in this rum and soda to stain the drink brown.

> 'WHY DOES MAN KILL? HE KILLS FOR FOOD. AND NOT ONLY FOR FOOD: FREQUENTLY THERE MUST BE A BEVERAGE.'
> WOODY ALLEN.

CUBAN ISLAND

Glass: Martini
Garnish: Orange zest twist
Method: **SHAKE** all ingredients with ice and fine strain into chilled glass.

2	shot(s)	Bacardi Superior rum
½	shot(s)	Noilly Prat dry vermouth
½	shot(s)	Freshly squeezed lemon juice
¼	shot(s)	Sugar syrup (2 sugar to 1 water)

Origin: Adapted from a drink discovered in 2005 at DiVino's, Hong Kong, China.
Comment: The Daiquiri meets the Wet Martini. Interesting!

CUBAN MASTER

Glass: Collins
Garnish: Pineapple wedge
Method: **SHAKE** all ingredients with ice and strain into ice-filled glass.

1½	shot(s)	Bacardi Superior rum
1	shot(s)	Courvoisier V.S.O.P. cognac
1½	shot(s)	Freshly squeezed orange juice
1½	shot(s)	Pressed pineapple juice
½	shot(s)	Freshly squeezed lemon juice
¼	shot(s)	Sugar syrup (2 sugar to 1 water)

Origin: A classic cocktail I discovered in 1999 during a trip to Cuba.
Comment: Well balanced, wonderfully fruity.

CUBAN SPECIAL

Glass: Old-fashioned
Garnish: Orange zest twist
Method: **SHAKE** ingredients with ice and strain into ice-filled glass.

1½	shot(s)	Bacardi Superior rum
¾	shot(s)	Cointreau triple sec
2	shot(s)	Pressed pineapple juice
¼	shot(s)	Freshly squeezed lime juice

Comment: Rum blends well with orange, pineapple and lime.

CUBANITA

Glass: Collins
Garnish: Lime wedge
Method: **SHAKE** all ingredients with ice and strain into ice-filled glass.

2	shot(s)	Bacardi Superior rum
3½	shot(s)	Pressed tomato juice
½	shot(s)	Freshly squeezed lemon juice
7	drops	Tabasco pepper sauce
4	dashes	Lea & Perrins Worcestershire sauce
½	spoon	Horseradish sauce
2	pinches	Celery salt
2	pinches	Black pepper

Comment: The Bloody Mary returns - this time with rum.

CUCUMBER & MINT MARTINI

Glass: Martini
Garnish: Cucumber slice
Method: **MUDDLE** cucumber and mint in base of shaker. Add other ingredients, **SHAKE** with ice and fine strain into chilled glass.

2	inches	Peeled diced cucumber
7	fresh	Mint leaves
2	shot(s)	Ketel One vodka
1	shot(s)	Pressed apple juice
¼	shot(s)	Sugar syrup (2 sugar to 1 water)

Origin: Created in 2004 by David Ramos in the Netherlands.
Comment: A well balanced fortified salad in a glass – almost healthy.

CUBA LIBRE

DAIQUIRI NATURAL

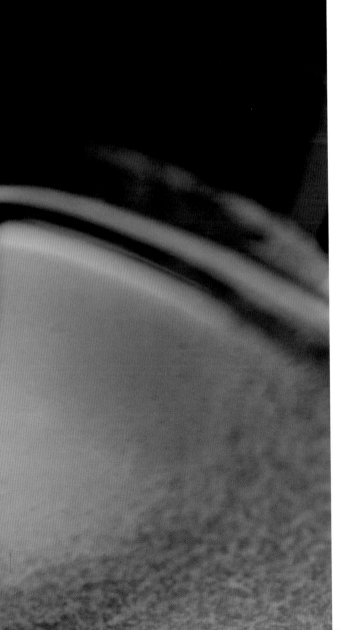

DAIQUIRI NATURAL NO.1 #1

D

Glass: Martini
Garnish: Lime wedge on rim
Method: SHAKE all ingredients with ice and fine strain into chilled glass.

2	shot(s)	**Bacardi Superior rum**
¾	shot(s)	**Freshly squeezed lime juice**
½	shot(s)	**Sugar syrup (2 sugar to 1 water)**
½	shot(s)	**Chilled mineral water**

Origin: Pronounced 'Dye-Ker-Ree',
Named after the town where it was first created, the Bacardi Daiquirí was invented by Jennings Stockton Cox, an American engineer who was working at a iron-ore mine near Santiago, Cuba, in 1898. Looking for a way to cool down in the relentless heat, Mr Cox started experimenting with his monthly ration of Bacardi Superior Rum which he had requested for his team. He finally perfected the recipe of lime, sugar, ice and Bacardi Superior rum and recorded it in his diary. The new drink quickly spread through the town of Daiquirí and nearby Santiago de Cuba. Wherever Cox went he taught the local bartenders how to make his sublime concoction. One day in late 1898 at the Hotel Venus, Mr Cox decided to finally baptise the cocktail - "I have it - we shall call it The Daiquiri!" - The legend was born!

During that summer of 1898, Jennings Stockton Cox had achieved something special. He had created the recipe for a drink that would soon become known for its perfect balance, its ability to test even the best bartenders, and – later in its life – its extraordinary versatility.

The Daiquirí is a mix of the four key elements of any cocktail: sweetness (from the sugar), sourness (the lime), strength (the rum) and dilution (the ice). To make the perfect Daiquirí, Cox believed that you had to have absolute balance of these four elements. He insisted that only Bacardi Superior Rum would do as it complemented rather than dominated the other ingredients. It was an essential part of his original recipe, recorded in his personal diary.

A hundred years after the Classic Daquirí was first conceived, it remains one of the cleanest and most refreshing cocktails. Despite the addition of fruit such as strawberries, watermelon and mango to make modern variants, some of which are included in this book, the essential ingredients of the genuine Daiquirí remain the same: lime, sugar, ice and Bacardi Superior Rum.

The Daiquirí seems to have come to America with US Admiral Lucius Johnson, who fought in the Spanish-American war of 1898. He introduced the drink to the Army & Navy Club in Washington DC and a plaque in their Daiquiri Lounge records his place in cocktail history.
Comment: This 'classic' Daiquirí is more correctly titled a 'Natural' Daiquirí, but both terms are generally recognised as denoting that the drink should be shaken and served 'straight-up' rather than blended with crushed ice.

DAIQUIRI NO.1 #2 (MODERN FORMULA)

Glass: Martini
Garnish: Lime wedge on rim
Method: SHAKE all ingredients with ice and fine strain into chilled glass.

2	shot(s)	**Bacardi Superior rum**
¼	shot(s)	**Freshly squeezed lime juice**
⅛	shot(s)	**Sugar syrup** (2 sugar to 1 water)
½	shot(s)	**Chilled mineral water** (omit if wet ice)

Origin: Throughout 2006 I kept encountering bartenders who favour this Daiquiri formula, particularly in London.
Comment: This modern style of Daiquiri emphasises the character of the rum. The influences of lime and sugar are very subtle.

DAIQUIRI NO.2

Glass: Martini
Garnish: Lime wedge on rim
Method: SHAKE all ingredients with ice and fine strain into chilled glass.

2	shot(s)	**Bacardi Superior rum**
⅛	shot(s)	**Cointreau triple sec**
¼	shot(s)	**Freshly squeezed orange juice**
½	shot(s)	**Freshly squeezed lime juice**
¼	shot(s)	**Sugar syrup** (2 sugar to 1 water)
½	shot(s)	**Chilled mineral water** (omit if wet ice)

Origin: Created circa 1915 by Constantino (Constante) Ribalaigua Vert at Floridita bar in Havana, Cuba.
Comment: Best described as a Daiquiri with subtle orange notes.

DAIQUIRI ON THE ROCKS

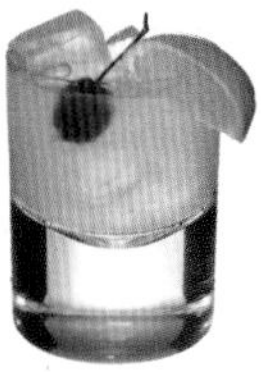

Glass: Old-fashioned
Garnish: Lime wedge & maraschino cherry
Method: SHAKE all ingredients with ice and strain into ice-filled glass.

2	shot(s)	**Bacardi Superior rum**
¾	shot(s)	**Freshly squeezed lime juice**
½	shot(s)	**Sugar syrup** (2 sugar to 1 water)

Comment: Some hardened Daiquiri-philes prefer their tipple served over ice in an old-fashioned glass, arguing that a Martini glass is too dainty.

DAISY DUKE

Glass: Old-fashioned
Garnish: Berries
Method: SHAKE all ingredients with ice and strain into glass filled with crushed ice. Serve with straws.

2	shot(s)	**Bulleit bourbon whiskey**
1	shot(s)	**Freshly squeezed lemon juice**
½	shot(s)	**Pomegranate (grenadine) syrup**

Origin: Created in 2002 by Jake Burger at Townhouse, Leeds, England.
Comment: This bright red drink tastes more adult than it looks.

DAMN-THE-WEATHER

Glass: Martini
Garnish: Orange zest twist
Method: SHAKE all ingredients with ice and fine strain into chilled glass.

1	shot(s)	**Tanqueray London dry gin**
1	shot(s)	**Martini Rosso sweet vermouth**
½	shot(s)	**Cointreau triple sec**
1½	shot(s)	**Freshly squeezed orange juice**

Comment: Gin and herbal notes emerge in this predominantly orange drink.

DELMONICO

Glass: Martini
Garnish: Orange zest twist
Method: STIR all ingredients with ice and strain into chilled glass.

1¼	shot(s)	**Courvoisier V.S.O.P. cognac**
1½	shot(s)	**Martini Rosso sweet vermouth**
1¼	shot(s)	**Noilly Prat dry vermouth**
3	dashes	**Angostura aromatic bitters**

Variant: If orange bitters are used in place of Angostura this becomes a Harvard.
Origin: A classic from the 1930s.
Comment: A Perfect Manhattan with cognac substituted for the whiskey.

DELMONICO SPECIAL

Glass: Martini
Garnish: Orange zest twist
Method: STIR all ingredients with ice and strain into chilled glass.

2¼	shot(s)	**Tanqueray London dry gin**
¼	shot(s)	**Courvoisier V.S.O.P. cognac**
¾	shot(s)	**Noilly Prat dry vermouth**
3	dashes	**Angostura aromatic bitters**

Origin: A classic from the 1930s.
Comment: A Wet Martini dried with a splash of cognac.

DAIQUIRI NO.1 #2

D

DETROIT

DERBY DAIQUIRI

Glass: Martini
Garnish: Orange zest twist
Method: **SHAKE** all ingredients with ice and fine strain into chilled glass.

2	shot(s)	**Bacardi Superior rum**
¾	shot(s)	**Freshly squeezed orange juice**
½	shot(s)	**Freshly squeezed lime juice**
¼	shot(s)	**Sugar syrup** (2 sugar to 1 water)

Comment: A fruity twist on the Classic Daiquiri.

D

DERBY FIZZ

Glass: Collins (8oz max)
Garnish: Lemon slice
Method: **SHAKE** first six ingredients with ice and strain into chilled glass. **TOP** with soda.

1¾	shot(s)	**Bulleit bourbon whiskey**
½	shot(s)	**Bacardi Superior rum**
¼	shot(s)	**Grand Marnier liqueur**
1	shot(s)	**Freshly squeezed lemon juice**
½	shot(s)	**Sugar syrup** (2 sugar to 1 water)
½	fresh	**Egg white** (optional)
Top up with		**Soda water** (from siphon)

Comment: An elongated sour with perfectly balanced strength, sweetness and sourness.

DETROIT MARTINI

Glass: Martini
Garnish: Float mint sprig
Method: **SHAKE** all ingredients (including mint) with ice and fine strain into chilled glass.

7	fresh	**Mint leaves**
3	shot(s)	**Ketel One vodka**
½	shot(s)	**Sugar syrup** (2 sugar to 1 water)
⅛	shot(s)	**Freshly squeezed lime juice**

Variant: Cowboy Hoof Martini
Origin: Created by Dick Bradsell in the mid 90s and based on his Cowboy Hoof Martini.
Comment: Vodka doused mint with the merest hint of lime. Clean and flavoursome.

DETROPOLITAN

Glass: Martini
Garnish: Flamed orange zest
Method: **SHAKE** all ingredients with ice and fine strain into chilled glass.

1	shot(s)	**Ketel One vodka**
½	shot(s)	**Cointreau triple sec**
¼	shot(s)	**Crème de cassis or Chambord**
1½	shot(s)	**Ocean Spray cranberry juice**
½	shot(s)	**Freshly squeezed lime juice**

Origin: Created at Detroit, London, England.
Comment: Yet another twist on the Cosmopolitan.

DIABLE ROUGE

Glass: Martini
Garnish: Berries on stick
Method: SHAKE all ingredients with ice and fine strain into chilled glass.

2	shot(s)	**Ketel One vodka**
2	shot(s)	**Pressed pineapple juice**
¼	shot(s)	**Crème de cassis or Chambord**

Comment: Not quite as rouge as the name would suggest. Hard to hate.

DIAMOND FIZZ

Glass: Collins (8oz max)
Garnish: Lemon slice
Method: SHAKE first three ingredients with ice and strain into chilled glass. **TOP** with champagne.

2	shot(s)	**Tanqueray London dry gin**
1	shot(s)	**Freshly squeezed lemon juice**
½	shot(s)	**Sugar syrup** (2 sugar to 1 water)
Top up with		**Brut champagne**

Origin: A long lost classic.
Comment: Why top a Fizz with soda when you can use champagne?

DICKENS' MARTINI

Glass: Martini
Garnish: None
Method: STIR vermouth with ice and strain to **DISCARD** excess, leaving the mixing glass and ice coated with vermouth. **POUR** gin over vermouth coated ice, **STIR** and strain into chilled glass.

¾	shot(s)	**Noilly Prat dry vermouth**
2½	shot(s)	**Tanqueray London dry gin**

Comment: A Dry Martini served without any garnish (i.e. no olive or twist). The name is a reference to Charles Dickens' novel Oliver Twist.

DIRTY MARTINI

Glass: Martini
Garnish: Olive on stick
Method: STIR all ingredients with ice and strain into a chilled glass.

2½	shot(s)	**Tanqueray London dry gin**
¼	shot(s)	**Brine from cocktail olives**
¼	shot(s)	**Noilly Prat dry vermouth**

AKA: F.D.R. Martini after the American president Franklin Delano Roosevelt.
Variant: Substitute vodka for gin.
Origin: Some attribute the creation of this drink to Roosevelt: the 32nd president was a keen home bartender, although his cocktails were reportedly 'horrendous', and there is no evidence that he used olive brine in his Martinis.
Comment: This drink varies from delicious to disgusting, depending on the liquid in your jar of olives. Oil will produce a revolting emulsion: make sure that your olives are packed in brine.

DNA

Glass: Martini
Garnish: Orange zest twist
Method: SHAKE all ingredients with ice and fine strain into chilled glass.

1½	shot(s)	**Tanqueray London dry gin**
¾	shot(s)	**Bols apricot brandy liqueur**
1	shot(s)	**Freshly squeezed lemon juice**
¼	shot(s)	**Sugar syrup** (2 sugar to 1 water)
2	dashes	**Fee Brothers orange bitters** (optional)

Origin: Created by Emmanuel Audermatte at The Atlantic Bar & Grill, London, England, in 1999.
Comment: Slightly sharp and very fruity, but pleasantly so.

DORIAN GRAY

Glass: Martini
Garnish: Orange zest twist
Method: SHAKE all ingredients with ice and fine strain into chilled glass.

1½	shot(s)	**Bacardi Superior rum**
¾	shot(s)	**Grand Marnier liqueur**
1	shot(s)	**Freshly squeezed orange juice**
¾	shot(s)	**Ocean Spray cranberry juice**

Origin: Discovered in 1999 at One Aldwych, London, England. This cocktail takes its name from Oscar Wilde's novel, in which a socialite's wish to remain as young and charming as his own portrait is granted. Lured by his depraved friend Lord Henry Wotton, Dorian Gray assumes a life of perversion and sin. But every time he sins the painting ages, while Gray stays young and healthy.
Comment: Fruity and rum laced, not overly sweet.

> 'I DRINK TO MAKE OTHER PEOPLE INTERESTING.'
> GEORGE JEAN NATHAN

DOWA

Glass: Old-fashioned
Garnish: Lime wedge
Method: STIR honey and vodka in base of shaker until honey dissolves. Add lime juice, **SHAKE** with ice and strain into glass filled with crushed ice. Serve with straws.

4	spoons	**Runny honey**
2½	shot(s)	**Ketel One vodka**
¼	shot(s)	**Freshly squeezed lime juice**

Origin: This cocktail is particularly popular in upscale hotel bars in Kenya where it is enjoyed by the safari set. The name translates as 'medicine'.
Comment: Very similar to the Caipirovska in its use of vodka, lime and crushed ice: the honey makes the difference.

DIRTY MARTINI

DRY MARTINI

DRY MARTINI #1
(TRADITIONAL)

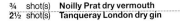

Glass: Martini

Garnish: The 'Oliver Twist' choice between an olive (stuffed or otherwise) or a lemon zest twist is traditional and these are the two most common garnishes for a Dry Martini. There are, however, a number of variants. A 'Dickens' is a Martini without a twist, a 'Gibson' is a Martini with two onions instead of an olive or a twist and a 'Franklin Martini' is named after Franklin Roosevelt and has two olives.

Method: STIR vermouth with ice and strain to discard excess, leaving the glass and ice coated with vermouth. **POUR** gin over vermouth coated ice, **STIR** and strain into a chilled glass.

¾	shot(s)	**Noilly Prat dry vermouth**
2½	shot(s)	**Tanqueray London dry gin**

Origin: The Martini and its origins is a topic that can raise temperatures among drinks aficionados and, as so often, no one really knows.

Today the drink is a blend of dry gin or vodka with a hint of Noilly Prat dry vermouth. Yet it seems to have evolved from the Manhattan via the Martinez, a rather sweet drink based on Dutch genever or Old Tom gin with the addition of Martini Rosso sweet vermouth, curaçao and orange bitters. The Martini, like the Martinez, was initially sweet, not dry (hence the need to specify that its descendant was a 'Dry' Martini), and very heavy on the vermouth by modern standards.

Martinis were known in the late 1880s but the Dry Martini most likely appeared with the emergence of the Tanqueray London dry gin style. In 1906 Louis Muckenstrum wrote about a Dry Martini Cocktail which, like the Martinez, benefited from curaçao and bitters as well as vermouth. Yet, unlike earlier versions, both the gin and the vermouth were dry. According to Gary Regan, the marketeers at Martini & Rossi vermouth were advertising a Dry Martini cocktail heavily at that time.

One myth attributes the creation of the Dry Martini to one Martini di Arma di Taggia, head bartender at New York's Knickerbocker Hotel, in 1911, although this is clearly too late. It is also no longer believed that the name relates to Martini & Henry rifles, the first of which was launched in 1871.

The Dry Martini seems to have got drier and drier over the years. Curaçao rapidly left the drink, but orange bitters remained a usual ingredient until the 1940s (interestingly, these are now coming back into vogue in some bars).

There is some debate as to whether a Martini should be shaken or stirred. It should be stirred. If shaken, it becomes a 'Bradford'. Shaking the drink increases the dilution and introduces air bubbles into the drink, making it taste fresher and colder but making the drink appear cloudy due to the introduction of tiny air bubbles.

The following are some of the most popular variations on the classic Dry Martini:

Dickens' Martini – without a twist.
Dirty Martini – with the brine from an olive jar.
Franklin Martini - named after Franklin Roosevelt and served with two olives.
Gibson Martini – with two onions.
Vesper Martini – James Bond's Martini, made with gin and vodka.
Vodkatini – very dry, vodka based Martini.
Wet Martini – heavy on the vermouth.

Comment: The proportion of gin to vermouth is a matter of taste, some say 7 to 1, others that one drop is sufficient. I recommend you ask the drinker how they would like their Martini, in the same manner that you might ask how they have their steak. If the drinker orders a 'Sweet Martini', use sweet red vermouth rather than dry and use a cherry as garnish instead of an olive.

DRY MARTINI #2 (NAKED)

Glass: Martini (frozen)
Garnish: Chilled olive on stick or lemon zest twist
Method: POUR water into glass, swirl around to coat and place in freezer for at least two hours, alongside gin, until the inside of the glass is covered in a thin layer of ice and the gin is frozen. POUR vermouth into icy glass and swirl to coat the ice with vermouth. POUR frozen gin into glass and serve immediately.

¼	shot(s)	Chilled mineral water
⅛	shot(s)	Noilly Prat dry vermouth
2½	shot(s)	Tanqueray London dry gin (frozen)

Variant: Use an atomiser to coat glass with vermouth. Based on vodka.
Origin: After the second world war, vermouth proportions in the classic Dry Martini dropped rapidly, and this 'Naked' style of serve began to appear. Traditionally both vermouth and gin had been stirred with ice. In a Naked Martini they are mixed by merely dousing a well chilled glass with a hint of vermouth and then pouring frozen gin into the vermouth coated glass.
 The trick to a good Naked Martini is still achieving some dilution by the addition of a splash of water in the glass before freezing. This is a trick I learnt from Salvatore Calabrese, originally from London's Duke's Hotel – famous for its Dry Martinis.
Comment: Dilution is achieved as the water you have frozen in the glass begins to melt. Both glass and gin must be freezing cold so that the temperature masks the strength of the alcohol. You have been warned!

DYEVITCHKA

Glass: Martini
Garnish: Orange zest twist
Method: SHAKE all ingredients with ice and fine strain into chilled glass.

1	shot(s)	Ketel One vodka
1	shot(s)	Cointreau triple sec
½	shot(s)	Freshly squeezed lime juice
¼	shot(s)	Sugar syrup (2 sugar to 1 water)
1½	shot(s)	Pressed pineapple juice

Comment: Pineapple replaces cranberry in this Cosmo-like cocktail.

EARL GREY MAR-TEA-NI

Glass: Martini
Garnish: Lemon zest twist
Method: SHAKE all ingredients with ice and fine strain into chilled glass.

2	shot(s)	Tanqueray London dry gin
1¼	shot(s)	Strong cold Earl Grey tea
¾	shot(s)	Freshly squeezed lemon juice
½	shot(s)	Sugar syrup (2 sugar to 1 water)
½	fresh	Egg white

Origin: Adapted from a drink created in 2000 by Audrey Saunders at Bemelmans Bar at The Carlyle, New York City.
Comment: A fantastic and very English drink created by a New Yorker. The botanicals of gin combine wonderfully with the flavours and tannins of the tea.

EAST INDIA #2

Glass: Martini
Garnish: Orange zest twist & nutmeg dust
Method: SHAKE all ingredients with ice and fine strain into chilled glass.

1½	shot(s)	Courvoisier V.S.O.P. cognac
1	shot(s)	Grand Marnier liqueur
2	shot(s)	Pressed pineapple juice
2	dashes	Angostura aromatic bitters

Origin: Another version of the East India classic, thought to originate with Frank Meier at the Ritz Bar, Paris.
Comment: A rich but bitter short drink based on cognac.

ECLIPSE

Glass: Collins
Garnish: Mint leaf & raspberry
Method: MUDDLE raspberries in base of shaker. Add other ingredients, SHAKE with ice and strain into glass filled with crushed ice. Serve with straws.

12	fresh	Raspberries
2	shot(s)	Bulleit bourbon whiskey
1	shot(s)	Crème de cassis or Chambord
½	shot(s)	Freshly squeezed lime juice
2	shot(s)	Ocean Spray cranberry juice

Origin: Signature cocktail at the chain of Eclipse Bars, London, England.
Comment: A fruity summer cooler which I challenge anyone not to like.

EGGNOG #1 (COLD)

Glass: Collins
Garnish: Dust with freshly grated nutmeg
Method: SHAKE all ingredients with ice and strain into ice-filled glass.

2½	shot(s)	Courvoisier V.S.O.P. cognac
½	shot(s)	Sugar syrup (2 sugar to 1 water)
½	shot(s)	Double (heavy) cream
1	fresh	Egg
2	shot(s)	Milk

Comment: Lightly flavoured alcoholic egg custard. Also try swapping dark rum for the cognac.

EGGNOG #2 (HOT)

Glass: Toddy
Garnish: Dust with freshly grated nutmeg
Method: POUR ingredients into heatproof glass and STIR thoroughly. HEAT in microwave oven for a minute (adjust time as appropriate to your oven) and STIR again. Alternatively, mix and warm in pan over heat – do not boil.

2½	shot(s)	Courvoisier V.S.O.P. cognac
½	shot(s)	Sugar syrup (2 sugar to 1 water)
½	shot(s)	Double (heavy) cream
1	fresh	Egg (white & yolk)
2	shot(s)	Milk

Comment: A warming, spicy and filling meal in a glass.

ECLIPSE

EL PRESIDENTE #3

EL PRESIDENTE NO. 1 (DAIQUIRI) #1

Glass: Martini
Garnish: Lime wedge on rim
Method: SHAKE all ingredients with ice and fine strain into chilled glass.

2	shot(s)	**Bacardi Superior rum**
¾	shot(s)	**Pressed pineapple juice**
½	shot(s)	**Freshly squeezed lime juice**
¼	shot(s)	**Pomegranate (grenadine) syrup**

Origin: Classic variation on the Daiquiri, of unknown origin.
Comment: Rum and pineapple combine wonderfully and the Daiquiri is the king of cocktails.

EL PRESIDENTE #2

Glass: Martini
Garnish: Lime zest twist
Method: SHAKE all ingredients with ice and fine strain into chilled glass.

2	shot(s)	**Bacardi Superior rum**
1	shot(s)	**Noilly Prat dry vermouth**
1	dash	**Angostura aromatic bitters**

Comment: Bone dry. Rather like a rum based, old school Martini.

EL PRESIDENTE #3

Glass: Martini
Garnish: Orange zest twist
Method: SHAKE all ingredients with ice and fine strain into chilled glass.

2	shot(s)	**Bacardi Superior rum**
1	shot(s)	**Noilly Prat dry vermouth**
½	shot(s)	**Cointreau triple sec**
¼	shot(s)	**Pomegranate (grenadine) syrup**

Origin: Adapted from Victor Bergeron's 'Trader Vic's Bartender's Guide' (1972 revised edition). Vic writes of this drink, "This is the real recipe".
Comment: A sweeter version of #2 above.

EL PRESIDENTE #4

Glass: Martini
Garnish: Orange zest twist
Method: STIR all ingredients with ice and strain into chilled glass.

1½	shot(s)	**Bacardi Superior rum**
¾	shot(s)	**Noilly Prat dry vermouth**
½	shot(s)	**Cointreau triple sec**

Comment: Dry but not bone dry, with balanced fruit from the triple sec and vermouth.

EL TORADO

Glass: Martini
Garnish: Float thin apple slice
Method: SHAKE all ingredients with ice and fine strain into chilled glass.

2	shot(s)	**Don Julio 100% agave tequila**
½	shot(s)	**Noilly Prat dry vermouth**
1½	shot(s)	**Pressed apple juice**

Origin: Popular throughout Mexico.
Comment: Dry, sophisticated and fruity, with tequila body.

EMBASSY COCKTAIL

Glass: Martini
Garnish: Orange zest twist
Method: SHAKE all ingredients with ice and fine strain into chilled glass.

1	shot(s)	**Courvoisier V.S.O.P. cognac**
1	shot(s)	**Bacardi Superior rum**
1	shot(s)	**Cointreau triple sec**
¾	shot(s)	**Freshly squeezed lime juice**
1	dash	**Angostura aromatic bitters**

Origin: Created in 1930 at the famous Embassy Club speakeasy in Hollywood, USA.
Comment: Bone dry – one for hardened palates.

EPESTONE DAIQUIRI

Glass: Martini
Garnish: Lime wedge
Method: SHAKE all ingredients with ice and fine strain into chilled glass.

2	shot(s)	**Bacardi Superior rum**
½	shot(s)	**Crème de cassis or Chambord**
½	shot(s)	**Freshly squeezed lime juice**
½	shot(s)	**Chilled mineral water** (omit if wet ice)

Comment: A pleasant, maroon coloured, blackcurrant flavoured Daiquiri.

EPIPHANY

Glass: Martini
Garnish: Berries on stick
Method: SHAKE all ingredients with ice and fine strain into chilled glass.

1¾	shot(s)	**Bulleit bourbon whiskey**
½	shot(s)	**Crème de cassis or Chambord**
2	shot(s)	**Pressed apple juice**

Origin: Created in 2004 by Naomi Young at Match, London, England.
Comment: Not sure what a fruity bourbon drink has to do with the manifestation of Christ.

ESQUIRE #1

Glass: Martini
Garnish: Orange zest twist
Method: SHAKE all ingredients with ice and fine strain into chilled glass.

2	shot(s)	**Bulleit bourbon whiskey**
¾	shot(s)	**Grand Marnier liqueur**
¾	shot(s)	**Freshly squeezed orange juice**
1	dash	**Angostura aromatic bitters**
½	shot(s)	**Chilled mineral water** (omit if wet ice)

Comment: Spicy bourbon laden with orange fruit.

THE ESTRIBO

Glass: Martini
Garnish: Berries on stick
Method: SHAKE all ingredients with ice and fine strain into chilled glass.

2	shot(s)	**Don Julio 100% agave tequila**
¼	shot(s)	**Crème de cassis or Chambord**
1	shot(s)	**Pressed pineapple juice**
½	shot(s)	**Double (heavy) cream**
½	shot	**Milk**

Origin: The signature drink at El Estribo, Mexico City, which sadly closed in 2005. The drink and this once legendary tequila bar's name translate as 'The Stirrup'.
Comment: Pink and creamy but with a tequila kick.

FAIR & WARMER COCKTAIL

Glass: Martini
Garnish: Orange zest twist
Method: SHAKE all ingredients with ice and fine strain into chilled glass.

2	shot(s)	**Bacardi Superior rum**
1	shot(s)	**Martini Rosso sweet vermouth**
½	shot(s)	**Cointreau triple sec**

Origin: Adapted from Harry Craddock's 1930 'The Savoy Cocktail Book'.
Comment: Sure to warm and fairly good.

FAIRBANKS COCKTAIL NO.1

Glass: Martini
Garnish: Maraschino cherry
Method: SHAKE all ingredients with ice and fine strain into chilled glass.

1	shot(s)	**Tanqueray London dry gin**
1	shot(s)	**Noilly Prat dry vermouth**
1	shot(s)	**Bols apricot brandy liqueur**
¼	shot(s)	**Freshly squeezed lemon juice**
¼	shot(s)	**Pomegranate (grenadine) syrup**
½	shot(s)	**Chilled mineral water** (omit if wet ice)

Origin: Adapted from Harry Craddock's 1930 'The Savoy Cocktail Book'.
Comment: Apricot liqueur dominates this cocktail but the Noilly Prat dry vermouth and dilution save it from excessive sweetness.

FIFTY FIFTY MARTINI

FANCY BRANDY

Glass: Martini
Garnish: Lemon peel zest
Method: SHAKE all ingredients with ice and fine strain into chilled glass.

2	shot(s)	**Courvoisier V.S.O.P. cognac**
¼	shot(s)	**Cointreau triple sec**
⅛	shot(s)	**Sugar syrup** (2 sugar to 1 water)
1	dash	**Angostura aromatic bitters**
½	shot(s)	**Chilled mineral water** (omit if wet ice)

Origin: Adapted from a recipe by Charles Schumann, Munich, Germany, and published in his 'American Bar'. Very similar to Jerry Thomas' Fancy Brandy Cocktail, published in his 1862 edition.
Comment: This appropriately named brandy based drink benefits from dilution, hence my addition of a splash of water.

FANTASIA (MOCKTAIL)

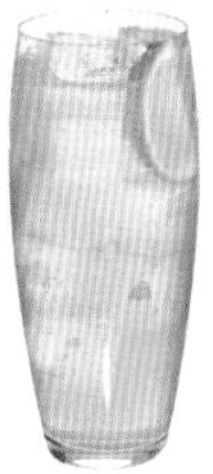

Glass: Collins
Garnish: Lime wedge
Method: SHAKE first four ingredients with ice and strain into ice-filled glass. **TOP** with lemonade, stir and serve with straws.

¼	shot(s)	**Freshly squeezed lime juice**
¼	shot(s)	**Freshly squeezed lemon juice**
¼	shot(s)	**Sugar syrup** (2 sugar to 1 water)
5	dashes	**Angostura aromatic bitters**
Top up with		**7-Up / lemonade / Sprite**

Origin: Discovered in 2004 at Claris Hotel, Barcelona, Spain.
Comment: A Spanish twist on the popular Australian LLB.

FIFTY-FIFTY MARTINI

Glass: Martini
Garnish: Olive on stick
Method: SHAKE all ingredients with ice and fine strain into chilled glass.

| 1½ | shot(s) | **Tanqueray London dry gin** |
| 1½ | shot(s) | **Noilly Prat dry vermouth** |

Origin: Adapted from Harry Craddock's 1930 'The Savoy Cocktail Book'.
Comment: A very 'wet' but wonderfully dry Martini which demands an olive, not a twist. Before you start – Craddock calls for it to be shaken.

FINE & DANDY

Glass: Martini
Garnish: Lemon zest twist
Method: SHAKE all ingredients with ice and fine strain into chilled glass.

1¾	shot(s)	**Tanqueray London dry gin**
¾	shot(s)	**Cointreau triple sec**
½	shot(s)	**Freshly squeezed lemon juice**
¼	shot(s)	**Sugar syrup** (2 sugar to 1 water)
½	shot(s)	**Chilled mineral water**
1	dash	**Angostura aromatic bitters**

Comment: A gin based drink that's soured with lemon and sweetened with orange liqueur.

FIREMAN'S SOUR

Glass: Old-fashioned
Garnish: Orange slice & cherry on stick (sail)
Method: SHAKE all ingredients with ice and strain into ice-filled glass.

2	shot(s)	**Bacardi Superior rum**
1	shot(s)	**Freshly squeezed lime juice**
½	shot(s)	**Pomegranate (grenadine) syrup**
½	fresh	**Egg white**

Origin: Circa 1930s, USA.
Comment: Smooth and balanced with great rum character. Lime fresh and fruity sweet.

FIX (GENERIC NAME)

Glass: Old-fashioned
Garnish: With fruit used in recipe
Method: SHAKE all ingredients with ice and strain into ice-filled glass.

2	shot(s)	**Liquor** (of your choice)
		Bacardi Superior rum
		Tanqueray London dry gin
		Bulleit bourbon whiskey
		Johnnie Walker Scotch whisky
1	shot(s)	**Freshly squeezed lemon juice**
1	shot(s)	**Sweet fruit juice** (often pineapple)
½	shot(s)	**Sugar syrup** (2 sugar to 1 water)

Origin: A Fix is a classic style of drink which constitutes of a spirit, lemon juice, and some kind of sweet fruit served short.
Comment: Match the juice and spirit and this formula works every time.

HOW TO MAKE SUGAR SYRUP

To make your own sugar syrup, gradually pour TWO cups of granulated sugar into a saucepan containing ONE cup of hot water. Stir as you pour and carry on stirring and simmering until the sugar is dissolved. Do not let the water even come close to boiling and only simmer for as long as it takes to dissolve the sugar. Allow syrup to cool and pour into an empty bottle. Ideally, you should finely strain your syrup into the bottle to remove any undissolved crystals which could otherwise encourage crystallisation. If kept in a refrigerator this mixture will last for a couple of months.

FIZZ

FIZZ
(GENERIC NAME)

F

Glass: Collins (8oz max)
Garnish: Lemon slice
Method: SHAKE first four ingredients with ice and strain into chilled glass (no ice in glass). **TOP** with soda dispensed from a siphon.

2	shot(s)	**Liquor** (of your choice)
		Bacardi Superior rum
		Tanqueray London dry gin
		Bulleit bourbon whiskey
		Johnnie Walker Scotch whisky
		Ketel One vodka
1	shot(s)	**Freshly squeezed lemon or lime juice**
½	shot(s)	**Sugar syrup** (2 sugar to 1 water)
½	fresh	**Egg white** (optional)
Top up with		**Soda water** (from siphon)

Origin: Like the Collins, this mid-19th century classic is basically a sour lengthened with charged water and at first glance there is little difference between a Fizz and a Collins. However, there are several distinguishing features. A Collins should be served in at least a twelve ounce, and ideally a fourteen ounce tall glass, while that used for a Fizz should be no bigger than eight ounces. A Collins should be served in an ice-filled glass, while a Fizz should be served in a chilled glass without ice. A Fizz should also be made using charged water from a siphon in preference to soda from bottles or cans. The burst of pressure from the siphon bulb generates tiny bubbles which give off carbonic acid, benefiting the flavour and the mouthfeel of the drink.

For the correct proportions I have turned to David A. Embury's seminal 'The Fine Art of Mixing Drinks'. He recommends "1 - or a little less – sweet (sugar, fruit syrup, or liqueur), 2 sour (lime or lemon juice), 3 - or a little more - strong (spirituous liquor), and 4 weak (charged water and ice). I interpret this as follows: 2 shots spirit (gin, whiskey, vodka, brandy), 1 shot lemon or lime juice, ½ shot sugar syrup, topped up with soda. I also like to add half a fresh egg white, which technically makes the drink a 'Silver Fizz'.

Comment: I recommend the Derby Fizz with its combination of liqueur and spirits over these more traditional versions.

FLIP
(GENERIC NAME)

Glass: Sour or Martini
Garnish: Dust with freshly grated nutmeg
Method: SHAKE all ingredients with ice and fine strain into chilled glass.

2	shot(s)	**Liquor** (of your choice)
		Bacardi Superior rum
		Courvoisier V.S.O.P cognac
		Tanqueray London dry gin
		Bulleit bourbon whiskey
		Johnnie Walker Scotch whisky
1	shot(s)	**Sugar syrup** (2 sugar to 1 water)
1	fresh	**Egg (white & yolk)**
½	shot(s)	**Double (heavy) cream**

Variant: Served hot in a toddy glass - heat in a microwave oven or mix in a pan over heat.
Origin: Flips basically consist of any fortified wine or liquor shaken with a whole egg and sweetened with sugar. They can also contain cream and are typically garnished with a dusting of nutmeg and served in a sour glass or small Martini glass. They can be served hot or cold.

The very first Flips, which emerged as early as the late 1600s, consisted of a tankard of ale to which a mixture made from sugar, eggs and spices was added before being heated with a red-hot iron poker from the fire. Later they came to mean any fortified wine or liquor shaken with a whole egg and sweetened with sugar.
Comment: I favour creamy, spicy, bourbon based Flips.

FLIP

THE FLIRT

Glass: Martini
Garnish: Lipstick on rim
Method: SHAKE all ingredients with ice and fine strain into chilled glass.

2	shot(s)	**Don Julio 100% agave tequila**
¾	shot(s)	**Bols apricot brandy liqueur**
¾	shot(s)	**Freshly squeezed lime juice**
1	shot(s)	**Ocean Spray cranberry juice**

Origin: Created in 2002 by Dick Bradsell at Lonsdale House, London, England.
Comment: A fruity drink to upset glass washers throughout the land.

FLIRTINI #1

Glass: Martini
Garnish: Pineapple wedge on rim
Method: SHAKE all ingredients with ice and fine strain into chilled glass.

2	shot(s)	**Ketel One vodka**
1½	shot(s)	**Pressed pineapple juice**
¼	shot(s)	**Crème de cassis or Chambord**

AKA: French Martini
Origin: Made famous on television's Sex And The City. Said to have been created in 2003 for Sarah Jessica Parker at Guastavinos, New York City, USA.
Comment: It's a French Martini! Hard not to like.

FLIRTINI #2

Glass: Martini
Garnish: Maraschino cherry
Method: SHAKE first three ingredients with ice and fine strain into chilled glass. **TOP** with champagne.

¾	shot(s)	**Ketel One vodka**
¾	shot(s)	**Cointreau triple sec**
2	shot(s)	**Pressed pineapple juice**
Top up with		**Brut champagne**

Origin: Adapted from a recipe by the New York bartender Dale DeGroff.
Comment: A flirtatious little number that slips down easily.

THE FLO ZIEGFELD

Glass: Martini
Garnish: Pineapple wedge on rim
Method: SHAKE all ingredients with ice and fine strain into chilled glass.

2	shot(s)	**Tanqueray London dry gin**
1	shot(s)	**Pressed pineapple juice**
¼	shot(s)	**Sugar syrup** (2 sugar to 1 water)

Origin: Named after Florenz Ziegfeld, the Broadway impresario, whose widow recalled the recipe for the 1946 'Stork Club Bar Book'.
Comment: The original recipe omits sugar but was probably made with sweetened pineapple juice.

FLORIDA COCKTAIL (MOCKTAIL)

Glass: Collins
Garnish: Orange slice & cherry on stick (sail)
Method: SHAKE first four ingredients with ice and strain into ice-filled glass, **TOP** with soda.

1	shot(s)	**Freshly squeezed grapefruit juice**
2	shot(s)	**Freshly squeezed orange juice**
½	shot(s)	**Freshly squeezed lemon juice**
¼	shot(s)	**Sugar syrup** (2 sugar to 1 water)
Top up with		**Soda water** (club soda)

Comment: The Florida sun shines through this fruity, refreshing drink.

FLORIDITA MARGARITA

Glass: Coupette
Garnish: Lime wedge & salted rim (optional)
Method: SHAKE all ingredients with ice and fine strain into chilled glass.

1½	shot(s)	**Don Julio 100% agave tequila**
½	shot(s)	**Cointreau triple sec**
½	shot(s)	**Ocean Spray cranberry juice**
¼	shot(s)	**Rose's lime cordial**
1½	shot(s)	**Freshly squeezed grapefruit juice**
¾	shot(s)	**Freshly squeezed lime juice**
½	shot(s)	**Sugar syrup** (2 sugar to 1 water)

Origin: Created in 1999 by Robert Plotkin and Raymon Flores of BarMedia, USA.
Comment: A blush coloured, Margarita-style drink with a well-matched amalgamation of flavours.

> **'I COULD NEVER QUITE ACCUSTOM MYSELF TO ABSINTHE, BUT IT SUITS MY STYLE SO WELL.'**
> OSCAR WILDE

FLYING SCOTSMAN

Glass: Old-fashioned
Garnish: Orange zest twist
Method: STIR all ingredients with ice and strain into ice-filled glass.

2	shot(s)	**Johnnie Walker Scotch whisky**
2	shot(s)	**Martini Rosso sweet vermouth**
¼	shot(s)	**Sugar syrup** (2 sugar to 1 water)
3	dashes	**Angostura aromatic bitters**

Comment: Sweetened Scotch with plenty of spice: like a homemade whisky liqueur.

FLYING TIGRE COCTEL

Glass: Martini
Garnish: Orange zest twist
Method: SHAKE all ingredients with ice and fine strain into chilled glass.

1¾	shot(s)	**Bacardi Superior rum**
¾	shot(s)	**Tanqueray London dry gin**
¼	shot(s)	**Sugar syrup** (2 sugar to 1 water)
⅛	shot(s)	**Pomegranate (grenadine) syrup**
3	dashes	**Angostura aromatic bitters**
¾	shot(s)	**Chilled mineral water** (omit if wet ice)

Origin: Adapted from a recipe in the 1949 edition of Esquire's 'Handbook For Hosts'. The drink is credited to an unnamed Captain serving in the US Marines, Amphibious Group Seven, at Santiago de Cuba in 1942.
Comment: Light, aromatic and complex – one to sip.

FOG CUTTER #2

Glass: Old-fashioned
Garnish: Orange slice
Method: SHAKE first five ingredients with ice and strain into glass filled with crushed ice. **DRIZZLE** liqueur over drink and serve with straws.

1	shot(s)	**Bacardi Superior rum**
½	shot(s)	**Courvoisier V.S.O.P. cognac**
½	shot(s)	**Tanqueray London dry gin**
½	shot(s)	**Freshly squeezed lime juice**
¼	shot(s)	**Sugar syrup** (2 sugar to 1 water)
¼	shot(s)	**Crème de cassis or Chambord**

Comment: A well balanced (neither too strong nor too sweet), short, fruity drink.

FOG HORN

Glass: Old-fashioned
Garnish: Lime wedge
Method: POUR ingredients into ice-filled glass and stir.

2	shot(s)	**Tanqueray London dry gin**
½	shot(s)	**Rose's lime cordial**
Top up with		**Ginger ale**

Comment: Different! Almost flowery in taste with the spice of ginger beer.

FORT LAUDERDALE

Glass: Martini
Garnish: Orange zest twist
Method: SHAKE all ingredients with ice and fine strain into chilled glass.

1½	shot(s)	**Bacardi Superior rum**
½	shot(s)	**Martini Rosso sweet vermouth**
1	shot(s)	**Freshly squeezed orange juice**
¼	shot(s)	**Freshly squeezed lime juice**

Comment: Rum, vermouth, lime and orange form a challenging combination in this golden drink.

FRANK SULLIVAN COCKTAIL

Glass: Martini
Garnish: Sugar rim & lemon zest twist
Method: SHAKE all ingredients with ice and fine strain into chilled glass.

1	shot(s)	**Courvoisier V.S.O.P. cognac**
1	shot(s)	**Cointreau triple sec**
1	shot(s)	**Noilly Prat dry vermouth**
1	shot(s)	**Freshly squeezed lemon juice**

Origin: Adapted from Harry Craddock's 1930 'The Savoy Cocktail Book'.
Comment: A Sidecar made dry with vermouth: it needs the sweet rim.

F

THE FRANKENJACK COCKTAIL

Glass: Martini
Garnish: Orange zest twist
Method: SHAKE all ingredients with ice and fine strain into chilled glass.

1½	shot(s)	**Tanqueray London dry gin**
1½	shot(s)	**Noilly Prat dry vermouth**
½	shot(s)	**Bols apricot brandy liqueur**
½	shot(s)	**Cointreau triple sec**

Origin: Adapted from Harry Craddock's 1930 'The Savoy Cocktail Book'.
Comment: Dry, sophisticated orange and apricot.

FRANKLIN MARTINI

Glass: Martini
Garnish: Two olives
Method: STIR vermouth with ice and strain to **DISCARD** excess, leaving the glass and ice coated with vermouth. **POUR** gin over vermouth coated ice, **STIR** and strain into chilled glass.

¾	shot(s)	**Noilly Prat dry vermouth**
2½	shot(s)	**Tanqueray London dry gin**

Comment: A Dry Martini garnished with two olives.

FRENCH 75

Glass: Flute
Garnish: Maraschino cherry
Method: SHAKE first three ingredients with ice and strain into chilled glass. **TOP** with champagne.

1½	shot(s)	**Tanqueray London dry gin**
½	shot(s)	**Freshly squeezed lemon juice**
¼	shot(s)	**Sugar syrup** (2 sugar to 1 water)
Top up with		**Brut champagne**

Origin: Legend has it that the drink was created by Harry MacElhone at his Harry's American Bar, Paris, and named after the 75mm field gun used by the French army during the First World War. However, he does not claim credit for the drink in his 1922 book.
Comment: Fresh, clean, sophisticated - very drinkable and hasn't dated.

FRENCH 76

Glass: Flute
Garnish: Maraschino cherry
Method: SHAKE first three ingredients with ice and strain into chilled glass. **TOP** with champagne.

1	shot(s)	**Ketel One vodka**
½	shot(s)	**Freshly squeezed lemon juice**
¼	shot(s)	**Sugar syrup** (2 sugar to 1 water)
Top up with		**Brut champagne**

Variant: Diamond Fizz
Comment: A Vodka Sour topped with champagne. Works well.

FRENCH DAIQUIRI

Glass: Martini
Garnish: Lime wedge on rim
Method: SHAKE all ingredients with ice and fine strain into chilled glass.

2	shot(s)	**Bacardi Superior rum**
1	shot(s)	**Crème de cassis or Chambord**
½	shot(s)	**Freshly squeezed lime juice**
¾	shot(s)	**Chilled mineral water** (omit if wet ice)

Comment: A classic Daiquiri with a hint of berry fruit.

FRENCH MARTINI

Glass: Martini
Garnish: Pineapple wedge on rim
Method: SHAKE all ingredients with ice and fine strain into chilled glass.

2	shot(s)	**Ketel One vodka**
1¾	shot(s)	**Pressed pineapple juice**
¼	shot(s)	**Crème de cassis or Chambord**

AKA: Flirtini
Comment: Raspberry and pineapple laced with vodka. Easy drinking and very fruity.

FRENCH MOJITO

Glass: Collins
Garnish: Raspberry & mint sprig
Method: Lightly **MUDDLE** mint in base of glass (just to bruise). Add rum, liqueur and lime juice. Half fill glass with crushed ice and **CHURN** (stir) with bar spoon. Continue to add crushed ice and churn until drink is level with glass rim.

12	fresh	**Mint leaves**
2	shot(s)	**Bacardi Superior rum**
½	shot(s)	**Crème de cassis or Chambord**
1	shot(s)	**Freshly squeezed lime juice**
¼	shot(s)	**Sugar syrup** (2 sugar to 1 water)

Comment: A classic Mojito with a hint of berry fruit.

FRENCH MULE

Glass: Collins
Garnish: Sprig of mint
Method: SHAKE first four ingredients with ice and strain into ice-filled glass. **TOP** with ginger beer, stir and serve with straws.

2	shot(s)	**Courvoisier V.S.O.P. cognac**
1	shot(s)	**Freshly squeezed lime juice**
1	shot(s)	**Sugar syrup** (2 sugar to 1 water)
3	dashes	**Angostura aromatic bitters**
Top up with		**Ginger beer**

Comment: This French answer to the vodka based Moscow Mule uses cognac to make a more flavoursome, long, refreshing drink.

FRENCH SHERBET

Glass: Martini
Garnish: Orange zest twist
Method: SHAKE all ingredients with ice and fine strain into chilled glass.

1	shot(s)	**Tanqueray London dry gin**
1	shot(s)	**Cointreau triple sec**
1	shot(s)	**Freshly squeezed orange juice**
1	shot(s)	**Freshly squeezed lime juice**

Comment: Not particularly French or sherbety – just a fresh orange wake-up call.

FRENCH SPRING PUNCH

Glass: Sling
Garnish: Strawberry
Method: SHAKE first four ingredients with ice and strain into ice-filled glass. **TOP** with champagne and serve with straws.

1	shot(s)	**Courvoisier V.S.O.P. cognac**
½	shot(s)	**Crème de cassis or Chambord**
1	shot(s)	**Freshly squeezed lemon juice**
½	shot(s)	**Sugar syrup** (2 sugar to 1 water)
Top up with		**Brut champagne**

Origin: Created by Dick Bradsell and Rodolphe Sorel at Match EC1, London, England, during the late 1990s.
Comment: Not as popular as the Russian Spring Punch but still a modern day London classic.

FRESCA NOVA

Glass: Flute
Garnish: Quarter orange slice
Method: SHAKE first four ingredients with ice and fine strain into chilled glass. Slowly **TOP** with champagne.

1½	shot(s)	**Grand Marnier liqueur**
¾	shot(s)	**Freshly squeezed orange juice**
¼	shot(s)	**Sugar syrup** (2 sugar to 1 water)
1	shot(s)	**Double (heavy) cream**
Top up with		**Brut champagne**

Origin: Created by Jamie Terrell for Philip Holzberg at Vinexpo 1999.
Comment: Cream, orange and champagne work surprisingly well.

FRENCH MULE

FROTH BLOWER COCKTAIL

FROTH BLOWER COCKTAIL

Glass: Martini
Garnish: Lemon zest twist (spray & discard)
Method: SHAKE all ingredients well with ice and fine strain into chilled glass.

2	shot(s)	Tanqueray London dry gin
¼	shot(s)	Pomegranate (grenadine) syrup
1	fresh	Egg white

Origin: Adapted from Harry Craddock's 1930 'The Savoy Cocktail Book'.
Comment: Salmon-pink and very frothy but surprisingly complex and tasty.

FRUIT SOUR

Glass: Old-fashioned
Garnish: Lemon zest twist
Method: SHAKE all ingredients with ice and strain into ice-filled glass.

1	shot(s)	Bulleit bourbon whiskey
1	shot(s)	Cointreau triple sec
1	shot(s)	Freshly squeezed lemon juice
½	fresh	Egg white

Comment: An orange influenced, sweet and sour whiskey cocktail.

FROZEN DAIQUIRI

Glass: Martini
Garnish: Maraschino cherry
Method: BLEND all ingredients with 6oz scoop of crushed ice. Serve heaped in the glass with straws.

2	shot(s)	Bacardi Superior rum
½	shot(s)	Freshly squeezed lime juice
¾	shot(s)	Sugar syrup (2 sugar to 1 water)

Variant: Floridita Daiquiri or with fruit and/or fruit liqueurs.
Origin: Emilio Gonzalez is said to have first adapted the Natural Daiquiri into this frozen version at the Plaza Hotel in Cuba.
Comment: A superbly refreshing drink on a hot day.

FRUIT TREE DAIQUIRI

Glass: Martini
Garnish: Half grapefruit wedge & cherry
Method: SHAKE all ingredients with ice and fine strain into chilled glass.

2	shot(s)	Bacardi Superior rum
¾	shot(s)	Bols apricot brandy liqueur
¾	shot(s)	Freshly squeezed grapefruit juice
¾	shot(s)	Freshly squeezed lime juice
¼	shot(s)	Maraschino syrup (from cherry jar)
½	shot(s)	Chilled mineral water (omit if wet ice)

Comment: A restrained Papa Doble with apricot liqueur.

FROZEN MARGARITA

Glass: Martini
Garnish: Maraschino cherry
Method: BLEND all ingredients with 6oz scoop of crushed ice. Serve heaped in the glass and with straws.

1½	shot(s)	Don Julio 100% agave tequila
¾	shot(s)	Cointreau triple sec
¾	shot(s)	Freshly squeezed lime juice
½	shot(s)	Sugar syrup (2 sugar to 1 water)

Variant: With fruit and/or fruit liqueurs.
Comment: Citrus freshness with the subtle agave of tequila served frozen.

FULL CIRCLE

Glass: Collins
Garnish: Pineapple wedge on rim
Method: Cut pomegranate in half and juice with a spinning citrus juicer. SHAKE all ingredients with ice and strain into ice-filled glass.

3	shot(s)	Freshly extracted pomegranate juice
2	shot(s)	Tanqueray London dry gin
¾	shot(s)	Pressed pineapple juice

Origin: Adapted from a drink discovered in 2004 at Mandarin Oriental, New York City, USA. The name is a reference to the bar's location - Columbus Circle, where the world's first one-way rotary system (roundabout) was implemented in 1904.
Comment: Fruity and easy drinking, yet with complexity from the gin.

FRUIT CUP

Glass: Collins
Garnish: Lemon, orange & strawberry slices, mint sprig & borage in drink
Method: SHAKE first three ingredients with ice and strain into ice-filled glass. Add garnish. TOP up with ginger ale and lightly stir.

1½	shot(s)	Tanqueray London dry gin
1	shot(s)	Martini Rosso sweet vermouth
½	shot(s)	Cointreau triple sec
Top with		Ginger ale (or lemonade)

Comment: A refreshing fruity long summery drink, reminiscent of home-made Pimms.

GENTLE BREEZE (MOCKTAIL)

Glass: Collins
Garnish: Lime wedge
Method: POUR ingredients into ice-filled glass, stir and serve with straws.

4	shot(s)	Ocean Spray cranberry juice
2	shot(s)	Freshly squeezed grapefruit juice

Comment: A Seabreeze without the hard stuff.

GIBSON

Glass: Martini
Garnish: Two chilled cocktail onions on stick
Method: **STIR** vermouth with ice in a mixing glass. Strain and discard excess vermouth to leave only a coating on the ice. **POUR** gin into mixing glass containing coated ice and **STIR**. Finally strain into chilled glass.

| ½ | shot(s) | Noilly Prat dry vermouth |
| 2½ | shot(s) | Tanqueray London dry gin |

Origin: Today a Gibson is a Dry Martini served with two onions. Charles Dana Gibson produced hugely popular pen-and-ink drawings between the 1890s and 1930s. His illustrations of girls were as iconic as modern-day supermodels, and it is said this drink was named after the well-endowed Gibson Girls - hence the two onions.

However, a cocktail book published in 1917 includes a Martini-like drink named Gibson but without the onions, and a separate Onion cocktail which we might today call a Gibson. Gibson was a member of New York's The Players' club and a bartender there by the name of Charley Connolly is credited for at least adding the garnish, if not actually creating the drink.
Comment: A classic Dry Martini with cocktail onions in place of an olive or twist.

GIBSON

GIMLET

GIMLET

Glass: Martini
Garnish: Lime wedge or cherry
Method: STIR all ingredients with ice and strain
into chilled glass.

2½	shot(s)	Tanqueray London dry gin
¾	shot(s)	Rose's lime cordial

Variant: Other spirits, particularly vodka, may be
substituted for gin.
Origin: In 1747, James Lind, a Scottish surgeon,
discovered that consumption of citrus fruits helped
prevent scurvy, one of the most common illnesses
on board ship. (We now understand that scurvy is
caused by a Vitamin C deficiency and that it is the
vitamins in citrus fruit which help ward off the
condition.) In 1867, the Merchant Shipping Act
made it mandatory for all British ships to carry
rations of lime juice for the crew.

Lauchlin Rose, the owner of a shipyard in Leith,
Scotland, had been working to solve the problem of
how to keep citrus juice fresh for months on board
ship. In 1867 he patented a process for preserving
fruit juice without alcohol. To give his product wider
appeal he sweetened the mixture, packaged it in an
attractive bottle and named it 'Rose's Lime Cordial'.
Once the benefits of drinking lime juice became
more broadly known, British sailors consumed so
much of the stuff, often mixed with their daily ration
of rum and water ('grog'), that they became affec-
tionately known as 'Limeys'. Naval officers mixed
Rose's lime cordial with gin to make Gimlets.

A 'gimlet' was originally the name of a small
tool used to tap the barrels of spirits which were
carried on British Navy ships: this could be the
origin of the drink's name. Another story cites a
naval doctor, Rear-Admiral Sir Thomas Desmond
Gimlette (1857-1943), who is said to have mixed
gin with lime 'to help the medicine go down'.
Although this is a credible story it is not substantiat-
ed in his obituary in The Times, 6 October 1943.
Comment: A simple blend of gin and sweet lime.

GIN & FRENCH

Glass: Old-fashioned
Garnish: Lemon slice
Method: STIR all ingredients with ice and strain into ice-filled glass.

2	shot(s)	**Tanqueray London dry gin**
2	shot(s)	**Noilly Prat dry vermouth**

Origin: Traditionally Italian vermouth was sweet while French vermouth was dry. Hence this drink is simply gin and Noilly Prat dry vermouth.
Comment: Bone dry but botanically rich.

GIN & IT

Glass: Old-fashioned
Garnish: Orange slice
Method: STIR all ingredients with ice and strain into ice-filled glass.

2	shot(s)	**Tanqueray London dry gin**
2	shot(s)	**Martini Rosso sweet vermouth**
1	dash	**Angostura aromatic bitters**

Origin: The name is short for 'Gin and Italian', a reference to the Martini Rosso sweet vermouth, which was traditionally Italian while French vermouth was dry. In his 'Craft of the Cocktail', Dale DeGroff states that this drink was originally known as a 'Sweet Martini' and as such was a popular drink during the 1880s and 1890s at the Hoffman House and other New York bars. Later it became known as "Gin & Italian", until during/post Prohibition it was shortened to "Gin & It".
Comment: Simple but tasty combination of botanicals, wine and spirit.

GIN & JUICE

Glass: Collins
Garnish: Orange slice
Method: SHAKE all ingredients with ice and strain into ice-filled glass.

2	shot(s)	**Tanqueray London dry gin**
2½	shot(s)	**Freshly squeezed orange juice**
1½	shot(s)	**Freshly squeezed grapefruit juice**

Origin: Possibly the inspiration behind the Top 10 single 'Gin and Juice' by rapper Snoop Doggy Dogg, from his debut album Doggystyle.
Comment: Gin and fruit juice. OK, but nothing to sing about.

GIN & SIN

Glass: Martini
Garnish: Orange zest twist
Method: SHAKE all ingredients with ice and fine strain into chilled glass.

2	shot(s)	**Tanqueray London dry gin**
1	shot(s)	**Freshly squeezed orange juice**
½	shot(s)	**Freshly squeezed lemon juice**
¼	shot(s)	**Pomegranate (grenadine) syrup**
½	shot(s)	**Chilled mineral water (omit if wet ice)**

Comment: This is one of those drinks that benefits from a little dilution to prevent the citrus and gin becoming too aggressive.

GIN & TONIC

Glass: Collins
Garnish: Run lime wedge around rim of glass.
Squeeze and drop into drink.
Method: POUR ingredients into ice-filled glass,
stir and serve without straws.

2 shot(s)	**Tanqueray London dry gin**
Top up with	**Tonic water**

Origin: The precise origin of the G&T is lost in the
mists of time. Gin (or at least a grain based juniper
spirit) was drunk for medicinal reasons from the
1600s onwards. Quinine, the pungent bark extract
which gives tonic its distinctive bitterness, had
been used against malaria for even longer. The first
known quinine-based tonics were marketed during
the 1850s.

The popularity of tonic in the British colonies,
especially India, is clear. Schweppes launched their
first carbonated quinine tonic in 1870, branding it
Indian Tonic Water. The ladies and gentlemen of the
Raj also drank phenomenal quantities of gin. It is
therefore accepted that gin and tonic emerged in
India during the second half of the nineteenth
century and was drunk partly to ward off malaria.
Comment: This might not be considered a cocktail
by most, but it is actually classified as a Highball.
Whatever, it's one of the simplest and best drinks
ever devised, hence its lasting popularity.

GIN & TONIC

GIN BERRY

Glass: Martini
Garnish: Lime zest twist
Method: **SHAKE** all ingredients with ice and fine strain into chilled glass.

1½	shot(s)	**Tanqueray London dry gin**
½	shot(s)	**Crème de cassis or Chambord**
½	shot(s)	**Freshly squeezed lime juice**
1½	shot(s)	**Ocean Spray cranberry juice**

Origin: Adapted from a drink created in 2004 by Chris Lacey, UK.
Comment: Berry flavours combine harmoniously with gin – what an appropriate name.

GIN FIX

Glass: Goblet
Garnish: Lemon slice
Method: **SHAKE** all ingredients with ice and strain into glass filled with crushed ice. **CHURN** (stir) drink with ice and serve with straws.

2	shot(s)	**Tanqueray London dry gin**
1	shot(s)	**Freshly squeezed lemon juice**
½	shot(s)	**Sugar syrup** (2 sugar to 1 water)

Origin: The Fix is an old classic that's very similar to the Daisy.
Comment: A Gin Sour served over crushed ice in a goblet.

G

'I HAVE DRUNK SINCE I WAS FIFTEEN AND FEW THINGS HAVE GIVEN ME MORE PLEASURE… THE ONLY TIME IT ISN'T GOOD FOR YOU IS WHEN YOU WRITE OR WHEN YOU FIGHT. YOU HAVE TO DO THAT COLD. BUT IT ALWAYS HELPS MY SHOOTING.'
ERNEST HEMINGWAY

GIN COCKTAIL

Glass: Martini
Garnish: Lemon peel twist
Method: **STIR** all ingredients with ice and strain into chilled glass.

2½	shot(s)	**Tanqueray London dry gin**
⅛	shot(s)	**Cointreau triple sec**
⅛	shot(s)	**Sugar syrup** (2 sugar to 1 water)
2	dashes	**Angostura aromatic bitters**

Origin: A classic that was already well-established when Jerry Thomas recorded his version of the recipe in 1862.
Comment: A pink gin made more approachable by a splash of triple sec and sugar syrup.

GIN FIXED

Glass: Martini
Garnish: Lemon slice
Method: **SHAKE** all ingredients with ice and strain into glass filled with crushed ice. **CHURN** (stir) drink with ice and serve with straws.

2	shot(s)	**Tanqueray London dry gin**
¼	shot(s)	**Cointreau triple sec**
1	shot(s)	**Pressed pineapple juice**
½	shot(s)	**Freshly squeezed lemon juice**
¼	shot(s)	**Sugar syrup** (2 sugar to 1 water)

Comment: Sweet and sour with a spirity pineapple twang.

GIN FIZZ

Glass: Collins (8oz max)
Garnish: Half slice of lemon & mint
Method: **SHAKE** first three ingredients with ice and strain into chilled glass (no ice in glass). **TOP** with soda.

2	shot(s)	**Tanqueray London dry gin**
1	shot(s)	**Freshly squeezed lemon juice**
½	shot(s)	**Sugar syrup** (2 sugar to 1 water)
Top up with		**Soda water** (from siphon)

Variants: With the addition of egg white this drink becomes a Silver Fizz; with egg yolk it becomes a Golden Fizz. A Royal Fizz includes one whole egg, a Diamond Fizz uses champagne instead of charged water, a Green Fizz has a dash of green crème de menthe and a Purple Fizz uses equal parts of sloe gin and grapefruit juice in place of gin and lemon juice.
Origin: A mid-19th century classic.
Comment: Everyone has heard of this clean, refreshing, long drink but few have actually tried it.

GIN DAISY

Glass: Collins
Garnish: Seasonal berries
Method: **SHAKE** first three ingredients with ice and strain into ice-filled glass. **TOP** with soda and serve with straws.

2	shot(s)	**Tanqueray London dry gin**
1	shot(s)	**Freshly squeezed lemon juice**
½	shot(s)	**Pomegranate (grenadine) syrup**
Top up with		**Soda water** (club soda)

Origin: Daisies can be served in a goblet filled with crushed ice, straight-up or as in this case in a Collins glass.
Comment: Fruit and botanicals served long and refreshing.

G

GIN DAISY

GIN PUNCH

GIN PUNCH

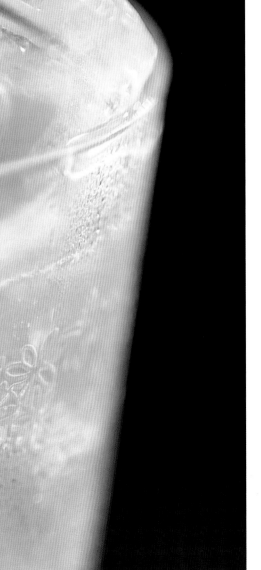

Glass: Collins
Garnish: Lemon slice
Method: SHAKE all ingredients with ice and fine strain into chilled glass.

2	shot(s)	**Tanqueray London dry gin**
¾	shot(s)	**Freshly squeezed lemon juice**
¾	shot(s)	**Sugar syrup** (2 sugar to 1 water)
2	shot(s)	**Chilled mineral water**
1	dash	**Angostura aromatic bitters**

Origin: This is a version of the drink for which Limmer's Hotel in London was most famed: a Captain Gronow recalled it in his 1860s memoirs as one of the top, if filthy and seedy, sporting hangouts of 1814, thanks in part to its 'famous gin-punch'. A bartender named John Collins worked there later in the 19th century, and was famous enough to inspire a limerick, so many believe he created the Collins, which is similar to gin punch, although the drink is not named in the rhyme which goes as follows:
My name is John Collins,
  head waiter at Limmer's,
Corner of Conduit Street,
  Hanover Square,
My chief occupation is filling
  brimmers
For all the young gentlemen
  frequenters there.
Comment: Light and refreshing – akin to alcoholic real lemonade.

G

GIN SLING

Glass: Sling
Garnish: Lemon slice and cherry on stick (sail)
Method: SHAKE first three ingredients with ice and strain into ice-filled glass. **TOP** with soda and serve with straws.

2	shot(s)	**Tanqueray London dry gin**
½	shot(s)	**Freshly squeezed lemon juice**
¼	shot(s)	**Sugar syrup** (2 sugar to 1 water)
Top with		**Soda water** (club soda)

Origin: 'Sling' comes from the German word 'schlingen', meaning 'to swallow' and is a style of drink which was popular from the late 1700s.
Comment: Sugar balances the citrus juice, the spirit fortifies and the carbonate lengthens.

GIN SOUR (CLASSIC FORMULA)

Glass: Old-fashioned
Garnish: Lemon slice & cherry on stick (sail)
Method: SHAKE all ingredients with ice and strain into ice-filled glass

2	shot(s)	**Tanqueray London dry gin**
¾	shot(s)	**Freshly squeezed lemon juice**
1	shot(s)	**Sugar syrup** (2 sugar to 1 water)
½	fresh	**Egg white**
3	dashes	**Angostura aromatic bitters**

Comment: This recipe follows the classic sour proportions: three quarter part of the sour ingredient (lemon juice), one part of the sweet ingredient (sugar syrup) and two parts of the strong ingredient (gin) - 3:4:8. I prefer mine sourer with one part lemon juice and half a part sugar (4:2:8) and that's the formula I tend to use in all 'sour' drinks.

GINA

Glass: Sling
Garnish: Berries on stick
Method: SHAKE first three ingredients with ice and strain into ice-filled glass. **TOP** with soda.

2	shot(s)	**Tanqueray London dry gin**
½	shot(s)	**Crème de cassis or Chambord**
½	shot(s)	**Freshly squeezed lemon juice**
Top up with		**Soda water** (club soda)

AKA: Cassis Collins
Comment: The lemon and blackcurrant mask the character of the gin.

GLOOM CHASER COCKTAIL #1

Glass: Martini
Garnish: Orange zest twist
Method: SHAKE all ingredients with ice and fine strain into chilled glass.

¾	shot(s)	**Grand Marnier liqueur**
¾	shot(s)	**Cointreau triple sec**
1	shot(s)	**Freshly squeezed lemon juice**
¼	shot(s)	**Pomegranate (grenadine) syrup**
1	shot(s)	**Chilled mineral water** (reduce if wet ice)

Origin: Adapted from Harry Craddock's 1930 'The Savoy Cocktail Book'.
Comment: A sunny coloured drink for happy souls. And sweet orange and pomegranate soured with lemon would make anyone happy.

GODFREY

Glass: Old-fashioned
Garnish: Three blackberries on drink
Method: MUDDLE blackberries in base of shaker. Add other ingredients, **SHAKE** with ice and fine strain into glass filled with crushed ice.

6	fresh	**Blackberries**
1½	shot(s)	**Courvoisier V.S.O.P. cognac**
½	shot(s)	**Grand Marnier liqueur**
¼	shot(s)	**Crème de cassis or Chambord**
¼	shot(s)	**Freshly squeezed lemon juice**
¼	shot(s)	**Sugar syrup** (2 sugar to 1 water)

Origin: Created by Salvatore Calabrese at the Library Bar, Lanesborough Hotel, London, England.
Comment: Well balanced with a rich blackberry flavour.

GOLDEN BRONX

Glass: Martini
Garnish: Maraschino cherry
Method: SHAKE all ingredients with ice and fine strain into chilled glass.

2	shot(s)	**Tanqueray London dry gin**
¼	shot(s)	**Noilly Prat dry vermouth**
¼	shot(s)	**Martini Rosso sweet vermouth**
1	shot(s)	**Freshly squeezed orange juice**
⅛	shot(s)	**Sugar syrup** (2 sugar to 1 water)
1	fresh	**Egg yolk**

Origin: A vintage cocktail adapted from the classic Bronx Cocktail, created in 1906 by Johnny Solon, a bartender at New York's Waldorf-Astoria Hotel, and named after the newly opened Bronx Zoo.
Comment: A Bronx made 'golden' by the addition of egg yolk.

HOW TO MAKE SUGAR SYRUP

To make your own sugar syrup, gradually pour TWO cups of granulated sugar into a saucepan containing ONE cup of hot water. Stir as you pour and carry on stirring and simmering until the sugar is dissolved. Do not let the water even come close to boiling and only simmer for as long as it takes to dissolve the sugar. Allow syrup to cool and pour into an empty bottle. Ideally, you should finely strain your syrup into the bottle to remove any undissolved crystals which could otherwise encourage crystallisation. If kept in a refrigerator this mixture will last for a couple of months.

GOLDEN FIZZ #1

Glass: Collins (8oz max)
Garnish: Lemon slice & mint
Method: **SHAKE** first four ingredients with ice and fine strain into chilled glass. **TOP** with soda.

2	shot(s)	Tanqueray London dry gin
1	shot(s)	Freshly squeezed lemon juice
½	shot(s)	Sugar syrup (2 sugar to 1 water)
1	fresh	Egg yolk
Top up with		Soda water (from siphon)

Variant: Gin Fizz
Origin: Mid-19th century classic.
Comment: You may have some raw egg inhibitions to conquer before you can enjoy this drink.

GOLDEN FIZZ #2

Glass: Collins
Garnish: Orange slice & mint sprig
Method: **STIR** honey with gin in base of shaker until honey dissolves. Add next three ingredients, **SHAKE** with ice and strain into ice-filled glass. **TOP** with lemonade.

2	spoons	Runny honey
1½	shot(s)	Tanqueray London dry gin
1	shot(s)	Cointreau triple sec
1	shot(s)	Freshly squeezed grapefruit juice
¼	shot(s)	Freshly squeezed lemon juice
Top up with		7-Up / lemonade / Sprite

Origin: Adapted from a drink created by Wayne Collins, UK.
Comment: More cloudy white than golden but a pleasant, refreshing long drink all the same.

GOLDEN SCREW

Glass: Flute
Garnish: Physalis fruit
Method: **POUR** all ingredients into chilled glass and lightly stir.

½	shot(s)	Courvoisier V.S.O.P. cognac
½	shot(s)	Bols apricot brandy liqueur
1	shot(s)	Freshly squeezed orange juice
Top up with		Brut champagne

Variant: With gin in place of brandy.
Comment: A favourite with Midas and others whose budgets extend beyond a Buck's Fizz or a Mimosa.

GOLF COCKTAIL

Glass: Martini
Garnish: Orange zest twist
Method: **STIR** all ingredients with ice and strain into chilled glass.

2	shot(s)	Tanqueray London dry gin
1	shot(s)	Noilly Prat dry vermouth
1	dash	Angostura aromatic bitters

Comment: A 'wet' Martini with bitters.

GLORIA

Glass: Flute
Garnish: Lemon zest twist
Method: **SHAKE** first three ingredients with ice and fine strain into chilled glass. **TOP** with champagne.

1	shot(s)	Don Julio 100% agave tequila
½	shot(s)	Freshly squeezed lemon juice
½	shot(s)	Sugar syrup (2 sugar to 1 water)
Top up with		Brut champagne

Comment: A tequila sour topped with champagne or a tequila French 75.

GRAND MARGARITA

Glass: Coupette
Garnish: Salt rim & lime wedge
Method: **SHAKE** all ingredients with ice and fine strain into chilled glass.

2	shot(s)	Don Julio 100% agave tequila
1	shot(s)	Grand Marnier liqueur
¾	shot(s)	Freshly squeezed lime juice

Comment: A balanced and flavoursome Margarita.

GRAND MIMOSA

Glass: Flute
Garnish: Strawberry on rim
Method: **SHAKE** first two ingredients with ice and strain into chilled glass. **TOP** with champagne.

1	shot(s)	Grand Marnier liqueur
2	shot(s)	Freshly squeezed orange juice
Top up with		Brut champagne

Origin: The Mimosa was created in 1925 at the Ritz Hotel, Paris, and named after the Mimosa plant - probably because of its trembling leaves, rather like the gentle fizz of this mixture. The Grand Mimosa as shown here benefits from the addition of Grand Marnier liqueur.
Comment: As the name suggests, the orange of Grand Marnier heavily influences this drink. Basically a Buck's Fizz with more oomph.

GRAND PASSION

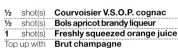

Glass: Martini
Garnish: Float half passion fruit
Method: Cut passion fruits in half and scoop flesh into shaker. Add other ingredients, **SHAKE** with ice and fine strain into chilled glass.

1	fresh	Passion fruit
2	shot(s)	Bacardi Superior rum
1	shot(s)	Pressed apple juice
½	shot(s)	Sugar syrup (2 sugar to 1 water)
3	dashes	Angostura aromatic bitters
½	fresh	Egg white

Comment: Are you lacking passion in your life? There's plenty in this fruity little number.

GRAND SIDECAR

Glass: Martini
Garnish: Orange zest twist
Method: SHAKE all ingredients with ice and fine strain into chilled glass.

2½	shot(s)	**Grand Marnier liqueur**
1	shot(s)	**Freshly squeezed lemon juice**
½	shot(s)	**Chilled mineral water** (omit if wet ice)

Origin: Created by yours truly in June 2005.
Comment: A twist on the classic, simple but very tasty. Also works well shaken and strained into an ice-filled old-fashioned glass.

GRANDE CHAMPAGNE COSMO

Glass: Martini
Garnish: Orange zest twist
Method: SHAKE all ingredients with ice and fine strain into chilled glass.

1½	shot(s)	**Courvoisier V.S.O.P. cognac**
¾	shot(s)	**Grand Marnier liqueur**
½	shot(s)	**Freshly squeezed lemon juice**
1	shot(s)	**Ocean Spray Cranberry juice**
½	fresh	**Egg white**

Comment: 'Grande Champagne' refers to the top cru of the Cognac region: this drink is suitably elite.

'I AM ONLY A BEER
TEETOTALLER, NOT A
CHAMPAGNE TEETOTALLER.'
GEORGE BERNARD SHAW

GRAPE ESCAPE

Glass: Collins
Garnish: Mint sprig
Method: MUDDLE grapes and mint in base of shaker. Add cognac and sugar, SHAKE with ice and strain into glass filled with crushed ice. TOP with champagne, stir and serve with straws.

8	fresh	**Seedless white grapes**
5	fresh	**Mint leaves**
2	shot(s)	**Courvoisier V.S.O.P. cognac**
½	shot(s)	**Sugar syrup** (2 sugar to 1 water)
Top up with		**Brut champagne**

Origin: Created in 2000 by Brian Lucas and Max Warner at Long Bar @ Sanderson, London, England.
Comment: A cracking drink – subtle and refreshing.

GRAPE MARTINI

Glass: Martini
Garnish: Grapes on stick
Method: MUDDLE grapes in base of shaker. Add other ingredients, SHAKE with ice and fine strain into chilled glass.

12	fresh	**Seedless white grapes**
2	shot(s)	**Ketel One vodka**
½	shot(s)	**Sugar syrup** (2 sugar to 1 water)

Origin: Formula by yours truly in 2004.
Comment: Simple but remarkably tasty.

GRAPEFRUIT JULEP

Glass: Collins
Garnish: Mint sprig
Method: STIR honey with vodka in base of shaker until honey dissolves. Add other ingredients, SHAKE with ice and strain into glass filled with crushed ice.

1	spoon	**Runny honey**
2	shot(s)	**Ketel One vodka**
4	fresh	**Mint leaves**
½	shot(s)	**Freshly squeezed lime juice**
½	shot(s)	**Pomegranate (grenadine) syrup**
¾	shot(s)	**Freshly squeezed grapefruit juice**

Origin: Created by Dale DeGroff, New York City, USA.
Comment: Wonderfully refreshing. Bring on the sun.

GREYHOUND

Glass: Collins
Garnish: Orange slice
Method: POUR ingredients into ice-filled glass and stir.

2	shot(s)	**Ketel One vodka**
Top up with		**Freshly squeezed grapefruit juice**

Comment: A sour Screwdriver.

HAIR OF THE DOG

Glass: Martini
Garnish: Grate fresh nutmeg
Method: STIR honey with Scotch until honey dissolves. Add other ingredients, SHAKE with ice and fine strain into chilled glass.

3	spoons	**Runny honey**
2	shot(s)	**Johnnie Walker Scotch whisky**
1	shot(s)	**Double (heavy) cream**
1	shot(s)	**Milk**

Origin: Traditionally drunk as a pick-me-up hangover cure.
Comment: This drink's name and reputation as a hangover cure may lead you to assume it tastes unpleasant. In fact, honey, whisky and cream combine wonderfully.

HAIR OF THE DOG

H

HARPOON

HARD LEMONADE

Glass: Collins
Garnish: Lemon slice in glass
Method: **SHAKE** first three ingredients with ice and strain into ice-filled glass. **TOP** with soda and serve with straws.

2	shot(s)	**Ketel One vodka**
2	shot(s)	**Freshly squeezed lemon juice**
1	shot(s)	**Sugar syrup** (2 sugar to 1 water)
Top up with		**Soda water** (club soda)

Variants: Vodka Collins, Ray's Hard Lemonade
Origin: Discovered in 2004 at Spring Street Natural Restaurant, New York City, USA.
Comment: Refreshing lemonade with a kick. Great for a hot afternoon.

HAVANATHEONE

Glass: Martini
Garnish: Mint leaf
Method: Lightly **MUDDLE** mint (just to bruise) in base of shaker. Add rum and honey and **STIR** until honey dissolves. Add other ingredients, **SHAKE** with ice and fine strain into chilled glass.

10	fresh	**Mint leaves**
2	spoons	**Runny honey**
2	shot(s)	**Bacardi Superior rum**
½	shot(s)	**Freshly squeezed lime juice**
1	shot(s)	**Pressed apple juice**

Origin: Discovered in 2003 at Hush, London, England.
Comment: A flavoursome Daiquiri featuring honey, apple and mint.

HARVARD

Glass: Martini
Garnish: Lemon zest twist
Method: **STIR** all ingredients with ice and strain into chilled glass. **TOP** with a shot or so of chilled soda.

1½	shot(s)	**Courvoisier V.S.O.P. cognac**
2	shot(s)	**Martini Rosso sweet vermouth**
2	dashes	**Fee Brother orange bitters** (optional)
Top up with		**Soda from siphon**

AKA: New Orleans Manhattan
Variant: Delmonico (with Angostura in place of orange bitters).
Origin: Recipe adapted from George J. Kappeler's 1895 'Modern American Drinks'. In his 1931 book 'Old Waldorf Bar Days', Albert Stevens Crockett, notes of this drink, "Named after a school for young men, whose site is contiguous to the Charles River, in a suburb of Boston. Alumni who drunk it sometimes lost the 'Harvard accent'.
Comment: Old-school, but approachably so. Dry and herbal. A great aperitif.

HARPOON

Glass: Old-fashioned
Garnish: Lime wedge
Method: **POUR** ingredients into ice-filled glass and stir.

1	shot(s)	**Ketel One vodka**
2	shot(s)	**Ocean Spray cranberry juice**
¼	shot(s)	**Freshly squeezed lime juice**

Origin: Though to be the forerunner to the Cosmopolitan. A 1968 bottle label from Ocean Spray's archives lists the Harpoon as a "new cocktail". It was originally launched as being 2 ounces Ocean Spray cranberry and 1 ounce vodka or light rum served "over the rocks or tall with soda. Suggested garnish: a splash of lime or lemon optional." In 1970, it was updated to also list gin as a possible base spirit.
Comment: Innocuously light in both flavour and alcohol. Add a shot of triple sec and you are well on your way to making a Cosmopolitan.

H

> 'IN NEVADA... THE CHEAPEST AND EASIEST WAY TO BECOME AN INFLUENTIAL MAN... WAS TO STAND BEHIND A BAR, WEAR A DIAMOND CLUSTER-PIN, AND SELL WHISKY.'
> MARK TWAIN

HAWAIIAN MARTINI

Glass: Martini
Garnish: Pineapple wedge & cherry
Method: **SHAKE** all ingredients with ice and fine strain into chilled glass.

1½	shot(s)	**Tanqueray London dry gin**
½	shot(s)	**Noilly Prat dry vermouth**
½	shot(s)	**Martini Rosso sweet vermouth**
1½	shot(s)	**Pressed pineapple juice**

Origin: Adapted from a drink discovered in 2005 at the Four Seasons, Milan, Italy.
Comment: An aptly named fruity twist on the classic Martini.

HIGHBALL
(GENERIC NAME)

H

Glass: Collins
Garnish: Slice of orange, lime or lemon as appropriate to the spirit and the carbonate
Method: POUR spirit into ice-filled glass and **TOP** with a carbonated soft drink (ginger ale, soda or tonic water). Stir gently so as not to kill the fizz.

2	shot(s)	**Liquor** (of your choice)
		Bacardi Superior rum
		Bulleit bourbon whiskey
		Johnnie Walker Scotch whisky
		Courvoisier V.S.O.P cognac
		Tanqueray London dry gin
Top up with		**Ginger ale, soda, tonic water or other carbonated mixer**

Origin: Scotch & Soda, Gin & Tonic, Whiskey & Ginger, Vodka & Tonic and Rum & Coke are all examples of Highball cocktails. Highballs are a type of simple cocktail with only two ingredients, normally a spirit and a carbonate, served in a tall ice-filled glass (often referred to as a highball glass). Unlike Rickeys, Collinses and Fizzes, Highballs do not contain citrus fruit juice.

In his 1934 'The Official Mixer's Guide', Patrick Gavin Duffy writes, "It is one of my fondest hopes that the highball will again take its place as the leading American Drink. I admit to being prejudiced about this - it was I who first brought the highball to America, in 1895. Although the distinction is claimed by the Parker House in Boston, I was finally given due credit for this innovation in the New York Times of not many years ago."

That New York Times reference appears to be a letter written by Duffy on 22 October 1927 to the Editor in response to an editorial piece in the paper. He starts, "An editorial in The Times says that the Adams House, Boston, claims to have served the first Scotch highball in this country. This claim is unfounded." He goes on to tell of how in 1894 he opened a little cafe next the old Lyceum in New York City and that in the Spring of that year, an English actor and regular patron, E. J. Ratcliffe, one day asked for a Scotch and soda. At that time Duffy did not carry Scotch but this request and the growing number of English actors frequenting his bar led Duffy to order five cases of Usher's from Park & Tilford. Duffy claims that when the shipment arrived he "sold little but Scotch highballs", consisting of "Scotch, a lump of ice and a bottle of club soda". His letter finishes, "Shortly afterward every actor along Broadway, and consequently every New Yorker who frequented the popular bars, was drinking Scotch highballs. In a few years other Scotch distillers introduced their brands and many were enriched by the quantity consumed in this country. Actors on tour, and members of the Ancient and Honorable Artillery of Boston, who came here annually to attend the Old Guard Ball, brought the new drink to the Adams House."

Duffy's letter to The New York Times mentions Adam House in Boston while the reference in his subsequent book talks of "Parker House". Both are plausible Boston locations but does this confusion mean we should not take any of Duffy's claims for being the first to make Scotch Highballs in America seriously? The Times merely published Duffy's letter to the editor, the paper did not substantiate or even "give credit" to his claims.

In his 2003 'The Joy of Mixology', Gary Regan explains that "Highball is an old railroad term for the ball indicator connected to a float inside a steam train's water tank which told the conductor that there was enough water in the tank and so the train could proceed. Apparently when the train was set to depart, the conductor would give the highball – two short whistle blows and one long. Gary explains that this term was apt as the drinks consist of 2 shots of liquor and a long pour of mixer.

Comment: Simple, but simplicity can be beautiful.

HIGHBALL

HOBSON'S CHOICE (MOCKTAIL)

Glass: Collins
Garnish: Lime wedge on rim
Method: SHAKE all ingredients with ice and strain into ice-filled glass.

2½	shot(s)	**Freshly squeezed orange juice**
2½	shot(s)	**Pressed apple juice**
1	shot(s)	**Freshly squeezed lime juice**
¼	shot(s)	**Pomegranate (grenadine) syrup**

Comment: A fruity, non-alcoholic cocktail.

HONEY & MARMALADE DRAM

Glass: Martini
Garnish: Strips of orange peel
Method: STIR honey with Scotch in base of shaker until honey dissolves. Add other ingredients, SHAKE with ice and fine strain into chilled glass.

2	shot(s)	**Johnnie Walker Scotch whisky**
4	spoons	**Runny honey**
1	shot(s)	**Freshly squeezed lemon juice**
1	shot(s)	**Freshly squeezed orange juice**

Origin: I adapted this recipe from the Honeysuckle Daiquiri.
Comment: This citrussy drink seems to enrich and enhance the flavour of Scotch.

HONEY BEE

Glass: Martini
Garnish: Lemon zest twist
Method: STIR honey with vodka in base of shaker until honey dissolves. Add other ingredients, SHAKE with ice and fine strain into chilled glass.

2	shot(s)	**Ketel One Vodka**
3	spoons	**Runny honey**
½	shot(s)	**Freshly squeezed lemon juice**
¾	shot(s)	**Chilled mineral water**

Origin: Adapted from 1949 Esquire's 'Handbook For Hosts'.
Comment: Honey balances lemon juice in this vodka cocktail.

HONEY DAIQUIRI

Glass: Martini
Garnish: Lime wedge on rim
Method: STIR honey with rum in base of shaker until honey dissolves. Add other ingredients, SHAKE with ice and fine strain into chilled glass.

2	spoons	**Runny honey**
2	shot(s)	**Bacardi Superior rum**
½	shot(s)	**Freshly squeezed lime juice**
½	shot(s)	**Chilled mineral water** (omit if wet ice)

Comment: Sweet honey replaces sugar syrup in this natural Daiquiri. Try experimenting with different honeys. I favour orange blossom honey.

HONEY LIMEAID (MOCKTAIL)

Glass: Collins
Garnish: Lime wedge
Method: STIR honey with lime juice in base of shaker until honey dissolves. SHAKE with ice and strain into ice-filled glass. TOP with soda.

1½	shot(s)	**Freshly squeezed lime juice**
7	spoons	**Runny honey**
Top up with		**Soda water** (club soda)

Origin: Discovered in 2005 at Hotel Quinta Real, Guadalajara, Mexico.
Comment: A refreshing Mexican variation on Real Lemonade.

HONEYSUCKLE DAIQUIRI

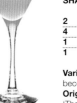

Glass: Martini
Garnish: Mint leaf
Method: STIR honey with rum in base of shaker until honey dissolves. Add lemon and orange juice, SHAKE with ice and fine strain into chilled glass.

2	shot(s)	**Bacardi Superior rum**
4	spoons	**Runny honey**
1	shot(s)	**Freshly squeezed lemon juice**
1	shot(s)	**Freshly squeezed orange juice**

Variant: Made with gin in place of rum this drink becomes the 'Bee's Knees Martini'.
Origin: Adapted from a recipe in David Embury's 'The Fine Art Of Mixing Drinks'.
Comment: Honey – I love it!

> 'NO WOMAN SHOULD MARRY A TEETOTALLER, OR A MAN WHO DOES NOT SMOKE.'
> ROBERT LOUIS STEVENSON

HONOLULU

Glass: Old-fashioned (or Tiki glass)
Garnish: Pineapple wedge and cherry
Method: BLEND all ingredients with 12oz scoop crushed ice and serve with straws.

1½	shot(s)	**Bacardi Superior rum**
1	shot(s)	**Pressed pineapple juice**
½	shot(s)	**Freshly squeezed lemon juice**
¼	shot(s)	**Pomegranate (grenadine) syrup**
¼	shot(s)	**Sugar syrup** (2 sugar to 1 water)

Origin: Adapted from Victor Bergeron's 'Trader Vic's Bartender's Guide' (1972 revised edition).
Comment: Cooling, fruity and pretty light on alcohol – perfect for a hot afternoon in Honolulu.

HONOLULU COCKTAIL NO.1

Glass: Martini
Garnish: Pineapple wedge & cherry on rim
Method: SHAKE all ingredients with ice and fine strain into chilled glass.

2	shot(s)	**Tanqueray London dry gin**
¼	shot(s)	**Freshly squeezed orange juice**
¼	shot(s)	**Pressed pineapple juice**
¼	shot(s)	**Freshly squeezed lemon juice**
¼	shot(s)	**Sugar syrup** (2 sugar to 1 water)

Origin: Adapted from Harry Craddock's 1930 'The Savoy Cocktail Book'.
Comment: Gin is hardly Hawaiian, but its bite works well in this tropically fruity cocktail.

HOOPLA

Glass: Martini
Garnish: Orange zest twist
Method: SHAKE all ingredients with ice and fine strain into chilled glass.

1	shot(s)	**Courvoisier V.S.O.P. cognac**
1	shot(s)	**Cointreau triple sec**
¾	shot(s)	**Noilly Prat dry vermouth**
¾	shot(s)	**Freshly squeezed lemon juice**
½	fresh	**Egg white**

Comment: Not far removed from a Sidecar.

HOP TOAD

Glass: Martini
Garnish: Apricot wedge on rim
Method: SHAKE all ingredients with ice and fine strain into chilled glass.

1¼	shot(s)	**Bacardi Superior rum**
1¼	shot(s)	**Bols apricot brandy liqueur**
1¼	shot(s)	**Freshly squeezed lime juice**
½	shot(s)	**Chilled mineral water** (omit if wet ice)

Variant: Made with brandy this is sometimes known as a Bullfrog.
Origin: First published in Tom Bullock's 'Ideal Bartender', circa 1917.
Comment: Resembles an apricot Daiquiri that's heavy on the lime yet balanced.

HORSE'S NECK WITH A KICK

Glass: Collins
Garnish: Peel rind of a large lemon in a spiral and place in glass with end hanging over rim.
Method: POUR ingredients into ice-filled glass and stir.

2	shot(s)	**Bulleit bourbon whiskey**
3	dashes	**Angostura aromatic bitters**
Top up with		**Ginger ale**

Variant: A Horse's Neck without a kick is simply ginger ale and bitters.
Comment: Whiskey and ginger with added shrubbery.

HOT BUTTERED WHISKEY

Glass: Toddy
Garnish: Grate nutmeg over drink
Method: Place bar spoon in warmed glass. Add ingredients and **STIR** until butter dissolves.

1	large	**Knob (pat) unsalted butter**
2	shot(s)	**Bulleit bourbon whiskey**
¾	shot(s)	**Sugar syrup** (2 sugar to 1 water)
Top up with		**Boiling water**

Comment: Warming and smooth – great on a cold day or whenever you fancy a warning treat.

HOT TODDY

Glass: Toddy
Garnish: Lemon slice & cinnamon stick
Method: Place bar spoon in warmed glass. Add ingredients and **STIR**.

2	shot(s)	**Courvoisier V.S.O.P. cognac**
½	shot(s)	**Freshly squeezed lemon juice**
¼	shot(s)	**Sugar syrup** (2 sugar to 1 water)
Top up with		**Boiling water**

Comment: Warms the cockles with cognac and a good dose of citrus.

HOT TUB

Glass: Martini
Garnish: Pineapple wedge on rim
Method: SHAKE first three ingredients with ice and fine strain into chilled glass. **TOP** with champagne.

1½	shot(s)	**Ketel One vodka**
¼	shot(s)	**Crème de cassis or Chambord**
1	shot(s)	**Pressed pineapple juice**
Top up with		**Brut Champagne**

Origin: Adapted from a drink discovered in 2004 at Teatro, Boston, USA.
Comment: Basically a French Martini with bubbles.

HOULA-HOULA COCKTAIL

Glass: Martini
Garnish: Orange zest twist
Method: SHAKE all ingredients with ice and fine strain into chilled glass.

2	shot(s)	**Tanqueray London dry gin**
1	shot(s)	**Freshly squeezed orange juice**
½	shot(s)	**Cointreau triple sec**
½	shot(s)	**Chilled mineral water** (omit if wet ice)

Origin: Adapted from Harry Craddock's 1930 'The Savoy Cocktail Book'.
Comment: Orange generously laced with gin.

HUAPALA COCKTAIL

Glass: Martini
Garnish: Lemon wedge on rim
Method: SHAKE all ingredients with ice and fine strain into chilled glass.

1	shot(s)	**Bacardi Superior rum**
1	shot(s)	**Tanqueray London dry gin**
½	shot(s)	**Freshly squeezed lemon juice**
¼	shot(s)	**Pomegranate (grenadine) syrup**
½	shot(s)	**Chilled mineral water** (omit if wet ice)

Origin: Adapted from Victor Bergeron's 'Trader Vic's Bartender's Guide' (1972 revised edition).
Comment: In his book Vic prefaces this cocktail with the comment, "Nice, easy drink". It's basically a lemon Daiquiri with gin and grenadine.

ICED TEA MARTINI

Glass: Martini
Garnish: Lemon zest twist
Method: SHAKE all ingredients with ice and strain into chilled glass.

2	shot(s)	**Tanqueray London dry gin**
½	shot(s)	**Noilly Prat dry vermouth**
1	shot(s)	**Cold Earl Grey tea**
½	shot(s)	**Sugar syrup** (2 sugar to 1 water)

Origin: Created in 2006 by yours truly.
Comment: Tannic and bittersweet - a very refreshing after dinner drink.

ICY PINK LEMONADE

Glass: Collins
Garnish: Lemon slice
Method: SHAKE first four ingredients with ice and strain into ice-filled glass. **TOP** with soda.

2	shot(s)	**Ketel One vodka**
½	shot(s)	**Crème de cassis or Chambord**
2	shot(s)	**Freshly squeezed lemon juice**
½	shot(s)	**Sugar syrup** (2 sugar to 1 water)
Top up with		**Soda water** (club soda)

Comment: Tangy, citrussy, fruity and refreshing - just not that butch.

INCOGNITO

Glass: Martini
Garnish: Apricot slice or physalis fruit on rim
Method: SHAKE all ingredients with ice and fine strain into chilled glass.

1½	shot(s)	**Courvoisier V.S.O.P. cognac**
1½	shot(s)	**Noilly Prat dry vermouth**
1	shot(s)	**Bols apricot brandy liqueur**
3	dashes	**Angostura aromatic bitters**

Comment: Dry with hints of sweet apricot – most unusual.

INCOME TAX COCKTAIL

Glass: Martini
Garnish: Orange zest twist
Method: SHAKE all ingredients with ice and fine strain into chilled glass.

2	shot(s)	**Tanqueray London dry gin**
¼	shot(s)	**Noilly Prat dry vermouth**
¼	shot(s)	**Martini Rosso sweet vermouth**
1	shot(s)	**Freshly squeezed orange juice**
2	dashes	**Angostura aromatic bitters**

Origin: A vintage cocktail adapted from the classic Bronx Cocktail, created in 1906 by Johnny Solon, a bartender at New York's Waldorf-Astoria Hotel, and named after the newly opened Bronx Zoo.
Comment: A Bronx with the addition of two dashes of Angostura.

JACK DEMPSEY

Glass: Martini
Garnish: Maraschino cherry
Method: SHAKE all ingredients with ice and fine strain into chilled glass.

1½	shot(s)	**Bacardi Superior rum**
1½	shot(s)	**Tanqueray London dry gin**
¼	shot(s)	**Freshly squeezed lemon juice**
¼	shot(s)	**Sugar syrup** (2 sugar to 1 water)
¾	shot(s)	**Chilled mineral water** (omit if wet ice)

Comment: Dilution makes or breaks this subtle, gin laced drink.

JA-MORA

Glass: Flute
Garnish: Float single raspberry
Method: SHAKE first four ingredients with ice and fine strain into chilled glass. **TOP** with champagne.

1	shot(s)	**Ketel One vodka**
½	shot(s)	**Crème de cassis or Chambord**
½	shot(s)	**Freshly squeezed orange juice**
½	shot(s)	**Pressed apple juice**
Top up with		**Brut champagne**

Origin: Created by Jamie Terrell and Andres Masso in 1998. Named after 'mora', the Spanish for blackberry. The 'j' and 'a' stand for the names of its two creators.
Comment: Ja-more of this fruity champagne cocktail you drink, ja-more you'll like it.

JODI MAY

Glass: Collins
Garnish: Orange slice
Method: SHAKE all ingredients with ice and fine strain into chilled glass.

1½	shot(s)	**Bulleit bourbon whiskey**
½	shot(s)	**Cointreau triple sec**
2½	shot(s)	**Freshly squeezed orange juice**
1½	shot(s)	**Ocean Spray cranberry juice**
¼	shot(s)	**Freshly squeezed lime juice**

Origin: Adapted from a drink discovered in 2003 at World Service, Nottingham, England.
Comment: Long, fruity and laced with whiskey.

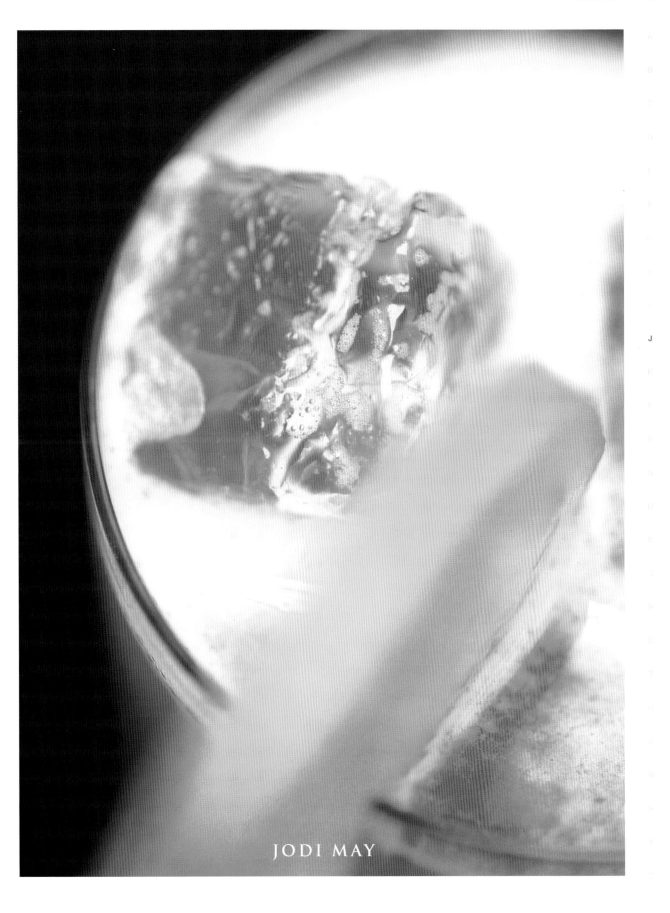

JODI MAY

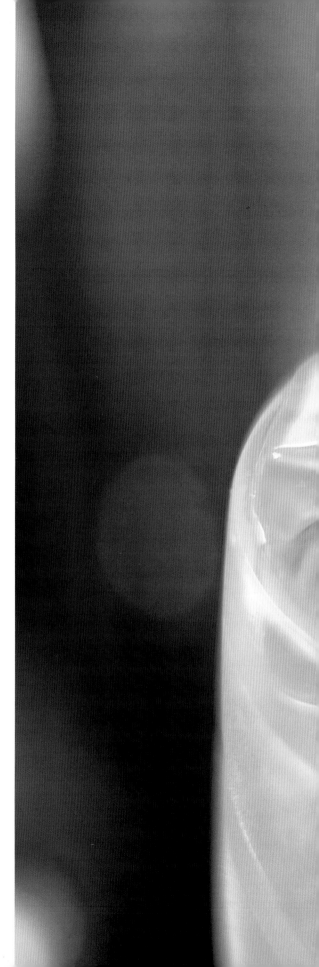

JOHN COLLINS

J

Glass: Collins
Garnish: Orange slice & cherry on stick (sail)
Method: SHAKE first three ingredients with ice and strain into ice-filled glass. **TOP** with soda, stir and serve with straws.

2	shot(s)	**Tanqueray London dry gin**
1	shot(s)	**Freshly squeezed lemon juice**
½	shot(s)	**Sugar syrup** (2 sugar to 1 water)
Top up with		**Soda water** (club soda)

Origin: In England, this drink is traditionally credited to John Collins, a bartender who worked at Limmer's Hotel, Conduit Street, London. The 'coffee house' of this hotel, a true dive bar, was popular with sporting types during the 19th century, and famous, according to the 1860s memoirs of a Captain Gronow, for its gin-punch as early as 1814.

John (or possibly Jim) Collins, head waiter of Limmer's, is immortalised in a limerick, which was apparently first printed in an 1892 book entitled 'Drinks of the World'. In 1891 a Sir Morell Mackenzie had identified John Collins as the creator of the Tom Collins, using this limerick, although both the words of the rhyme and the conclusions he drew from it were disputed. But, according to this version of the story, the special gin-punch for which John Collins of Limmer's was famous went on to become known as the Tom Collins when it was made using Old Tom gin.

The original Collins was probably based on genever gin, but there is also debate as to whether it was Old Tom or London Dry. To further complicate the issue a 'John Collins' appears to be exactly the same drink as a 'Tom Collins'. Thus I make a 'Collins' with genever gin, a 'Tom Collins' with old tom gin, and a 'John Collins' with Tanqueray London dry gin. Confused? Then you should also check out the 'Gin Punch' (which has the addition of bitters) and a 'Gin Fizz' which is topped with soda from a siphon.

Comment: A refreshing balance of sour lemon and sugar, laced with gin and lengthened with soda.

JOHN COLLINS

JOSÉ COLLINS

Glass: Collins
Garnish: Orange slice & cherry on stick (sail)
Method: SHAKE first three ingredients with ice and strain into ice-filled glass. **TOP** with soda, stir and serve with straws.

2	shot(s)	**Don Julio 100% agave tequila**
1	shot(s)	**Freshly squeezed lemon juice**
½	shot(s)	**Sugar syrup** (2 sugar to 1 water)
Top up with		**Soda water** (club soda)

AKA: Juan Collins
Comment: The classic long balance of sweet and sour with tequila adding Mexican spirit.

THE JOURNALIST

Glass: Martini
Garnish: Maraschino cherry in drink
Method: SHAKE all ingredients with ice and fine strain into chilled glass.

2	shot(s)	**Tanqueray London dry gin**
½	shot(s)	**Noilly Prat dry vermouth**
½	shot(s)	**Martini Rosso sweet vermouth**
¼	shot(s)	**Cointreau triple sec**
¼	shot(s)	**Freshly squeezed lemon juice**
2	dashes	**Angostura aromatic bitters**

AKA: Periodista ('journalist' in Spanish).
Comment: Like some journalists I've met, this is bitter and sour.

JULEP (GENERIC NAME)

Glass: Collins
Garnish: Mint sprig
Method: Lightly **MUDDLE** mint leaves with spirit in base of shaker (just enough to bruise). (At this stage, if time allows, you should refrigerate the shaker, mint and spirit, and the glass in which the drink is to be served, for at least two hours.) Add other ingredients to shaker, **SHAKE** with ice and strain into glass filled with crushed ice. **CHURN** (stir) the drink using a bar spoon. Top with more crushed ice to fill glass and churn again. Serve with straws.

12	fresh	**Mint leaves**
2½	shot(s)	**Liquor** (of your choice)
		Bulleit bourbon whiskey
		Bacardi Superior rum
		Tanqueray London dry gin
		Courvoisier V.S.O.P cognac
¾	shot(s)	**Sugar syrup** (2 sugar to 1 water)
3	dashes	**Angostura aromatic bitters**

Comment: Adjust sugar to balance if using a fortified wine in place of a spirit.

JULEP MARTINI

Glass: Martini
Garnish: Mint leaf
Method: Lightly **MUDDLE** mint in base of shaker (just to bruise). Add other ingredients, **SHAKE** with ice and fine strain into chilled glass.

8	fresh	**Mint leaves**
2½	shot(s)	**Bulleit bourbon whiskey**
½	shot(s)	**Sugar syrup** (2 sugar to 1 water)
¾	shot(s)	**Chilled mineral water** (omit if wet ice)

Origin: Adapted from a recipe created in the mid 1990s by Dick Bradsell.
Comment: A short variation on the classic Julep: sweetened bourbon and mint.

JUNGLE JUICE

Glass: Collins
Garnish: Orange slice
Method: SHAKE all ingredients with ice and strain into ice-filled glass.

1	shot(s)	**Ketel One vodka**
1	shot(s)	**Bacardi Superior rum**
½	shot(s)	**Cointreau triple sec**
1	shot(s)	**Ocean Spray cranberry juice**
1	shot(s)	**Freshly squeezed orange juice**
1	shot(s)	**Pressed pineapple juice**
¾	shot(s)	**Freshly squeezed lime juice**
¼	shot(s)	**Sugar syrup** (2 sugar to 1 water)

Comment: If this is the juice of the jungle, I'm a monkey's uncle. That said, as fruity long drinks go this is not bad at all.

KAMIKAZE

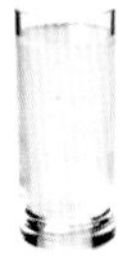

Glass: Shot
Method: SHAKE all ingredients with ice and fine strain into chilled glass.

1	shot(s)	**Don Julio 100% agave tequila**
½	shot(s)	**Cointreau triple sec**
½	shot(s)	**Freshly squeezed lime juice**

Variant: With vodka in place of tequila.
Comment: A bite-sized Margarita.

KATINKA

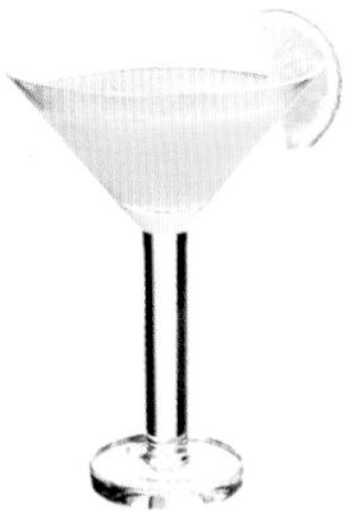

Glass: Martini
Garnish: Lime wedge on rim
Method: SHAKE all ingredients with ice and fine strain into chilled glass.

1½	shot(s)	**Ketel One vodka**
1	shot(s)	**Bols apricot brandy liqueur**
1	shot(s)	**Freshly squeezed lime juice**
½	shot(s)	**Sugar syrup** (2 sugar to 1 water)

Comment: Medium sweet, yet also tart and tangy.

JULEP

KENTUCKY JEWEL

Glass: Martini
Garnish: Berries on stick
Method: SHAKE all ingredients with ice and fine strain into chilled glass.

1½	shot(s)	**Bulleit bourbon whiskey**
¼	shot(s)	**Crème de cassis or Chambord**
¼	shot(s)	**Cointreau triple sec**
2	shot(s)	**Ocean Spray cranberry juice**

Origin: Adapted from a drink created in 2004 by Jonathan Lamm, The Admirable Crichton, London, England.
Comment: Easy sipping, fruity bourbon.

KENTUCKY MUFFIN

Glass: Old-fashioned
Garnish: Blueberries
Method: MUDDLE blueberries in base of shaker. Add other ingredients, **SHAKE** with ice and strain into glass filled with crushed ice. Stir and serve with straws.

12	fresh	**Blueberries**
2	shot(s)	**Bulleit bourbon whiskey**
1	shot(s)	**Pressed apple juice**
½	shot(s)	**Freshly squeezed lime juice**
½	shot(s)	**Sugar syrup** (2 sugar to 1 water)

Origin: Created in 2000 at Mash, London, England.
Comment: Blueberries, lime and apple combine with and are fortified by bourbon.

KENTUCKY TEA

Glass: Collins
Garnish: Lime wedge
Method: SHAKE first four ingredients with ice and strain into ice-filled glass. **TOP** with ginger ale.

2	shot(s)	**Bulleit bourbon whiskey**
1	shot(s)	**Cointreau triple sec**
1	shot(s)	**Freshly squeezed lime juice**
½	shot(s)	**Sugar syrup** (2 sugar to 1 water)
Top up with		**Ginger ale**

Comment: Spicy whiskey and ginger.

KIR ROYALE

Glass: Flute
Method: POUR cassis into glass and **TOP** with champagne.

½	shot(s)	**Crème de cassis or Chambord**
Top up with		**Brut champagne**

Variant: Kir
Comment: Easy to make, easy to drink.

KLONDIKE

Glass: Collins
Garnish: Orange slice
Method: POUR ingredients into ice-filled glass and stir.

2	shot(s)	**Bulleit bourbon whiskey**
2	shot(s)	**Freshly squeezed orange juice**
Top up with		**Ginger ale**

Origin: Recipe adapted from A. S. Crockett's 1935 'The Old Waldorf-Astoria Bar Book'.
Comment: A simple drink but the three ingredients combine well.

KNICKERBOCKER MARTINI

Glass: Martini
Garnish: Orange zest twist
Method: STIR all ingredients with ice and strain into chilled glass.

1¾	shot(s)	**Tanqueray London dry gin**
¾	shot(s)	**Noilly Prat dry vermouth**
½	shot(s)	**Martini Rosso sweet vermouth**

Origin: Thought to have been created at the Knickerbocker Hotel, New York City, USA.
Comment: Aromatic vermouth dominates this flavoursome Martini variant.

LARCHMONT

Glass: Martini
Garnish: Orange zest twist
Method: SHAKE all ingredients with ice and fine strain into chilled glass.

1½	shot(s)	**Bacardi Superior rum**
½	shot(s)	**Grand Marnier liqueur**
½	shot(s)	**Freshly squeezed lime juice**
¼	shot(s)	**Sugar syrup** (2 sugar to 1 water)
½	shot(s)	**Chilled mineral water** (omit if wet ice)

Origin: Created by David A. Embury, who in his 1948 'Fine Art of Mixing Drinks' writes of this drink: "As a grand finale to cocktails based on the Rum Sour, I give you one of my favorites which I have named after my favorite community."
Comment: I share Embury's appreciation of this fine drink, although I think of it more as a type of Orange Daiquiri.

LEAP YEAR MARTINI

Glass: Martini
Garnish: Lemon peel twist
Method: SHAKE all ingredients with ice and fine strain into chilled glass.

2	shot(s)	**Tanqueray London dry gin**
½	shot(s)	**Grand Marnier liqueur**
½	shot(s)	**Martini Rosso sweet vermouth**
¼	shot(s)	**Freshly squeezed lemon juice**

Origin: Harry Craddock created this drink for the Leap Year celebrations at the Savoy Hotel, London, on 29th February 1928 and recorded it in his 1930 Savoy Cocktail Book.
Comment: This drink, which is on the dry side, needs to be served ice-cold.

LEAVE IT TO ME MARTINI

Glass: Martini
Garnish: Lemon zest twist
Method: SHAKE all ingredients with ice and fine strain into chilled glass.

1½	shot(s)	**Tanqueray London dry gin**
½	shot(s)	**Bols apricot brandy liqueur**
¾	shot(s)	**Martini Rosso sweet vermouth**
½	shot(s)	**Freshly squeezed lemon juice**
¼	shot(s)	**Pomegranate (grenadine) syrup**

Origin: Adapted from a recipe in Harry Craddock's 1930 Savoy Cocktail Book.
Comment: Gin, apricot, vermouth and lemon create an old fashioned but well balanced drink.

'SO LONG AS ANY MAN DRINKS WHEN HE WANTS TO AND STOPS WHEN HE WANTS TO, HE ISN'T A DRUNKARD, NO MATTER HOW MUCH HE DRINKS OR HOW OFTEN HE FALLS UNDER THE TABLE.'
WILLIAM BUEHLER SEABROOK

THE LEGEND

Glass: Martini
Garnish: Lime wedge on rim
Method: SHAKE all ingredients with ice and fine strain into chilled glass.

2	shot(s)	**Ketel One vodka**
1	shot(s)	**Freshly squeezed lime juice**
½	shot(s)	**Crème de cassis or Chambord**
½	shot(s)	**Sugar syrup** (2 sugar to 1 water)
2	dashes	**Fee Brothers orange bitters** (optional)

Origin: Created in the late 1990s by Dick Bradsell for Karen Hampsen at Legends, London, England.
Comment: The quality of orange bitters and blackberry liqueur used dramatically affect the flavour of this blush coloured cocktail.

LEMON DROP

Glass: Shot
Garnish: Sugar coated slice of lemon
Method: SHAKE all ingredients with ice and fine strain into chilled glass.

½	shot(s)	**Ketel One vodka**
½	shot(s)	**Cointreau triple sec**
½	shot(s)	**Freshly squeezed lemon juice**

Comment: Lemon and orange combine to make a fresh tasting citrus shot.

LEMON LIME & BITTERS

Glass: Collins
Garnish: Lime wedge
Method: POUR lime and bitters into ice-filled glass. **TOP** with lemonade, lightly stir and serve with straws.

½	shot(s)	**Freshly squeezed lime juice**
4	dashes	**Angostura aromatic bitters**
Top up with		**Sprite/lemonade/7-Up**

AKA: LLB
Origin: Very popular in its homeland, Australia.
Comment: If you're unlucky enough to be the driver, this refreshing long drink is a good low alcohol option.

LIMEADE (MOCKTAIL)

Glass: Collins
Garnish: Lime wedge
Method: SHAKE all ingredients with ice and fine strain into ice filled glass.

2	shot(s)	**Freshly squeezed lime juice**
1	shot(s)	**Sugar syrup** (2 sugar to 1 water)
3	shot(s)	**Chilled mineral water**

Variant: Shake first two ingredients & top with sparkling water.
Comment: A superbly refreshing alternative to lemonade.

L

LIVINGSTONE

Glass: Martini
Garnish: Lemon peel twist
Method: SHAKE all ingredients with ice and fine strain into chilled glass.

2	shot(s)	**Tanqueray London dry gin**
1	shot(s)	**Noilly Prat dry vermouth**
¼	shot(s)	**Sugar syrup** (2 sugar to 1 water)

Variant: Use pomegranate syrup in place of sugar and you have a Red Livingstone, named after London's 'lefty' ex-mayor, Ken.
Origin: This 1930s classic was named after Doctor Livingstone, the famous African missionary.
Comment: The classic gin and vermouth Martini made more approachable with a dash of sugar.

LOLITA MARGARITA

Glass: Coupette
Garnish: Lime wedge on rim
Method: STIR honey with tequila in base of shaker to dissolve honey. Add other ingredients, **SHAKE** with ice and fine strain into chilled glass.

2	spoons	**Runny honey**
2	shot(s)	**Don Julio 100% agave tequila**
1	shot(s)	**Freshly squeezed lime juice**
2	dashes	**Angostura aromatic bitters**

Origin: Named after the novel by Vladimir Nabokov which chronicles a middle-aged man's infatuation with a 12 year old girl. Nabokov invented the word 'nymphet' to describe her seductive qualities.
Comment: A fittingly seductive Margarita.

LONG ISLAND ICED TEA

Glass: Sling
Garnish: Lemon slice
Method: SHAKE first seven ingredients with ice and strain into ice-filled glass. **TOP** with cola, stir and serve with straws.

½	shot(s)	**Bacardi Superior rum**
½	shot(s)	**Tanqueray London dry gin**
½	shot(s)	**Ketel One vodka**
½	shot(s)	**Don Julio 100% agave tequila**
½	shot(s)	**Cointreau triple sec**
1	shot(s)	**Freshly squeezed lime juice**
½	shot(s)	**Sugar syrup** (2 sugar to 1 water)
Top up with		**Cola**

Origin: This infamous drink reached the height of its popularity in the early 1980s of the many stories surrounding its origin, perhaps the most credible attributes its creation to sometime in the late 1970s by Robert (rosebud) Butt at Oak Beach Inn in Babylon, New York . This area of New York State is known as 'Long Island' and the drink looks like iced tea disguising its contents – a fact that has many claiming its true origins lie with Prohibition.
Comment: A cooling, combination of five different spirits with a hint of lime and a splash of cola.

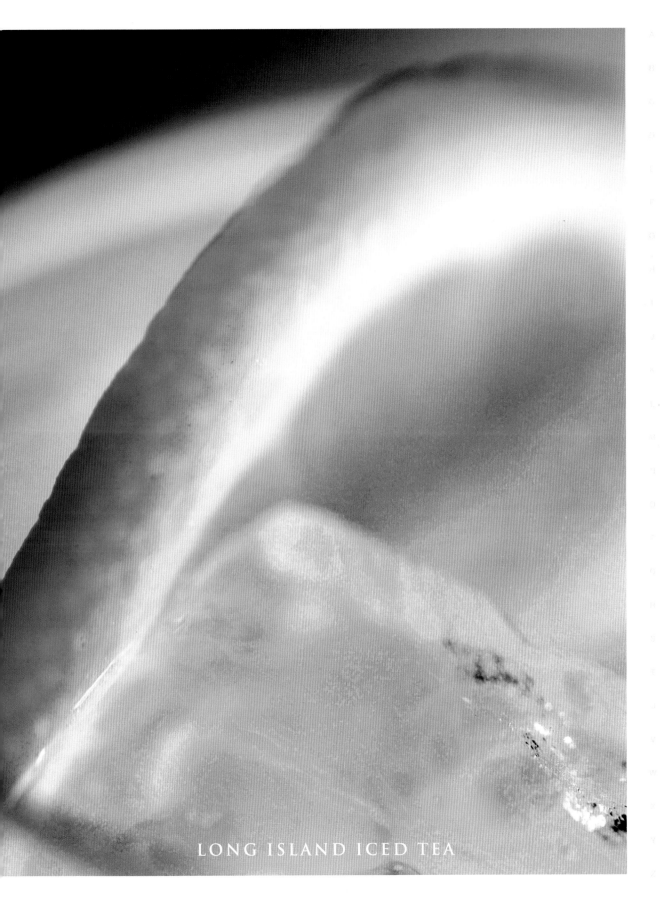

LONG ISLAND ICED TEA

LONDON COSMOPOLITAN

Glass: Martini
Garnish: Orange zest twist (flamed)
Method: SHAKE all ingredients with ice and fine strain into chilled glass.

1	shot(s)	**Tanqueray London dry gin**
1	shot(s)	**Cointreau triple sec**
1½	shot(s)	**Ocean Spray cranberry juice**
½	shot(s)	**Freshly squeezed lime juice**

Comment: Basically a Cosmopolitan but made with Tanqueray London dry gin instead of citrus vodka.

LOUD SPEAKER MARTINI

Glass: Martini
Garnish: Lemon peel twist
Method: SHAKE all ingredients with ice and fine strain into chilled glass.

1½	shot(s)	**Tanqueray London dry gin**
1½	shot(s)	**Courvoisier V.S.O.P. cognac**
½	shot(s)	**Martini Rosso sweet vermouth**
¼	shot(s)	**Freshly squeezed lemon juice**
¼	shot(s)	**Sugar syrup** (2 sugar to 1 water)

Origin: Adapted from a recipe in the 1930 Savoy Cocktail Book by Harry Craddock.
Comment: I've added a dash of sugar to the original recipe which I found too dry.

LOVED UP

Glass: Martini
Garnish: Berries on stick
Method: SHAKE all ingredients with ice and fine strain into chilled glass.

1½	shot(s)	**Don Julio 100% agave tequila**
½	shot(s)	**Cointreau triple sec**
½	shot(s)	**Crème de cassis or Chambord**
½	shot(s)	**Freshly squeezed lime juice**
1	shot(s)	**Freshly squeezed orange juice**
¼	shot(s)	**Sugar syrup** (2 sugar to 1 water)

Origin: Adapted from a cocktail discovered in 2002 at the Merc Bar, New York City, where the original name was listed as simply 'Love'.
Comment: Tequila predominates in this rusty coloured drink, which also features orange and berry fruit.

LUCKY LILY MARGARITA

Glass: Coupette
Garnish: Pineapple wedge dusted with pepper
Method: STIR honey with tequila in base of shaker to dissolve honey. ADD other ingredients, SHAKE with ice and fine strain into chilled glass.

2	spoons	**Runny honey**
2	shot(s)	**Don Julio 100% agave tequila**
1	shot(s)	**Pressed pineapple juice**
¾	shot(s)	**Freshly squeezed lime juice**
5	grinds	**Black pepper**

Origin: Adapted from a drink discovered in 2006 at All Star Lanes, London, England.
Comment: Spicy tequila and pineapple tingle with balance and flavour.

LUCKY LINDY

Glass: Collins
Garnish: Lemon slice
Method: STIR honey with bourbon in base of shaker so as to dissolve honey. Add lemon juice, SHAKE with ice and strain into ice-filled glass. TOP with lemonade, lightly stir and serve with straws.

3	spoon(s)	**Runny honey**
2	shot(s)	**Bulleit bourbon whiskey**
½	shot(s)	**Freshly squeezed lemon juice**
Top up with		**Sprite/lemonade/7-Up**

Origin: Adapted from a drink discovered in 2003 at The Grange Hall, New York City, USA.
Comment: A long refreshing drink that combines whisky, citrus and honey – a long chilled toddy without the spice.

LUSH

Glass: Flute
Garnish: Raspberry in glass
Method: POUR vodka and liqueur into chilled glass, TOP with champagne and lightly stir.

1	shot(s)	**Ketel One vodka**
½	shot(s)	**Crème de cassis or Chambord**
Top up with		**Brut champagne**

Origin: Created in 1999 by Spike Marchant at Alphabet, London, England.
Comment: It is, are you?

LUTKINS SPECIAL MARTINI

Glass: Martini
Garnish: Orange zest twist
Method: SHAKE all ingredients with ice and fine strain into chilled glass.

1½	shot(s)	**Tanqueray London dry gin**
1	shot(s)	**Noilly Prat dry vermouth**
½	shot(s)	**Bols apricot brandy liqueur**
¾	shot(s)	**Freshly squeezed orange juice**

Origin: Adapted from a recipe in Harry Craddock's 1930 Savoy Cocktail Book.
Comment: I've tried many variations on the above formula and none are that special.

MACKA

Glass: Collins
Garnish: Lemon slice
Method: SHAKE first four ingredients with ice and strain into ice-filled glass. TOP with soda.

2	shot(s)	**Tanqueray London dry gin**
½	shot(s)	**Noilly Prat dry vermouth**
½	shot(s)	**Martini Rosso sweet vermouth**
½	shot(s)	**Crème de cassis or Chambord**
Top up with		**Soda water** (club soda)

Comment: A long fruity drink for parched palates.

L

MADRAS

Glass: Collins
Garnish: Orange slice
Method: SHAKE all ingredients with ice and strain into ice-filled glass.

2	shot(s)	Ketel One vodka
3	shot(s)	Ocean Spray cranberry juice
2	shot(s)	Freshly squeezed orange juice

Comment: A Seabreeze with orange juice in place of grapefruit juice, making it slightly sweeter.

MADROSKA

Glass: Collins
Garnish: Orange slice
Method: SHAKE all ingredients with ice and strain into ice-filled glass.

2	shot(s)	Ketel One vodka
2½	shot(s)	Pressed apple juice
1½	shot(s)	Ocean Spray cranberry juice
1	shot(s)	Freshly squeezed orange juice

Origin: Created in 1998 by Jamie Terrell, London, England.
Comment: A Madras with more than a hint of apple juice.

MAHUKONA

Glass: Sling (10oz Pilsner glass)
Garnish: Pineapple cubes & cherry on stick, mint sprig
Method: BLEND all ingredients with 6oz scoop crushed ice and strain into glass half-filled with crushed ice. Serve with straws.

1	shot(s)	Bacardi Superior rum
½	shot(s)	Cointreau triple sec
1	shot(s)	Pressed pineapple juice
½	shot(s)	Freshly squeezed lemon juice
¼	shot(s)	Sugar syrup (2 sugar to 1 water)
2	dashes	Angostura aromatic bitters

Origin: Adapted from Victor Bergeron's 'Trader Vic's Bartender's Guide' (1972 revised edition).
Comment: Citrus fresh and refreshing, not at all a sweetie.

MAIDEN'S BLUSH

Glass: Martini
Garnish: Lemon peel twist
Method: SHAKE all ingredients with ice and fine strain into chilled glass.

2	shot(s)	Tanqueray London dry gin
½	shot(s)	Cointreau triple sec
½	shot(s)	Pomegranate (grenadine) syrup
¼	shot(s)	Freshly squeezed lemon juice
½	shot(s)	Chilled mineral water (omit if wet ice)

Origin: Adapted from a recipe in Harry Craddock's 1930 Savoy Cocktail Book.
Comment: Pale pink, subtle and light.

MAIDEN'S PRAYER

Glass: Martini
Garnish: Orange zest twist
Method: SHAKE all ingredients with ice and fine strain into chilled glass.

1½	shot(s)	Tanqueray London dry gin
1	shot(s)	Cointreau triple sec
1	shot(s)	Freshly squeezed orange juice
½	shot(s)	Freshly squeezed lemon juice

Origin: Adapted from a recipe in Harry Craddock's 1930 Savoy Cocktail Book.
Comment: Fresh, zesty orange with a pleasing twang of alcohol.

MAINBRACE

Glass: Martini
Garnish: Orange zest twist
Method: SHAKE all ingredients with ice and fine strain into chilled glass.

1¼	shot(s)	Tanqueray London dry gin
1¼	shot(s)	Cointreau triple sec
1¼	shot(s)	Freshly squeezed grapefruit juice

Comment: Tangy grapefruit laced with gin and a hint of orange. Tart finish.

MAJOR BAILEY #1

M

Glass: Sling
Garnish: Mint sprig
Method: Lightly MUDDLE (only to bruise) mint with gin in base of shaker. Add other ingredients, SHAKE with ice and fine strain into glass half filled with crushed ice. CHURN (stir) drink with the ice using a barspoon. Top the glass to the brim with more crushed ice and churn again. Serve with straws.

12	fresh	Mint leaves
2	shot(s)	Tanqueray London dry gin
¼	shot(s)	Freshly squeezed lime juice
¼	shot(s)	Freshly squeezed lemon juice
½	shot(s)	Sugar syrup (2 sugar to 1 water)

Origin: Adapted from a recipe in the 1947 Trader Vic's Bartender's Guide by Victor Bergeron.
Comment: As Victor says of this gin based Julep, "This is a hell of a drink."

MAJOR BAILEY #2

Glass: Sling
Garnish: Mint sprig
Method: BLEND all ingredients with one 12oz scoop of crushed ice and serve with straws.

2	shot(s)	Bacardi Superior rum
1	shot(s)	Cointreau triple sec
1	shot(s)	Pressed pineapple juice
½	shot(s)	Freshly squeezed lemon juice
¼	shot(s)	Sugar syrup (2 sugar to 1 water)

Origin: Adapted from a drink created by Victor Bergeron.
Comment: Made well, this is a long, fruity, brilliant frozen Daiquiri.

MANHATTAN
DRY

M

Glass: Martini
Garnish: Twist of orange (discarded) & two maraschino cherries
Method: STIR all ingredients with ice and strain into chilled glass.

2½	shot(s)	**Bulleit bourbon whiskey**
1	shot(s)	**Noilly Prat dry vermouth**
3	dashes	**Angostura aromatic bitters**

Variant: Manhattan Perfect and Manhattan Sweet. Also served over ice in an old-fashioned glass.
Origin: Like so many cocktails, the origins of the Manhattan are lost in time. And, as neither the name nor the ingredients are so unusual as to prevent inadvertent duplication, the mystery is likely to remain unsolved. The Democrat newspaper remarked in 1882 that, 'It is but a short time ago that a mixture of whiskey, vermouth and bitters came into vogue' and observed that it had been known as a Turf Club cocktail, a Jockey Club cocktail and a Manhattan cocktail.

Until fairly recently, the most popular story was that the drink was created in November 1874 at New York City's Manhattan Club for Lady Randolph Churchill (née Jenny Jerome), while she was celebrating the successful gubernatorial campaign of Samuel Jones Tilden. (The Manhattan Club was opposite the site which now houses the Empire State Building.) However, David Wondrich has pointed out that the banquet in question was held in November 1874, when Lady C was otherwise engaged, in England, giving birth to Winston.

A 1945 article claims that a drink under the name of the Manhattan appeared in an 1860 bar guide; it certainly appears in Harry Johnson's book of 1884.

A plausible story comes from a book published in 1923, 'Valentine's Manual of New York'. In this a William F. Mulhall who was a bartender at New York's Hoffman House in the 1880s recounts, "The Manhattan cocktail was invented by a man named Black who kept a place ten doors below Houston Street on Broadway in the [eighteen] sixties - probably the most famous drink in the world in its time."

Yet another story involves a Col. Joe Walker on a yachting trip in New York but as this specifically refers to Martini Rosso sweet vermouth I have recounted it under 'Manhattan Sweet'.
Comment: A bone dry Manhattan for those with dry palates.

MANHATTAN DRY

MANHATTAN PERFECT

Glass: Martini
Garnish: Twist of orange (discarded) & two maraschino cherries
Method: STIR all ingredients with ice and strain into chilled glass.

2½	shot(s)	**Bulleit bourbon whiskey**
½	shot(s)	**Martini Rosso sweet vermouth**
½	shot(s)	**Noilly Prat dry vermouth**
3	dashes	**Angostura aromatic bitters**

Origin: Whatever the truth of its invention (see Manhattan Dry), the Manhattan was probably originally made with rye whiskey, rather than bourbon, as New York was a rye-drinking city, although early bar books just state 'whiskey'. Today it is common to use bourbon, although purists are beginning to revive rye.

When Scotch is substituted for bourbon the Manhattan becomes a Rob Roy, with brandy (cognac) it becomes a Harvard and with applejack it is a Star Cocktail.

Some time in 2005 it became conventional in some New York bars to garnish a Manhattan with two cherries as a 9/11 tribute.

Comment: The Manhattan version most popularly served – medium dry.

MANHATTAN SWEET

Glass: Martini **Garnish:** Twist of orange (discarded) & two maraschino cherries
Method: STIR all ingredients with ice and strain into chilled glass.

2½	shot(s)	**Bulleit bourbon whiskey**
1	shot(s)	**Martini Rosso sweet vermouth**
⅛	shot(s)	**Syrup from jar of maraschino cherries**
3	dashes	**Angostura aromatic bitters**

Origin: Various origins for this drink abound. The most recent I have come across and comes courtesy of Barry Popik's website barrypopik.com where Barry notes an entry in the Daily Journal, Racine, Wisconsin, 8 March 1899. The article purports that Col. Joe Walker ran the then-famous Crescent Hall Saloon in New Orleans, at the corner of Canal and St. Charles Streets and that some years before he went on a little yachting trip with a party of friends while in New York. "By some oversight the liquid refreshments in the icebox were confined to Italian vermouth and plain whisky, and it occurred to the colonel that a palatable drink might be made by mixing the two.

The results were so good that he experimented a little on his return to New Orleans, and soon perfected the Manhattan cocktail, as it is known today. It was christened in honor of his friends on Manhattan island, and the fame of the decoction soon spread all over the country. The true Manhattan cocktail is always made with Italian vermouth, but at half the places where they undertake to serve them, French [dry] vermouth is substituted, and the fine flavor is altogether destroyed. French vermouth is a sort of wine, while Italian vermouth is a cordial, pure and simple. They are as different as milk and molasses. A cocktail made from the French brand is no more a Manhattan cocktail than it is a Spanish omelette."

Comment: I must confess to preferring my Manhattans served sweet, or perfect at a push. The Manhattan is complex, challenging and moreish. Best of all, it's available in a style to suit every palate.

MARGARITA #1
(STRAIGHT-UP)

Glass: Coupette
Garnish: Salt rim & lime wedge
Method: SHAKE all ingredients with ice and fine strain into chilled glass.

2	shot(s)	**Don Julio 100% agave tequila**
1	shot(s)	**Cointreau triple sec**
1	shot(s)	**Freshly squeezed lime juice**

Variant: Margaritas made with premium tequilas are sometimes referred to as 'Deluxe' or 'Cadillac' Margaritas.

Origin: The Margarita can be considered a Tequila Sour, or a Tequila Sidecar, and two variations of this classic cocktail date back to the 1930s: the Tequila Daisy and the Picador. Both, however, lack the distinctive salt rim.

There are many people who claim to have invented the Margarita, which, as Spanish for 'daisy' and a popular woman's name, would have been a very common name for a drink. A brief summary of the top claimants:
Francisco 'Pancho' Morales, while working in a bar called Tommy's Place in Ciudad Juarez, Mexico, was asked to make a 'Magnolia' on the 4th July 1942, but couldn't remember it so created this drink. The customer's name may even have been Margarita.

Carlos 'Danny' Herrera created the cocktail either in 1947 or 1948 at his Rancho La Gloria bar in Rosarito, Mexico, for an actress called Marjorie King who drank no spirit but tequila. He added Cointreau and lime, and the unique salt rim which caught people's attention at the bar, then named his creation Margarita, the Spanish for Marjorie.

Daniel (Danny) Negrete created the drink in 1936 when he was the manager of Garci Crespo Hotel in Puebla, Mexico. His girlfriend, Margarita, apparently liked salt in her drinks and he is said to have created the drink for her as a present. In 1944 Danny moved to Tijuana, Mexico, and became a bartender at the Agua Caliente Racetrack, a place which has some claim to be the birthplace of the Margarita in the early 1930s.

Vernon Underwood was president of Young's Market Company, who in the 1930s had started distributing Cuervo tequila. He went to Johnny Durlesser, head bartender of the Tail O' The Cock in LA, and asked him to create something using his spirit, then named it after his wife Margaret (Margarita).

Sara Morales, an expert in Mexican folklore, claimed the Margarita was created in 1930 by Doña Bertha, owner of Bertha's Bar in Taxco, Mexico. The socialite Margaret Sames held a Christmas party in Acapulco, Mexico, in 1948, and created the first Margarita. She thought nothing of it until, when flying home to San Antonio from Acapulco airport, she saw a bar advertising 'Margarita's Drink', a cocktail with exactly the same ingredients as her own. So… Plenty of Margarets and even Margaritas: there is also a popular holiday destination called Margarita Island, located in the Caribbean north of Venezuela, two-and-a-half hours from Miami.

It could simply be a twist on the 'Daisy', a classic cocktail dating back to Victorian times and made with citrus juice, sweetened with a syrup or liqueur, and fortified with a base spirit. Margarita is the Spanish word for daisy. A British antecedent of the Margarita called a 'Picador' has recently been unearthed.

Comment: For the perfect salt rim, liquidise sea salt to make it finer, then run a lime wedge around the outside edge of the glass before dipping the rim in salt. Rimming only half the glass with salt gives the drinker the option of enjoying the cocktail with or without salt.

M

MARGARITA

MARGARITA #2 (ON THE ROCKS)

Glass: Old-fashioned
Garnish: Salt rim & lime wedge
Method: SHAKE all ingredients with ice and strain into ice-filled glass.

2	shot(s)	**Don Julio 100% agave tequila**
1	shot(s)	**Cointreau triple sec**
1	shot(s)	**Freshly squeezed lime juice**

Comment: Tangy citrus, tequila and salt.

MARGARITA #3 (FROZEN)

Glass: Martini
Garnish: Maraschino cherry
Method: BLEND all ingredients with 6oz scoop of crushed ice. Serve heaped in the glass and with straws.

1½	shot(s)	**Don Julio 100% agave tequila**
¾	shot(s)	**Cointreau triple sec**
¾	shot(s)	**Freshly squeezed lime juice**
½	shot(s)	**Sugar syrup** (2 sugar to 1 water)

Variant: With fruit and/or fruit liqueurs.
Comment: Citrus freshness with the subtle agave of tequila served frozen.

M

MARIA THERESA MARGARITA

Glass: Martini
Garnish: Lime wedge on rim
Method: STIR honey with tequila in base of shaker to dissolve honey. **ADD** other ingredients, **SHAKE** with ice and fine strain into chilled glass.

2	spoons	**Runny honey**
2	shot(s)	**Don Julio 100% agave tequila**
1	shot(s)	**Ocean Spray cranberry juice**
½	shot(s)	**Freshly squeezed lime juice**

Origin: Adapted from a Tiki drink created by Victor Bergeron (Trader Vic).
Comment: Originally sweetened with sugar syrup, this is better smoothed with honey.

MAPLE LEAF

Glass: Old-fashioned
Garnish: Lemon zest twist
Method: SHAKE all ingredients with ice and strain into ice-filled glass.

2	shot(s)	**Bulleit bourbon whiskey**
½	shot(s)	**Freshly squeezed lemon juice**
¼	shot(s)	**Maple syrup**

Comment: This trio combine wonderfully with maple to the fore.

MAPLE POMME

Glass: Collins
Garnish: Apple wedge
Method: SHAKE first four ingredients with ice and strain into ice-filled glass. **TOP** with ginger ale, lightly stir and serve with straws.

2	shot(s)	**Johnnie Walker Scotch whisky**
½	shot(s)	**Freshly squeezed lemon juice**
1	shot(s)	**Pressed apple juice**
½	shot(s)	**Maple syrup**
Top up with		**Ginger ale**

Origin: Adapted from a short drink created in 2005 by Tonin Kacaj at Maze, London, England.
Comment: Scotch based drink for warm weather.

> 'A MEDIUM VODKA DRY MARTINI — WITH A SLICE OF LEMON PEEL. SHAKEN AND NOT STIRRED.'
> IAN FLEMING

MARMALADE COCKTAIL

Glass: Martini
Garnish: Orange zest twist
Method: STIR marmalade with gin until the marmalade dissolves. **SHAKE** other ingredients with ice and fine strain into chilled glass.

4	spoons	**Orange marmalade**
2	shot(s)	**Tanqueray London dry gin**
½	shot(s)	**Freshly squeezed lemon juice**

Origin: Adapted from a recipe in the 1930 'Savoy Cocktail Book' by Harry Craddock (the original recipe serves six people).
Comment: Harry wrote of his own drink, "By its bitter-sweet taste this cocktail is especially suited to be a luncheon aperitif."

MARMARITA

Glass: Coupette
Garnish: Wipe Marmite (yeast extract) around rim
Method: SHAKE all ingredients with ice and fine strain into chilled glass.

2	shot(s)	**Don Julio 100% agave tequila**
1	shot(s)	**Cointreau triple sec**
1	shot(s)	**Freshly squeezed lime juice**

Origin: Created in 2005 by Simon (Ginger) Warneford at Blanch House, Brighton, England.
Comment: A Margarita with a Marmite rim. After all yeast extract is slightly salty.

MARQUEE

Glass: Martini
Garnish: Raspberries on stick
Method: SHAKE all ingredients with ice and fine strain into chilled glass.

1½	shot(s)	**Bulleit bourbon whiskey**
1½	shot(s)	**Ocean Spray cranberry juice**
½	shot(s)	**Crème de cassis or Chambord**
½	shot(s)	**Freshly squeezed lemon juice**
¼	shot(s)	**Sugar syrup** (2 sugar to 1 water)

Origin: Created in 1998 by Giovanni Burdi at Match EC1, London, England.
Comment: Raspberry and bourbon combine perfectly in this short, slightly sweet, fruity drink.

MATADOR

Glass: Collins
Garnish: Pineapple wedge on rim
Method: SHAKE all ingredients with ice and strain into ice-filled glass.

2	shot(s)	**Don Julio 100% agave tequila**
1	shot(s)	**Cointreau triple sec**
1	shot(s)	**Freshly squeezed lime juice**
2	shot(s)	**Pressed pineapple juice**

Comment: A long Margarita with pineapple juice. The lime and tequila work wonders with the sweet pineapple.

MARTINEZ

Glass: Martini
Garnish: Orange zest twist
Method: STIR all ingredients with ice and strain into chilled glass.

2	shot(s)	**Tanqueray London dry gin**
1	shot(s)	**Martini Rosso sweet vermouth**
¼	shot(s)	**Cointreau triple sec**
2	dashes	**Fee Brother orange bitters** (optional)

Origin: Probably the forerunner of the Martini, the first known recipe for this drink appears in 1884. Drinks historian David Wondrich and others believe it was first made using Dutch oude genever as this was the style of exported to America long before English Old Tom gin or Tanqueray London dry gins. Although the drink appears in his 1887 Bartenders' Guide, there is no evidence that Jerry Thomas invented the Martinez and the town of Martinez in California claims that Julio Richelieu created it for a gold miner in 1874.
Comment: Stir well as dilution helps to tame this old-school classic in which bitter orange predominates.

MEDIUM MARTINI

Glass: Martini
Garnish: Orange zest twist
Method: STIR all ingredients with ice and strain into chilled glass.

1½	shot(s)	**Tanqueray London dry gin**
¾	shot(s)	**Noilly Prat dry vermouth**
¾	shot(s)	**Martini Rosso sweet vermouth**

Origin: Adapted from a recipe in Harry Craddock's 1930 Savoy Cocktail Book.
Comment: A classic Martini served perfect and very wet. I prefer mine shaken which is the method Harry specifies in his guide.

M

MESA FRESCA

Glass: Collins
Garnish: Lime wedge
Method: SHAKE all ingredients with ice and strain into ice-filled glass.

2	shot(s)	**Don Julio 100% agave tequila**
3	shot(s)	**Freshly squeezed grapefruit juice**
1	shot(s)	**Freshly squeeezed lime juice**
½	shot(s)	**Sugar syrup** (2 sugar to 1 water)

Origin: Discovered in 2005 at Mesa Grill, New York City, USA.
Comment: Sweet and sour tequila and grapefruit.

> 'IT'S BEEN SO LONG SINCE I'VE HAD CHAMPAGNE.'
> LAST WORDS OF ANTON CHEKHOV

MARTINI ROYALE

Glass: Martini
Garnish: Lemon zest twist
Method: STIR vodka and crème de cassis with ice and strain into chilled glass. **TOP** with chilled champagne.

1½	shot(s)	**Ketel One vodka**
½	shot(s)	**Crème de cassis or Chambord**
Top up with		**Brut champagne**

Origin: Created in 2001 by Dick Bradsell at Monte's, London, England.
Comment: The Kir Royale meets the vodkatini in this pink but powerful drink.

MERRY-GO-ROUND MARTINI

Glass: Martini
Garnish: Olive & lemon zest twist
Method: STIR all ingredients with ice and fine strain into chilled glass.

2	shot(s)	**Tanqueray London dry gin**
½	shot(s)	**Noilly Prat dry vermouth**
½	shot(s)	**Martini Rosso sweet vermouth**

Origin: Long lost classic variation on the Dry Martini.
Comment: Stir this 'perfect' Martini around and then get merry.

MEXICAN

Glass: Martini
Garnish: Pineapple wedge on rim
Method: SHAKE all ingredients with ice and fine strain into chilled glass.

2	shot(s)	**Don Julio 100% agave tequila**
1½	shot(s)	**Pressed pineapple juice**
¼	shot(s)	**Pomegranate (grenadine) syrup**

Variant: Substitute sugar syrup for pomegranate syrup.
Comment: Fresh pineapple makes this drink.

'FRANKLY, I WAS HORRIFIED BY LIFE, AT WHAT A MAN HAD TO DO SIMPLY IN ORDER TO EAT, SLEEP AND KEEP HIMSELF CLOTHED. SO I STAYED IN BED AND DRANK.'
CHARLES BUKOWSKI

M

MEXICAN 55

Glass: Collins
Garnish: Lime wedge
Method: SHAKE first four ingredients with ice and strain into ice-filled glass. **TOP** with champagne.

1½	shot(s)	**Don Julio 100% agave tequila**
1	shot(s)	**Freshly squeezed lemon juice**
½	shot(s)	**Sugar syrup** (2 sugar to 1 water)
2	dashes	**Angostura aromatic bitters**
Top up with		**Brut champagne**

Origin: An adaptation of the classic French '75 created in 1988 at La Perla, Paris, France. The name comes from Fidel Castro's statement that bullets, like wine, came in vintages and Mexican '55 was a good year [for bullets].
Comment: Suitably hard, yet surprisingly refreshing and sophisticated.

MEXICAN MANHATTAN

Glass: Martini
Garnish: Maraschino cherry
Method: STIR all ingredients with ice and strain into chilled glass.

2	shot(s)	**Don Julio 100% agave tequila**
1	shot(s)	**Martini Rosso sweet vermouth**
3	dashes	**Angostura aromatic bitters**

Comment: You've tried this with bourbon, now surprise yourself with an aged tequila.

MEXICAN MARTINI

Glass: Martini
Garnish: Pineapple leaf on rim
Method: SHAKE all ingredients with ice and fine strain into chilled glass.

2	shot(s)	**Don Julio 100% agave tequila**
¼	shot(s)	**Crème de cassis or Chambord**
2	shot(s)	**Pressed pineapple juice**

Origin: Discovered in 2004 at Indigo Yard, Edinburgh, Scotland.
Comment: Tequila, pineapple and blackcurrant combine in this medium dry cocktail.

MEXICAN TEA (HOT)

Glass: Toddy
Garnish: Lime slice
Method: Place bar spoon in warmed glass. **POUR** all ingredients into glass and stir.

2	shot(s)	**Don Julio 100% agave tequila**
½	shot(s)	**Sugar syrup** (2 sugar to 1 water)
Top up with		**Hot black breakfast tea**

Comment: Tiffin will never be the same again.

MIAMI BEACH

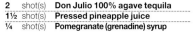

Glass: Martini
Garnish: Pineapple wedge & cherry
Method: SHAKE all ingredients with ice and fine strain into chilled glass.

2	shot(s)	**Tanqueray London dry gin**
1½	shot(s)	**Pressed pineapple juice**
¼	shot(s)	**Sugar syrup** (2 sugar to 1 water)

Comment: Fruity and well proportioned – like the babes on Miami Beach. Sorry.

THE MILLION DOLLAR COCKTAIL

Glass: Martini
Garnish: Lemon zest twist (round like an egg yolk in the foam)
Method: SHAKE all ingredients with ice and fine strain into chilled glass.

2	shot(s)	**Tanqueray London dry gin**
1	shot(s)	**Martini Rosso sweet vermouth**
½	shot(s)	**Pressed pineapple juice**
¼	shot(s)	**Pomegranate (grenadine) syrup**
½	fresh	**Egg white**

Origin: This classic cocktail is thought to have been created around 1910 by Ngiam Tong Boon at The Long Bar, Raffles Hotel, Singapore. Boon is more famous for the Singapore Sling.
Comment: Serious, yet superbly smooth and a bit fluffy.

MILLION DOLLAR MARGARITA

Glass: Old-fashioned
Garnish: Lime wedge
Method: SHAKE all ingredients with ice and strain into ice-filled glass.

1½	shot(s)	**Don Julio 100% agave tequila**
1½	shot(s)	**Grand Marnier (Cuvée du Centenaire)**
½	shot(s)	**Freshly squeezed lime juice**

Origin: Discovered in 2006 at Maison 140 Hotel, Los Angeles, USA where I paid a mere $41.14 plus tip for the drink.
Comment: The proportions of this Margarita accentuate the liqueur.

MINT & HONEY DAIQUIRI

Glass: Martini
Garnish: Mint sprig
Method: STIR honey and rum in base of shaker until honey dissolves. Add other ingredients, **SHAKE** with ice and fine strain into chilled glass.

2	spoons	**Runny honey**
2	shot(s)	**Bacardi Superior rum**
3	torn	**Mint leaves**
½	shot(s)	**Freshly squeezed lime juice**
½	shot(s)	**Chilled mineral water** (omit if wet ice)

Origin: Created in 2006 by yours truly.
Comment: A fresh-breath-tastic twist on the Daiquiri.

MILLIONAIRE

Glass: Martini
Garnish: Quarter orange slice on rim
Method: SHAKE all ingredients with ice and fine strain into chilled glass.

2	shot(s)	**Bulleit bourbon whiskey**
½	shot(s)	**Cointreau triple sec**
½	shot(s)	**Freshly squeezed lemon juice**
¼	shot(s)	**Pomegranate (grenadine) syrup**
½	fresh	**Egg white**

Comment: Rust coloured tangy citrus smoothed and served straight-up.

MINT COLLINS

Glass: Collins
Garnish: Mint sprig
Method: Lightly **MUDDLE** (just to bruise) mint in base of shaker. Add next three ingredients, **SHAKE** with ice and fine strain into chilled glass. **TOP** with soda, lightly stir and serve with straws.

12	fresh	**Mint leaves**
2	shot(s)	**Tanqueray London dry gin**
1	shot(s)	**Freshly squeezed lemon juice**
½	shot(s)	**Sugar syrup** (2 sugar to 1 water)
Top up with		**Soda water** (club soda)

Origin: Adapted from a recipe in the 1947-72 Trader Vic's Bartender's Guide by Victor Bergeron.
Comment: Exactly what the name promises.

M

MIMOSA

Glass: Flute
Garnish: Orange zest twist
Method: POUR ingredients into chilled glass and gently stir.

½	shot(s)	**Grand Marnier liqueur**
1¾	shot(s)	**Freshly squeezed orange juice**
Top up with		**Brut champagne**

Variant: When made with mandarin juice this becomes a Puccini.
Origin: Created in 1925 at the Ritz Hotel in Paris and named after the tropical flowering shrub.
Comment: A liqueur-infused take on the Buck's Fizz.

MINT DAIQUIRI

Glass: Martini
Garnish: Mint leaf
Method: Lightly **MUDDLE** (just to bruise) mint in base of shaker. Add other ingredients, **SHAKE** with ice and fine strain into chilled glass.

12	fresh	**Mint leaves**
2	shot(s)	**Bacardi Superior rum**
½	shot(s)	**Freshly squeezed lime juice**
¼	shot(s)	**Sugar syrup** (2 sugar to 1 water)
½	shot(s)	**Chilled mineral water** (omit if wet ice)

Origin: Created in 2006 by yours truly.
Comment: A short, concentrated Mojito.

HOW TO MAKE SUGAR SYRUP

To make your own sugar syrup, gradually pour TWO cups of granulated sugar into a saucepan containing ONE cup of hot water. Stir as you pour and carry on stirring and simmering until the sugar is dissolved. Do not let the water even come close to boiling and only simmer for as long as it takes to dissolve the sugar. Allow syrup to cool and pour into an empty bottle. Ideally, you should finely strain your syrup into the bottle to remove any undissolved crystals which could otherwise encourage crystallisation. If kept in a refrigerator this mixture will last for a couple of months.

MINT JULEP

Glass: Collins (or metal Julep cup)
Garnish: Mint sprig and slice of lemon
Method: Lightly **MUDDLE** (just to bruise) mint in base of shaker. Add other ingredients, **SHAKE** with ice and strain into glass half filled with crushed ice. **CHURN** (stir) the drink with the crushed ice using a bar spoon. Top up the glass with more crushed ice and **CHURN** again. Repeat this process until the drink fills the glass and serve.

12	fresh	**Mint leaves**
2½	shot(s)	**Bulleit bourbon whiskey**
¾	shot(s)	**Sugar syrup** (2 sugar to 1 water)
3	dashes	**Angostura aromatic bitters**

Origin: Like so many cocktails, the humble Mint Julep's origins are the subject of heated debate. Today it is closely identified with America's Deep South, famously served at the Kentucky Derby. However, the name derives from the Arabic word 'julab', meaning rosewater, and the first known written reference to a cocktail-style Julep was by a Virginia gentleman in 1787. At that time it could be made with rum, brandy or whiskey, but by 1900 whiskey had become the preferred base spirit.

Common perceived wisdom has it that the Julep originated in Persia, or there abouts, and it travelled to Europe (some say Southern France) where the rose petals were substituted for indigenous mint. The drink is then believed to have crossed the Atlantic where cognac was replaced with peach brandy and then whiskey – the Mint Julep we recognise today.

The remodelled US style Mint Julep reached Britain in 1837, thanks to the novelist Captain Frederick Marryat, who complained of being woken at 7am by a slave brandishing a Julep. He popularised it through his descriptions of American Fourth of July celebrations.

When making a Mint Julep it is important to only bruise the mint as crushing the leaves releases the bitter, inner juices. Also be sure to discard the stems, which are also bitter.

It is imperative that the drink is served ice cold. Cocktail etiquette dictates that the shaker containing the mint and other ingredients should be placed in a refrigerator with the serving vessel (preferably made of metal rather than glass) for at least two hours prior to adding ice, shaking and serving.

Variations on the Mint Julep include substituting the bourbon for rye whiskey, rum, gin, brandy, calvados or applejack brandy. Another variation calls for half a shot of aged rum to be floated on top of the bourbon-based julep.

Comment: This superb drink is better if the shaker and its contents are placed in the refrigerator for several hours prior to mixing with ice. This allows the mint flavours to infuse in the bourbon.

M

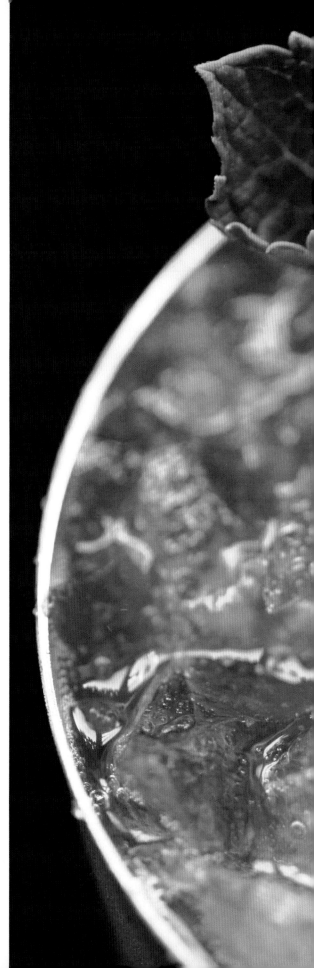

T JULEP

MINT LIMEADE (MOCKTAIL)

Glass: Collins
Garnish: Mint sprig
Method: Lightly **MUDDLE** (just to bruise) mint in base of shaker. Add next three ingredients, **SHAKE** with ice and fine strain into ice-filled glass. **TOP** with lemonade, lightly stir and serve with straws.

12	fresh	**Mint leaves**
1½	shot(s)	**Freshly squeezed lime juice**
1	shot(s)	**Pressed apple juice**
¾	shot(s)	**Sugar syrup** (2 sugar to 1 water)
Top up with		**Sprite/lemonade/7-Up**

Origin: Created in 2006 by yours truly.
Comment: Superbly refreshing - mint and lime served long.

MISS MARTINI

Glass: Martini
Garnish: Raspberries on stick
Method: **MUDDLE** raspberries in base of shaker. Add other ingredients, **SHAKE** with ice and fine strain into chilled glass.

7	fresh	**Raspberries**
2	shot(s)	**Ketel One vodka**
½	shot(s)	**Crème de cassis or Chambord**
¼	shot(s)	**Double (heavy) cream**
¼	shot(s)	**Milk**
⅛	shot(s)	**Sugar syrup** (2 sugar to 1 water)

Origin: Created in 1997 by Giovanni Burdi at Match EC1, London, England.
Comment: A pink, fruity and creamy concoction.

MISSISSIPPI PUNCH

Glass: Collins
Garnish: Lemon slice
Method: **SHAKE** all ingredients with ice and strain into glass filled with crushed ice.

1½	shot(s)	**Bulleit bourbon whiskey**
¾	shot(s)	**Courvoisier V.S.O.P. cognac**
¾	shot(s)	**Freshly squeezed lemon juice**
¾	shot(s)	**Sugar syrup** (2 sugar to 1 water)
2	shot(s)	**Chilled mineral water**

Comment: Balanced and refreshing.

DRINKS ARE GRADED AS FOLLOWS:

● DISGUSTING   ●● PRETTY AWFUL   ●● BEST AVOIDED
●●○ DISAPPOINTING   ●●● ACCEPTABLE   ●●●●○ GOOD
●●●● RECOMMENDED   ●●●●○ HIGHLY RECOMMENDED
●●●●● OUTSTANDING / EXCEPTIONAL

MOJITO

Glass: Collins
Garnish: Mint sprig
Method: Lightly **MUDDLE** (just to bruise) mint in base of glass. Add rum, lime juice and sugar. Half fill glass with crushed ice and **CHURN** (stir) with bar spoon. Fill glass with more crushed ice and **CHURN** some more. **TOP** with soda, stir and serve with straws.

M

12	fresh	**Mint leaves**
2	shot(s)	**Bacardi Superior rum**
¾	shot(s)	**Freshly squeezed lime juice**
½	shot(s)	**Sugar syrup** (2 sugar to 1 water)
Top up with		**Soda water** (club soda)

Variant: Add two dashes Angostura aromatic bitters.
Origin: Although the exact origins of the Mojito – and its name – are unclear, it's thought to go back to a medicinal drink called the 'Draque'. Named after Sir Francis Drake, the Draque was originally a mix of raw cane spirit (the crude forerunner of rum), sugar, lime and mint, and was said to drive out fever and colds. In the late 1890s, the raw cane spirit was replaced with Bacardi Superior Rum, made light and long with a splash of soda and the drink was re-named The Mojito.

It appealed to rich and poor alike and by the 1920's it had become Cuba's unofficial national drink. In fact, Ernest Hemmingway wrote that drinking a Mojito was like wearing a badge of Cuban heritage: it was not just a drink, it was a symbol of national pride.

The Bodeguita del Medio bar in Havana is usually credited with the first Mojito and this is apparently where Hemingway went for his. The earliest known recorded recipes of the Mojito call for a 'jigger' of Bacardi rum in the ingredients – so nothing much has changed really!

As for the origins of the name 'Mojito', no one knows for sure. Some say it comes from 'mojar', a Spanish verb that suggests wetness. Others say it comes from the African word 'mojo', meaning to place a little spell. Either way, Cuba's oldest cocktail continues to refresh and cast a spell on all those who drink it.
Comment: When well made, this Cuban cousin of the Mint Julep is one of the world's greatest and most refreshing cocktails.

MOJITO

MOSCOW MULE

M

Glass: Collins (or copper mug)
Garnish: Lime wedge & mint sprig
Method: **SHAKE** first three ingredients with ice and strain into ice-filled glass. **TOP** with ginger beer and stir.

2	shot(s)	**Ketel One vodka**
½	shot(s)	**Freshly squeezed lime juice**
3	dashes	**Angostura aromatic bitters**
Top up with		**Ginger beer**

Origin: This classic combination was born in 1941. John G. Martin had acquired the rights to Smirnoff vodka for Heublein, a small Connecticut based liquor and food distributor. Jack Morgan, the owner of Hollywood's famous Cock'n'Bull Saloon, was trying to launch his own brand of ginger beer. The two men met at New York City's Chatham Bar and hit on the idea of mixing Martin's vodka with Morgan's ginger beer and adding a dash of lime to create a new cocktail, the Moscow Mule.

To help promote the drink, and hence their respective products, Morgan had the idea of marketing the Moscow Mule using specially engraved mugs. The five ounce mugs were embossed with a kicking mule and made at a copper factory a friend of his had recently inherited. The promotion helped turn Smirnoff into a major brand.

Comment: A long, vodka based drink with spice provided by ginger beer and Angostura.

MOSCOW MULE

MOUNTAIN

Glass: Martini
Garnish: Maraschino cherry
Method: SHAKE all ingredients with ice and fine strain into chilled glass.

2	shot(s)	**Bulleit bourbon whiskey**
¾	shot(s)	**Noilly Prat dry vermouth**
¾	shot(s)	**Martini Rosso sweet vermouth**
½	fresh	**Egg white**

Comment: A perfect Manhattan smoothed by egg white.

'ALCOHOL IS LIKE LOVE. THE FIRST KISS IS MAGIC, THE SECOND IS INTIMATE, THE THIRD IS ROUTINE. AFTER THAT YOU TAKE THE GIRL'S CLOTHES OFF.'
RAYMOND CHANDLER

M

MOUNTAIN SIPPER

Glass: Old-fashioned
Garnish: Orange zest twist
Method: SHAKE all ingredients with ice and strain into ice-filled glass.

2	shot(s)	**Bulleit bourbon whiskey**
1	shot(s)	**Cointreau triple sec**
1	shot(s)	**Ocean Spray cranberry juice**
1	shot(s)	**Freshly squeezed grapefruit juice**
⅛	shot(s)	**Sugar syrup** (2 sugar to 1 water)

Comment: Fruity citrus flavours balance the richness of the whiskey.

NACIONAL DAIQUIRI #1

Glass: Martini
Garnish: Maraschino cherry
Method: SHAKE all ingredients with ice and fine strain into chilled glass.

2	shot(s)	**Bacardi Superior rum**
¾	shot(s)	**Bols apricot brandy liqueur**
½	shot(s)	**Freshly squeezed lime juice**
¾	shot(s)	**Chilled mineral water** (omit if wet ice)

Origin: An old classic named after the Hotel Nacional, Havana, Cuba, where it was created.
Comment: A sophisticated complex apricot Daiquiri.

NACIONAL DAIQUIRI #2

Glass: Martini
Garnish: Maraschino cherry
Method: SHAKE all ingredients with ice and fine strain into chilled glass.

2	shot(s)	**Bacardi Superior rum**
½	shot(s)	**Bols apricot brandy liqueur**
1½	shot(s)	**Pressed pineapple juice**
½	shot(s)	**Freshly squeezed lime juice**

Comment: An apricot Daiquiri with extra interest courtesy of pineapple.

NANTUCKET

Glass: Collins
Garnish: Lime wedge
Method: SHAKE all ingredients with ice and strain into ice-filled glass.

2	shot(s)	**Bacardi Superior rum**
3	shot(s)	**Ocean Spray cranberry juice**
2	shot(s)	**Freshly squeezed grapefruit juice**

Origin: Popularised by the Cheers bar chain, this is named after the beautiful island off Cape Cod.
Comment: Essentially a Seabreeze with rum in place of vodka.

NARANJA DAIQUIRI

Glass: Martini
Garnish: Orange slice on rim
Method: SHAKE all ingredients with ice and fine strain into chilled glass.

1¾	shot(s)	**Bacardi Superior rum**
¾	shot(s)	**Grand Marnier liqueur**
1	shot(s)	**Freshly squeezed orange juice**
½	shot(s)	**Freshly squeezed lime juice**
⅛	shot(s)	**Sugar syrup** (2 sugar to 1 water)

Comment: The Latino version of an orange Daiquiri.

NATURAL DAIQUIRI

Glass: Martini
Garnish: Lime wedge
Method: SHAKE all ingredients with ice and fine strain into chilled glass.

2	shot(s)	**Bacardi Superior rum**
½	shot(s)	**Freshly squeezed lime juice**
¼	shot(s)	**Sugar syrup** (2 sugar to 1 water)
½	shot(s)	**Chilled mineral water** (omit if wet ice)

Origin: Created in 1896 by Jennings Cox, an American engineer who was working at a mine near Santiago, Cuba.
Comment: A deliciously simple, clean, refreshing sour drink.

NAUTILUS

Glass: Collins (or Nautilus seashell)
Garnish: Mint sprig
Method: SHAKE all ingredients with ice and strain into ice-filled glass. Serve with straws.

2	shot(s)	**Don Julio 100% agave tequila**
2	shot(s)	**Ocean Spray cranberry juice**
1	shot(s)	**Freshly squeezed lime juice**
½	shot(s)	**Sugar syrup** (2 sugar to 1 water)

Origin: Adapted from a drink created by Victor Bergeron (Trader Vic).
Comment: Basically a Margarita lengthened with cranberry juice.

NO. 10 LEMONADE

Glass: Collins
Garnish: Lemon slice
Method: MUDDLE blueberries in base of shaker. Add next three ingredients, **SHAKE** with ice and fine strain into ice filled glass. **TOP** with soda, lightly stir and serve with straws.

12	fresh	**Blueberries**
2	shot(s)	**Bacardi Superior rum**
1½	shot(s)	**Freshly squeezed lemon juice**
¾	shot(s)	**Sugar syrup** (2 sugar to 1 water)
Top up with		**Soda water** (club soda)

Origin: Adapted from a drink discovered in 2006 at Double Seven, New York City, USA.
Comment: Basically a long blueberry Daiquiri.

NEVINS COCKTAIL

Glass: Martini
Garnish: Lemon zest twist
Method: SHAKE all ingredients with ice and fine strain into chilled glass.

1½	shot(s)	**Bulleit bourbon whiskey**
½	shot(s)	**Bols apricot brandy liqueur**
½	shot(s)	**Freshly squeezed grapefruit juice**
¼	shot(s)	**Freshly squeezed lemon juice**
1	dash	**Angostura aromatic bitters**

Comment: Whiskey and apricot combine beautifully with a light burst of citrus in this easy sipper.

NOON

Glass: Martini
Garnish: Orange zest twist
Method: SHAKE all ingredients with ice and strain into chilled glass.

1½	shot(s)	**Tanqueray London dry gin**
¾	shot(s)	**Noilly Prat dry vermouth**
¾	shot(s)	**Martini Rosso sweet vermouth**
¾	shot(s)	**Freshly squeezed orange juice**
2	dashes	**Angostura aromatic bitters**
½	fresh	**Egg white**

Comment: This classic cocktail is smooth and aromatic.

N

NIAGARA FALLS

Glass: Flute
Garnish: Physalis
Method: SHAKE first four ingredients with ice and strain into chilled glass. **TOP** with ginger ale and lightly stir.

1	shot(s)	**Ketel One vodka**
1	shot(s)	**Grand Marnier liqueur**
½	shot(s)	**Freshly squeezed lemon juice**
¼	shot(s)	**Sugar syrup** (2 sugar to 1 water)
Top up with		**Ginger ale**

Comment: Ginger ale and orange complement each other, fortified by vodka.

ONE UNIT OF ALCOHOL CONTAINS MORE THAN 100 TRILLION BILLION (100,000,000,000,000,000,000,000) MOLECULES OF ALCOHOL.

NOT SO COSMO (MOCKTAIL)

Glass: Martini
Garnish: Orange zest twist
Method: SHAKE all ingredients with ice and fine strain into chilled glass.

1	shot(s)	**Freshly squeezed orange juice**
1	shot(s)	**Ocean Spray cranberry juice**
1	shot(s)	**Freshly squeezed lime juice**
1	shot(s)	**Freshly squeezed lemon juice**

Origin: Discovered in 2003 at Claridge's Bar, London, England.
Comment: This non-alcoholic cocktail may look like a Cosmo but it doesn't taste like one.

NICKY'S FIZZ

Glass: Collins
Garnish: Orange slice
Method: SHAKE first two ingredients with ice and strain into ice-filled glass. **TOP** with soda, lightly stir and serve with straws.

2	shot(s)	**Tanqueray London dry gin**
2	shot(s)	**Freshly squeezed grapefruit juice**
Top up with		**Soda water** (from siphon)

Comment: A dry, refreshing, long drink.

NOVEMBER SEABREEZE (MOCKTAIL)

Glass: Collins
Garnish: Lime wedge
Method: SHAKE first three ingredients with ice and strain into ice-filled glass. **TOP** with soda, gently stir and serve with straws.

2	shot(s)	**Ocean Spray cranberry juice**
2	shot(s)	**Pressed apple juice**
1	shot(s)	**Freshly squeezed lime juice**
Top up with		**Soda water** (club soda)

Comment: A superbly refreshing fruity drink, whatever the time of year.

'WORK IS THE CURSE OF THE DRINKING CLASSES.'
OSCAR WILDE

OCEANBREEZE

Glass: Collins
Garnish: Lime wedge
Method: POUR cranberry juice into ice-filled glass. **SHAKE** other ingredients with ice and carefully strain into glass to **LAYER** over the cranberry juice. Serve with straws so drinker can mix layers prior to drinking.

2½	shot(s)	**Ocean Spray cranberry juice**
2	shot(s)	**Ketel One vodka**
1½	shot(s)	**Freshly squeezed grapefruit juice**
½	shot(s)	**Pressed pineapple juice**

Origin: Created in 2007 by yours truly for Ocean Spray cranberry juice.
Comment: It's juicy!

OH GOSH!

Glass: Martini
Garnish: Lemon zest twist
Method: SHAKE all ingredients with ice and fine strain into chilled glass.

1½	shot(s)	**Bacardi Superior rum**
1	shot(s)	**Cointreau triple sec**
½	shot(s)	**Freshly squeezed lime juice**
¼	shot(s)	**Sugar syrup** (2 sugar to 1 water)
½	shot(s)	**Chilled mineral water** (omit if wet ice)

Origin: Created by Tony Conigliaro in 2001 at Isola, London, England. A customer requested a Daiquiri with a difference – when this was served he took one sip and exclaimed "Oh gosh!".
Comment: A very subtle orange twist on the classic Daiquiri.

OLD FASHIONED

(CLASSIC VERSION)

Glass: Old-fashioned
Garnish: Orange (or lemon) twist
Method: STIR one shot of bourbon with two ice cubes in a glass. ADD sugar syrup and Angostura and two more ice cubes. **STIR** some more and add another two ice cubes and the rest of the bourbon. **STIR** lots more and add more ice.

2½	shot(s)	**Bulleit bourbon whiskey**
¼	shot(s)	**Sugar syrup (2 sugar to 1 water)**
3	dashes	**Angostura aromatic bitters**

Origin: As with the Martini, the glass this cocktail is served in has taken the name of the drink. Supposedly the cocktail was created at the Pendennis Club in Louisville, Kentucky, for a Kentucky Colonel (and bourbon distiller) named James E. Pepper. As the drink predates the club, this cannot be true, but Pepper seems to have promoted it heavily to help market his product and the story is given credence by appearing verbatim in A. S. Crockett's 1935 'The Old Waldorf-Astoria Bar Book'.
Comment: The melting and stirring in of ice cubes is essential to the dilution and taste of this sublime classic.

OLD FASHIONED

OLYMPIC

Glass: Martini
Garnish: Orange zest twist
Method: SHAKE all ingredients with ice and fine strain into chilled glass.

1¼	shot(s)	**Courvoisier V.S.O.P. cognac**
1¼	shot(s)	**Grand Marnier liqueur**
1¼	shot(s)	**Freshly squeezed orange juice**

Origin: Adapted from a recipe in Harry Craddock's 1930 Savoy Cocktail Book.
Comment: The perfect balance of cognac and orange juice. One to celebrate the 2012 Games perhaps.

OPENING SHOT

Glass: Shot
Method: SHAKE all ingredients with ice and fine strain into chilled glass.

1	shot(s)	**Bulleit bourbon whiskey**
½	shot(s)	**Martini Rosso sweet vermouth**
⅛	shot(s)	**Pomegranate (grenadine) syrup**

Variant: Double the quantities and strain into a Martini glass and you have the 1920s classic I based this drink on.
Comment: Basically a miserly Sweet Manhattan.

ORANGE BLOOM MARTINI

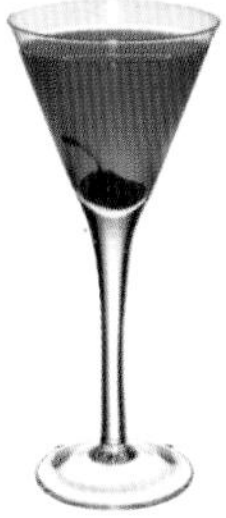

Glass: Martini
Garnish: Maraschino cherry
Method: SHAKE all ingredients with ice and fine strain into chilled glass.

2	shot(s)	**Tanqueray London dry gin**
1	shot(s)	**Cointreau triple sec**
1	shot(s)	**Martini Rosso sweet vermouth**

Origin: Adapted from a recipe in the 1930s edition of the Savoy Cocktail Book by Harry Craddock.
Comment: Strong, fruity zesty orange laced with gin.

ORANGE BLOSSOM

Glass: Old-fashioned
Garnish: Orange zest twist
Method: SHAKE all ingredients with ice and strain into ice-filled glass.

1½	shot(s)	**Tanqueray London dry gin**
½	shot(s)	**Cointreau triple sec**
1½	shot(s)	**Freshly squeezed orange juice**
½	shot(s)	**Freshly squeezed lime juice**
⅛	shot(s)	**Pomegranate (grenadine) syrup**

Variant: Served long in a Collins glass this becomes a Harvester.
Comment: Gin sweetened with liqueur and grenadine, and soured with lime.

PAISLEY MARTINI

Glass: Martini
Garnish: Lemon zest twist
Method: STIR all ingredients with ice and strain into chilled glass.

2½	shot(s)	**Tanqueray London dry gin**
½	shot(s)	**Noilly Prat dry vermouth**
¼	shot(s)	**Johnnie Walker Scotch whisky**

Comment: A dry Martini for those with a penchant for Scotch.

PALM BEACH

Glass: Martini
Garnish: Maraschino cherry
Method: SHAKE all ingredients with ice and fine strain into chilled glass.

2½	shot(s)	**Tanqueray London dry gin**
½	shot(s)	**Martini Rosso sweet vermouth**
1	shot(s)	**Freshly squeezed grapefruit juice**

Origin: A classic from the 1940s.
Comment: Dry, aromatic and packs one hell of a punch.

> SIR, IF YOU WERE MY HUSBAND, I WOULD POISON YOUR DRINK. LADY ASTOR TO WINSTON CHURCHILL
>
> MADAM, IF YOU WERE MY WIFE, I WOULD DRINK IT. HIS REPLY.

PARADISE #1

Glass: Martini
Garnish: Orange zest twist
Method: SHAKE all ingredients with ice and fine strain into chilled glass.

2	shot(s)	**Tanqueray London dry gin**
1	shot(s)	**Bols apricot brandy liqueur**
1	shot(s)	**Freshly squeezed orange juice**
¼	shot(s)	**Freshly squeezed lemon juice**

Origin: Proportioned according to a recipe in the 1930 edition of the Savoy Cocktail Book by Harry Craddock.
Comment: Orange predominates in this strong complex cocktail.

ORANGE BLOOM

PARADISE #2

Glass: Martini
Garnish: Orange zest twist
Method: Cut passion fruit in half and scoop flesh into shaker. Add other ingredients, **SHAKE** with ice and fine strain into chilled glass.

1	fresh	**Passion fruit**
2	shot(s)	**Tanqueray London dry gin**
¾	shot(s)	**Bols apricot brandy liqueur**
¾	shot(s)	**Freshly squeezed orange juice**

Comment: Thick, almost syrupy. Rich and fruity.

PARISIAN MARTINI #1

Glass: Martini
Garnish: Lemon peel twist
Method: **SHAKE** all ingredients with ice and fine strain into chilled glass.

1¼	shot(s)	**Tanqueray London dry gin**
1¼	shot(s)	**Crème de cassis or Chambord**
1¼	shot(s)	**Noilly Prat dry vermouth**

Origin: A drink created in the 1920s to promote crème de cassis. This recipe is adapted from one in Harry Craddock's Savoy Cocktail Book.
Comment: Full-on rich cassis is barely tempered by gin and Noilly Prat dry vermouth.

PARK AVENUE

Glass: Martini
Garnish: Maraschino cherry
Method: **SHAKE** all ingredients with ice and fine strain into chilled glass.

2	shot(s)	**Tanqueray London dry gin**
½	shot(s)	**Grand Marnier liqueur**
½	shot(s)	**Martini Rosso sweet vermouth**
1	shot(s)	**Pressed pineapple juice**

Origin: A classic from the 1940s.
Comment: Very fruity and well-balanced rather than dry or sweet.

PARK LANE

Glass: Martini
Garnish: Orange zest twist
Method: **SHAKE** all ingredients with ice and strain into chilled glass.

2	shot(s)	**Tanqueray London dry gin**
¾	shot(s)	**Bols apricot brandy liqueur**
¾	shot(s)	**Freshly squeezed orange juice**
⅛	shot(s)	**Pomegranate (grenadine) syrup**
½	fresh	**Egg white**

Comment: This smooth, frothy concoction hides a mean kick.

PASSION FRUIT DAIQUIRI

Glass: Martini
Garnish: Lime wedge on rim
Method: Cut passion fruit in half and scoop out flesh into shaker. Add other ingredients, **SHAKE** with ice and fine strain into chilled glass.

2	fresh	**Passion fruit**
2	shot(s)	**Bacardi Superior rum**
½	shot(s)	**Freshly squeezed lime juice**
½	shot(s)	**Sugar syrup** (2 sugar to 1 water)

Origin: Formula by yours truly in 2004.
Comment: The rum character comes through in this fruity cocktail.

PASSION FRUIT MARGARITA

Glass: Coupette
Garnish: Salt rim & lime wedge
Method: Cut passion fruit in half and scoop out flesh into shaker. Add other ingredients, **SHAKE** with ice and fine strain into chilled glass.

1	fresh	**Passion fruit**
2	shot(s)	**Don Julio 100% agave tequila**
1	shot(s)	**Cointreau triple sec**
1	shot(s)	**Freshly squeezed lime juice**
¼	shot(s)	**Passion fruit syrup**

Origin: Formula by yours truly in 2004.
Comment: The flavour of tequila is very evident in this fruity adaptation.

PASSION FRUIT MARTINI #1

Glass: Martini
Garnish: Physalis (cape gooseberry)
Method: Cut passion fruit in half and scoop out flesh into shaker. Add other ingredients, **SHAKE** with ice and fine strain into chilled glass.

1	fresh	**Passion fruit**
2	shot(s)	**Ketel One vodka**
½	shot(s)	**Sugar syrup** (2 sugar to 1 water)

Origin: Formula by yours truly in 2004.
Comment: A simple but tasty cocktail that wonderfully harnesses the flavour of passion fruit.

PASSION FRUIT MARTINI #2

Glass: Martini
Garnish: Star fruit on rim
Method: Cut passion fruit in half and scoop out flesh into shaker. Add other ingredients, **SHAKE** with ice and fine strain into chilled glass.

2	fresh	**Passion fruit**
2	shot(s)	**Ketel One vodka**
½	shot(s)	**Passion fruit syrup**

Origin: Formula by yours truly in 2004.
Comment: Not for Martini purists, but a fruity, easy drinking concoction for everyone else.

> 'THE SECRET TO A LONG LIFE IS TO STAY BUSY, GET PLENTY OF EXERCISE AND DON'T DRINK TOO MUCH. THEN AGAIN, DON'T DRINK TOO LITTLE.'
> HERMANN SMITH-JOHANNSON

PERIODISTA DAIQUIRI

Glass: Martini
Garnish: Lime wedge
Method: SHAKE all ingredients with ice and fine strain into chilled glass.

1½	shot(s)	**Bacardi Superior rum**
½	shot(s)	**Freshly squeezed lime juice**
½	shot(s)	**Grand Marnier liqueur**
½	shot(s)	**Bols apricot brandy liqueur**
½	shot(s)	**Chilled mineral water** (omit if wet ice)

Comment: Basically an orange and apricot Daiquiri.

PAVLOVA SHOT

Glass: Shot
Method: Refrigerate ingredients then **LAYER** in chilled glass by carefully pouring in the following order.

¾	shot(s)	**Crème de cassis or Chambord**
¾	shot(s)	**Ketel One vodka**

Comment: Pleasant, sweet shot.

PICADOR

Glass: Martini
Garnish: Lime zest twist
Method: SHAKE all ingredients with ice and fine strain into chilled glass.

2	shot(s)	**Don Julio 100% agave tequila**
1	shot(s)	**Freshly squeezed lime juice**
1	shot(s)	**Cointreau triple sec**

Origin: Yes, you're right! This drink is exactly the same as a classically proportioned Margarita. But… it was published in W. J. Tarling's 1937 'Café Royal Cocktail Book', 16 years before the first known written reference to a Margarita. Was the British recipe copied? Or did the Margarita independently evolve?
Comment: The name might be more masculine but it still tastes exactly like a classic Margarita.

PEDRO COLLINS

Glass: Collins
Garnish: Lime wedge
Method: SHAKE first three ingredients with ice and strain into ice-filled glass. **TOP** with soda, lightly stir and serve with straws.

2	shot(s)	**Bacardi Superior rum**
1	shot(s)	**Freshly squeezed lime juice**
½	shot(s)	**Sugar syrup** (2 sugar to 1 water)
Top up with		**Soda water** (club soda)

Comment: This rum based Tom Collins is basically a long Daiquiri with soda.

PIERRE COLLINS

Glass: Collins
Garnish: Orange slice & cherry on stick (sail)
Method: SHAKE first three ingredients with ice and strain into ice-filled glass. **TOP** with soda, lightly stir and serve with straws.

2	shot(s)	**Courvoisier V.S.O.P. cognac**
1	shot(s)	**Freshly squeezed lemon juice**
½	shot(s)	**Sugar syrup** (2 sugar to 1 water)
Top up with		**Soda water** (club soda)

Comment: A Tom Collins made with cognac. The cognac's character shines through.

PERFECT MARTINI

Glass: Martini
Garnish: Orange zest twist
Method: SHAKE all ingredients with ice and fine strain into chilled glass.

1¼	shot(s)	**Tanqueray London dry gin**
1¼	shot(s)	**Noilly Prat dry vermouth**
1¼	shot(s)	**Martini Rosso sweet vermouth**
1	dash	**Fee Brothers orange bitters** (optional)

Variant: Merry-Go-Round Martini
Origin: Adapted from a recipe in the 1930 edition of the Savoy Cocktail Book by Harry Craddock.
Comment: The high proportion of vermouth makes this Martini almost sherry-like.

PIÑA MARTINI

Glass: Martini
Garnish: Pineapple wedge on rim
Method: SHAKE all ingredients with ice and fine strain into chilled glass.

2	shot(s)	**Ketel One vodka**
1¾	shot(s)	**Pressed pineapple juice**
¼	shot(s)	**Freshly squeezed lime juice**
⅛	shot(s)	**Sugar syrup** (2 sugar to 1 water)

Origin: Created in 2005 by yours truly.
Comment: Rich pineapple but not too sweet.

PINK GIN & TONIC

PINEAPPLE BLOSSOM

Glass: Martini
Garnish: Pineapple wedge on rim
Method: SHAKE all ingredients with ice and fine strain into chilled glass.

2	shot(s)	**Johnnie Walker Scotch whisky**
1	shot(s)	**Pressed pineapple juice**
½	shot(s)	**Freshly squeezed lemon juice**
½	shot(s)	**Sugar syrup** (2 sugar to 1 water)

Origin: My interpretation of a classic.
Comment: Richly flavoured but drier than you might expect.

PINEAPPLE DAIQUIRI #1 (ON-THE-ROCKS)

Glass: Old-fashioned
Garnish: Pineapple wedge & cherry
Method: SHAKE all ingredients with ice and fine strain into ice-filled glass.

2	shot(s)	**Bacardi Superior rum**
1	shot(s)	**Pressed pineapple juice**
½	shot(s)	**Freshly squeezed lime juice**
¼	shot(s)	**Sugar syrup** (2 sugar to 1 water)

Origin: Formula by yours truly.
Comment: Rum and pineapple are just meant to go together.

PINEAPPLE DAIQUIRI #2 (FROZEN)

Glass: Martini (Large)
Garnish: Pineapple wedge & cherry
Method: BLEND all ingredients with two 6oz scoops crushed ice and serve with straws.

2	shot(s)	**Bacardi Superior rum**
1½	shot(s)	**Pressed pineapple juice**
½	shot(s)	**Freshly squeezed lime juice**
¾	shot(s)	**Sugar syrup** (2 sugar to 1 water)

Origin: Formula by yours truly.
Comment: Fluffy but very tasty.

PINEAPPLE MARGARITA

Glass: Coupette
Garnish: Pineapple wedge on rim
Method: SHAKE all ingredients with ice and fine strain into chilled glass.

2	shot(s)	**Don Julio 100% agave tequila**
¾	shot(s)	**Cointreau triple sec**
1½	shot(s)	**Pressed pineapple juice**

Variant: Add half a shot of pineapple syrup, blend with 12oz scoop of crushed ice and serve frozen.
Comment: A Tequila Margarita with a pineapple fruit kick.

PINEAPPLE SMOOTHIE (MOCKTAIL)

Glass: Collins
Garnish: Pineapple wedge
Method: BLEND all ingredients with 12oz scoop crushed ice. Serve with straws.

2	tblspoon	**Natural yoghurt**
2	tblspoon	**Runny honey**
4	shot(s)	**Pressed pineapple juice**

Comment: Fluffy in every sense of the word.

PINK GIN #1 (TRADITIONAL)

Glass: Martini
Garnish: Lemon zest twist
Method: RINSE chilled glass with Angostura bitters. **POUR** gin and water into rinsed glass and stir.

2	dashes	**Angostura aromatic bitters**
2	shot(s)	**Tanqueray London dry gin** (frozen)
2	shot(s)	**Chilled mineral water**

Origin: Gin was a favourite of the Royal Navy – along with rum, which was served as a daily ration right up until the 70s. It was often mixed with healthy ingredients to make them more palatable. Pink gin was originally used against stomach upsets, as Angostura aromatic bitters were considered medicinal.
Comment: A traditionally made Pink Gin without ice.

PINK GIN #2 (MODERN)

Glass: Martini
Garnish: Lemon zest twist
Method: STIR all ingredients with ice and strain into chilled glass.

2	shot(s)	**Tanqueray London dry gin**
2	shot(s)	**Chilled mineral water (reduce if wet ice)**
1	dash	**Angostura aromatic bitters**

Comment: Normally I'd advocate liberal use of Angostura bitters but this refined and subtle drink benefits from frugality.

PINK GIN & TONIC

Glass: Collins
Garnish: Lime slice
Method: POUR gin and Angostura bitters into ice-filled glass, top with tonic, lightly stir and serve with straws.

2	shot(s)	**Tanqueray London dry gin**
4	dashes	**Angostura aromatic bitters**
Top up with		**Tonic water**

Comment: Basically a G&T with an extra pep of flavour from Angostura, this has a wider appeal than the original Pink Gin.

PINK GRAPEFRUIT MARGARITA

Glass: Coupette
Garnish: Lime wedge on rim
Method: SHAKE all ingredients with ice and fine strain into chilled glass.

2	shot(s)	**Don Julio 100% agave tequila**
1	shot(s)	**Freshly squeezed pink grapefruit juice**
½	shot(s)	**Freshly squeezed lime juice**
¼	shot(s)	**Sugar syrup** (2 sugar to 1 water)

Comment: Delivers exactly what the name promises.

PINK HOUND

Glass: Martini
Garnish: Lemon zest twist
Method: SHAKE all ingredients with ice and fine strain into chilled glass.

2	shot(s)	**Tanqueray London dry gin**
1¾	shot(s)	**Freshly squeezed pink grapefruit juice**
¼	shot(s)	**Sugar syrup** (2 sugar to 1 water)

Comment: A flavoursome balance of sweet and sour.

PINK LADY

Glass: Martini
Garnish: Lemon zest twist
Method: SHAKE all ingredients with ice and fine strain into chilled glass.

2	shot(s)	**Tanqueray London dry gin**
½	shot(s)	**Freshly squeezed lemon juice**
½	shot(s)	**Pomegranate (grenadine) syrup**
½	fresh	**Egg white** (optional)

Variant: With the addition of half a shot apple brandy.
Origin: A classic cocktail named after a successful 1912 stage play.
Comment: Despite the colour, this is sharp and alcoholic.

PINK LEMONADE (MOCKTAIL)

Glass: Collins
Garnish: Lemon slice
Method: SHAKE first three ingredients with ice and strain into ice-filled glass. **TOP** with soda and serve with straws.

2	shot(s)	**Freshly squeezed lemon juice**
½	shot(s)	**Pomegranate (grenadine) syrup**
¼	shot(s)	**Sugar syrup** (2 sugar to 1 water)
Top up with		**Soda water** (club soda)

Origin: Discovered in 2004 in New York City.
Comment: A tall, pink, tangy, alcohol free cocktail.

PINK PALACE

Glass: Martini
Garnish: Lemon twist
Method: SHAKE all ingredients with ice and fine strain into chilled glass.

2	shot(s)	**Tanqueray London dry gin**
½	shot(s)	**Grand Marnier liqueur**
½	shot(s)	**Freshly squeezed lemon juice**
¼	shot(s)	**Pomegranate (grenadine) syrup**

Origin: The signature drink at The Polo Lounge, Beverly Hills Hotel, Los Angeles, USA. The hotel, which is lovingly termed the 'Pink Palace', inspired The Eagles' Hotel California and graces the album cover.
Comment: A great drink but rarely done justice at the Polo Lounge.

> **'A MAN YOU DON'T LIKE WHO DRINKS AS MUCH AS YOU DO.'** DYLAN THOMAS DEFINES AN ALCOHOLIC

PINO PEPE

Glass: Sling (or pineapple shell)
Garnish: Mint sprig
Method: BLEND all ingredients with 12oz scoop crushed ice. Pour into glass (or pineapple shell) and serve with straws. If using a pineapple shell, serve with ice cubes.

1	shot(s)	**Bacardi Superior rum**
1	shot(s)	**Ketel One vodka**
½	shot(s)	**Cointreau triple sec**
2	shot(s)	**Pressed pineapple juice**
½	shot(s)	**Freshly squeezed lime juice**
¼	shot(s)	**Freshly squeezed lemon juice**
½	shot(s)	**Sugar syrup** (2 sugar to 1 water)

Origin: Adapted from a recipe in the 1947-72 Trader Vic's Bartender's Guide by Victor Bergeron.
Comment: To quote Trader Vic, "Lethal but smooth – pineapple at its best".

PLANTER'S PUNCHLESS (MOCKTAIL)

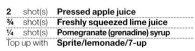

Glass: Collins
Garnish: Lime wedge
Method: SHAKE first three ingredients with ice and strain into ice-filled glass. **TOP** with lemonade, lightly stir and serve with straws.

2	shot(s)	**Pressed apple juice**
¾	shot(s)	**Freshly squeezed lime juice**
¼	shot(s)	**Pomegranate (grenadine) syrup**
Top up with		**Sprite/lemonade/7-up**

Comment: A pleasant, if uninspiring, driver's option.

PLAYA DEL MAR

Glass: Martini
Garnish: Pineapple wedge on rim
Method: SHAKE all ingredients with ice and fine strain into chilled glass.

1	shot(s)	**Don Julio 100% agave tequila**
½	shot(s)	**Cointreau triple sec**
1	shot(s)	**Ocean Spray cranberry juice**
¾	shot(s)	**Pressed pineapple juice**
½	shot(s)	**Freshly squeezed lime juice**
¼	shot(s)	**Sugar syrup** (2 sugar to 1 water)

Origin: This cocktail was created in 1997 by Wayne Collins at Navajo Joe, London, England. The name translates as 'Beach of the Sea'.
Comment: A fruity complex taste with a hint of tequila.

PLAYMATE MARTINI

Glass: Martini
Garnish: Orange zest twist
Method: SHAKE all ingredients with ice and fine strain into chilled glass.

1	shot(s)	**Courvoisier V.S.O.P. cognac**
1	shot(s)	**Grand Marnier liqueur**
1	shot(s)	**Bols apricot brandy liqueur**
1	shot(s)	**Freshly squeezed orange juice**
½	fresh	**Egg white**
3	dashes	**Angostura aromatic bitters**

Comment: Smooth and easy drinking.

POGO STICK

Glass: Martini (large)
Garnish: Mint sprig
Method: BLEND all ingredients with 6oz scoop crushed ice. Serve with straws.

2	shot(s)	**Tanqueray London dry gin**
½	shot(s)	**Pressed pineapple juice**
½	shot(s)	**Freshly squeezed grapefruit juice**
½	shot(s)	**Freshly squeezed lime juice**
½	shot(s)	**Sugar syrup** (2 sugar to 1 water)

Origin: Adapted from a recipe in the 1947-72 Trader Vic's Bartender's Guide by Victor Bergeron.
Comment: To quote Trader Vic, "A refreshing blend of gin with pineapple and grapefruit juice… a real romper".

POINSETTIA

Glass: Flute
Garnish: Quarter slice of orange on rim
Method: POUR first two ingredients into chilled glass. TOP with champagne.

½	shot(s)	**Cointreau triple sec**
1	shot(s)	**Ocean Spray cranberry juice**
Top up with		**Brut champagne**

Comment: Fruity champagne.

POLLY'S SPECIAL

Glass: Martini
Garnish: Grapefruit wedge on rim
Method: SHAKE all ingredients with ice and fine strain into chilled glass.

1¾	shot(s)	**Johnnie Walker Scotch whisky**
1	shot(s)	**Freshly squeezed grapefruit juice**
1	shot(s)	**Grand Marnier liqueur**
¼	shot(s)	**Sugar syrup** (2 sugar to 1 water)

Origin: I adapted this recipe from a 1947 edition of Trader Vic's Bartender's Guide.
Comment: Sweet, sour, flavoursome and balanced – for grown-ups who like the taste of alcohol.

POMPANSKI MARTINI

Glass: Martini
Garnish: Orange zest twist
Method: SHAKE all ingredients with ice and fine strain into chilled glass.

1¾	shot(s)	**Ketel One vodka**
½	shot(s)	**Cointreau triple sec**
1½	shot(s)	**Freshly squeezed grapefruit juice**
¼	shot(s)	**Sugar syrup** (2 sugar to 1 water)
⅛	shot(s)	**Noilly Prat dry vermouth**

Comment: Dry and zesty with the sharp freshness of grapefruit and a hint of orange.

> THE USSR'S MIG-25 FIGHTER-BOMBER CARRIED HALF A TON OF ALCOHOL FOR BRAKE FLUID. IT WAS NICKNAMED THE 'FLYING RESTAURANT' BY ITS SOVIET CREWS.

PONTBERRY MARTINI

Glass: Martini
Garnish: Blackberries
Method: SHAKE all ingredients with ice and fine strain into chilled glass.

1½	shot(s)	**Ketel One vodka**
½	shot(s)	**Crème de cassis or Chambord**
2	shot(s)	**Ocean Spray cranberry juice**

Origin: Created by Dick Bradsell in the late 90s for the opening of Agent Provocateur in Pont Street, London, England.
Comment: A light, fruity, easy drinking cocktail.

PORT LIGHT

Glass: Martini
Garnish: Passion fruit half
Method: STIR honey with bourbon in base of shaker to dissolve honey. Cut passion fruit in half and scoop flesh into shaker. Add other ingredients, SHAKE with ice and fine strain into chilled glass.

2	spoons	Runny honey
2	shot(s)	Bulleit bourbon whiskey
1	fresh	Passion fruit
1	shot(s)	Freshly squeezed lemon juice
½	shot(s)	Pomegranate (grenadine) syrup
½	fresh	Egg white

Origin: Adapted from a drink created by Victor Bergeron (Trader Vic).
Comment: Strong and very fruity. Too many will put your lights out.

PRAIRIE OYSTER #2 (MODERN & ALCOHOLIC)

Glass: Coupette
Method: Taking care not to break the egg yolk, PLACE it in the centre of the glass. SHAKE the rest of the ingredients with ice and strain over egg. Instruct drinker to down in one.

1	raw	Egg yolk
1	shot(s)	Courvoisier V.S.O.P. cognac
¼	shot(s)	Worcestershire sauce
½	shot(s)	Tomato juice
3	drops	Tabasco hot pepper sauce
2	pinches	Pepper
2	pinches	Salt
½	spoon	Malt vinegar

Variation: Use another spirit such as vodka in place of cognac.
Comment: This "pick-me-up" (A.K.A. hangover cure) may be a somewhat daunting prospect irrespective of the present state of your constitution.

PRESIDENT

Glass: Martini
Garnish: Orange zest twist
Method: SHAKE all ingredients with ice and fine strain into chilled glass.

2	shot(s)	Bacardi Superior rum
1	shot(s)	Freshly squeezed orange juice
¼	shot(s)	Freshly squeezed lemon juice
¼	shot(s)	Pomegranate (grenadine) syrup
½	shot(s)	Chilled mineral water (omit if wet ice)

Origin: Adapted from a recipe in Harry Craddock's 1930 Savoy Cocktail Book.
Comment: A delicately fruity orange Daiquiri.

PRESIDENT VINCENT

Glass: Martini
Garnish: Lime zest twist
Method: SHAKE all ingredients with ice and fine strain into chilled glass.

2	shot(s)	Bacardi Superior rum
½	shot(s)	Noilly Prat dry vermouth
½	shot(s)	Freshly squeezed lime juice
¼	shot(s)	Sugar syrup (2 sugar to 1 water)

Origin: Probably 1930s.
Comment: A dry, spicy take on the Daiquiri.

PRESIDENTE

Glass: Martini
Garnish: Orange zest twist
Method: SHAKE all ingredients with ice and fine strain into chilled glass.

1½	shot(s)	Bacardi Superior rum
¾	shot(s)	Cointreau triple sec
¾	shot(s)	Noilly Prat dry vermouth
⅛	shot(s)	Pomegranate (grenadine) syrup
½	shot(s)	Chilled mineral water (omit if wet ice)

Variant: El Presidente #3
Origin: This classic was created during the 1920s in Vista Alegre, Havana, Cuba.
Comment: A lightly flavoured classic cocktail.

'ABSINTHE MAKES THE TART GROW FONDER.'
ERNEST DOWSON

PRESIDENTE MENOCAL SPECIAL

Glass: Coupette
Garnish: Mint sprig and two cherries
Method: SHAKE all ingredients with ice and fine strain into glass filled with crushed ice.

7	fresh	Mint leaves
2	shot(s)	Bacardi Superior rum
¼	shot(s)	Sugar syrup (2 sugar to 1 water)
⅛	shot(s)	Freshly squeezed lime juice

Origin: Created by Constantino (Constante) Ribalaigua Vert at the Floridita bar in Havana, Cuba. This recipe is adapted from a 1937 Bar Florida (later renamed Floridita) menu. The name refers to Mario García Menocal, who was president of Cuba from 1912 to 1920.
Comment: What hot Cuban summers are made for.

PRESIDENT

P

PUNCH

PUNCH

(GENERIC NAME - USUALLY RUM)

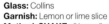

Glass: Collins
Garnish: Lemon or lime slice
Method: SHAKE all ingredients with ice and fine strain into glass filled with crushed ice.

¾	shot(s)	**Freshly squeezed lemon or lime juice** (1 x sour)
1½	shot(s)	**Sugar syrup** (2 x sweet)
2¼	shot(s)	**Bacardi Superior rum** (3 x strong) (can be made with other spirits)
3	shot(s)	**Water or fruit juice** (4 x weak)
3	dashes	**Angostura aromatic bitters**

Long before the Martini, the V-shaped glass and the cocktail shaker, the drink of choice at society gatherings was punch and the punch bowl was the centre of activity at every party.

Punch had existed in India for centuries before colonialists brought it back to Europe some time in the latter half of the 1600s. The name derives from the Hindi word for five, 'panch', and refers to the five key ingredients: alcohol, citrus, sugar, water and spices.

In India, it was made with arrack (the Arabic word for liquor and a local spirit distilled from palm sap or sugar cane). Back in Britain it was common for punches to be spiced with nutmeg or tea. The classic proportions of a punch follow a mnemonic, 'one of sour, two of sweet, three of strong and four of weak.' It refers to lime juice, sugar, rum and water - the fifth element, spice was added to taste.

The basic punch principle of balancing sweet and sour with spirit and dilution remains key to making a good cocktail to this day. Indeed, the essential punch ingredients - spirit, citrus, sugar and water - lie at the centre of most modern day cocktails including the Daiquiri, Sour, Margarita, Caipirinha and Sidecar. Today's bartenders are now also reintroducing the fifth punch ingredient by muddling or macerating herbs and spices in their cocktails.

Comment: Two traditional punches remain on today's cocktail lists, the 'Rum Punch' and the 'Hot Whisky Punch', now better known as the 'Hot Toddy'. Also bear in mind that the Gin Punch probably led to the creation of the Collins.

P

PURPLE HAZE

Glass: Shot
Method: SHAKE first three ingredients with ice and strain into glass. **POUR** liqueur down the inside of the glass. This will fall to the bottom and form the purple haze.

1½	shot(s)	**Ketel One vodka**
½	shot(s)	**Freshly squeezed lime juice**
¼	shot(s)	**Sugar syrup** (2 sugar to 1 water)
⅛	shot(s)	**Crème de cassis or Chambord**

Comment: A sweet and sour shot with a sweet, berry base.

PURPLE HOOTER

Glass: Collins
Garnish: Lime wedge
Method: SHAKE first three ingredients with ice and strain into ice-filled glass. **TOP** with soda.

2	shot(s)	**Ketel One vodka**
1	shot(s)	**Crème de cassis or Chambord**
1	shot(s)	**Freshly squeezed lime juice**
Top up with		**Soda water** (club soda)

Comment: Tangy, fruity, long and refreshing.

PUSSYFOOT (MOCKTAIL)

Glass: Collins
Garnish: Orange slice
Method: MUDDLE (just to brusie) mint in base of shaker. Add other ingredients, **SHAKE** with ice and fine strain into ice-filled glass.

7	fresh	**Mint leaves**
4	shot(s)	**Freshly squeezed orange juice**
½	shot(s)	**Freshly squeezed lemon juice**
½	shot(s)	**Freshly squeezed lime juice**
½	shot(s)	**Pomegranate (grenadine) syrup**
1	fresh	**Egg yolk**

Origin: Created in 1920 by Robert Vermeire at the Embassy Club, London, England. This non-alcoholic cocktail is named after 'Pussyfoot' (William E.) Johnson who was an ardent supporter of Prohibition.
Comment: Probably the best non-alcoholic cocktail ever.

QUEEN MARTINI

Glass: Martini
Garnish: Maraschino cherry
Method: SHAKE all ingredients with ice and fine strain into chilled glass.

1½	shot(s)	**Tanqueray London dry gin**
½	shot(s)	**Noilly Prat dry vermouth**
½	shot(s)	**Martini Rosso sweet vermouth**
½	shot(s)	**Freshly squeezed orange juice**
½	shot(s)	**Pressed pineapple juice**

Comment: A 'perfectly' fruity Martini that's fit for a…

RASPBERRY COLLINS

Glass: Collins
Garnish: Three raspberries & lemon slice
Method: MUDDLE raspberries in base of shaker. Add next five ingredients, **SHAKE** with ice and strain into ice-filled glass. **TOP** with soda, lightly stir and serve with straws.

10	fresh	**Raspberries**
2	shot(s)	**Tanqueray London dry gin**
1½	shot(s)	**Freshly squeezed lemon juice**
½	shot(s)	**Crème de cassis or Chambord**
½	shot(s)	**Sugar syrup** (2 sugar to 1 water)
3	dashes	**Fee Brothers orange bitters** (optional)
Top up with		**Soda water** (club soda)

Variant: Raspberry Debonnaire
Origin: Created in 1999 by Cairbry Hill, London, England.
Comment: This fruity drink is the most popular modern adaptation of the classic Collins.

RASPBERRY COOLER

Glass: Collins
Garnish: Raspberries on drink
Method: SHAKE first three ingredients with ice and strain into ice-filled glass. **TOP** with lemonade and **DRIZZLE** liqueur around surface of drink. It will fall through the drink, leaving coloured threads.

2	shot(s)	**Bulleit bourbon whiskey**
¾	shot(s)	**Freshly squeezed lime juice**
¼	shot(s)	**Sugar syrup** (2 sugar to 1 water)
Top up with		**Sprite/lemonade/7-Up**
½	shot(s)	**Crème de cassis or Chambord**

Origin: Created in 1992 by Wayne Collins at Roadhouse, London, England.
Comment: This variation on a Lynchburg Lemonade has a sweet and sour flavour laced with whiskey.

HOW TO MAKE SUGAR SYRUP

To make your own sugar syrup, gradually pour TWO cups of granulated sugar into a saucepan containing ONE cup of hot water. Stir as you pour and carry on stirring and simmering until the sugar is dissolved. Do not let the water even come close to boiling and only simmer for as long as it takes to dissolve the sugar. Allow syrup to cool and pour into an empty bottle. Ideally, you should finely strain your syrup into the bottle to remove any undissolved crystals which could otherwise encourage crystallisation. If kept in a refrigerator this mixture will last for a couple of months.

RASPBERRY MARGARITA

Glass: Coupette
Garnish: Lime wedge on rim
Method: MUDDLE raspberries in base of shaker. Add other ingredients, **SHAKE** with ice and fine strain into chilled glass.

7	fresh	**Raspberries**
2	shot(s)	**Don Julio 100% agave tequila**
1	shot(s)	**Cointreau triple sec**
1	shot(s)	**Freshly squeezed lime juice**
⅛	shot(s)	**Sugar syrup** (2 sugar to 1 water)

Comment: Just as it says – a raspberry flavoured Margarita.

RASPBERRY MARTINI

Glass: Martini
Garnish: Three raspberries on stick
Method: MUDDLE raspberries in base of shaker. Add other ingredients, **SHAKE** with ice and fine strain into chilled glass.

10	fresh	**Raspberries**
2½	shot(s)	**Ketel One vodka**
½	shot(s)	**Sugar syrup** (2 sugar to 1 water)

Comment: The simplest of raspberry Martinis but still tastes good.

RASPBERRY WATKINS

Glass: Sling
Garnish: Three raspberries
Method: MUDDLE raspberries in base of shaker. Add other ingredients except soda, **SHAKE** with ice and strain into ice-filled glass. **TOP** with soda, lightly stir and serve with straws.

7	fresh	**Raspberries**
2	shot(s)	**Ketel One vodka**
½	shot(s)	**Crème de cassis or Chambord**
½	shot(s)	**Freshly squeezed lime juice**
¼	shot(s)	**Pomegranate (grenadine) syrup**
Top up with		**Soda water** (club soda)

Comment: A light, long, fizzy and refreshing drink.

RAT PACK MANHATTAN

Glass: Martini
Garnish: Orange zest twist & maraschino cherry
Method: Chill glass, add Grand Marnier, swirl to coat and then **DISCARD. STIR** other ingredients with ice and strain into liqueur coated glass.

½	shot(s)	**Grand Marnier liqueur**
1½	shot(s)	**Bulleit bourbon whiskey**
¾	shot(s)	**Martini Rosso sweet vermouth**
¾	shot(s)	**Noilly Prat dry vermouth**
3	dashes	**Angostura aromatic bitters**

Origin: Created in 2000 by Wayne Collins at High Holborn, London, England. Originally Wayne used different whiskies to represent each of the Rat Pack crooners. The wash of Grand Marnier was for Sammy Davis, the wild card of the bunch.
Comment: A twist on the classic Manhattan.

REAL LEMONADE (MOCKTAIL)

Glass: Collins
Garnish: Lemon slice
Method: POUR ingredients into ice-filled glass and lightly **STIR**. Serve with straws.

2	shot(s)	**Freshly squeezed lemon juice**
1	shot(s)	**Sugar syrup** (2 sugar to 1 water)
Top up with		**Soda water** (club soda)

Comment: The classic English summertime refresher.

RED LION #1 (MODERN FORMULA)

Glass: Martini
Garnish: Orange slice on rim
Method: SHAKE all ingredients with ice and fine strain into chilled glass.

1¼	shot(s)	**Tanqueray London dry gin**
1¼	shot(s)	**Grand Marnier liqueur**
1	shot(s)	**Freshly squeezed orange juice**
1	shot(s)	**Freshly squeezed lemon juice**
⅛	shot(s)	**Pomegranate (grenadine) syrup**

Origin: This classic drink is said to have been created for the Chicago World Fair in 1933. However, it won the British Empire Cocktail Competition that year and was more likely created by W J Tarling for Booth's gin and named after the brand's Red Lion Distillery in London.
Comment: The colour of a summer's twilight with a rich tangy orange flavour.

RED LION #2 (EMBURY'S FORMULA)

Glass: Martini
Garnish: Orange slice on rim
Method: SHAKE all ingredients with ice and fine strain into chilled glass.

2	shot(s)	**Tanqueray London dry gin**
¼	shot(s)	**Grand Marnier liqueur**
½	shot(s)	**Freshly squeezed lime juice**
¼	shot(s)	**Pomegranate (grenadine) syrup**
¾	shot(s)	**Chilled mineral water** (reduce if wet ice)

Origin: Recipe adapted from one originally published in The Fine Art of Mixing Drinks by David Embury.
Comment: Embury is a Daiquiri fan and this is reminiscent of a Daiquiri in both style and proportions.

RED MARAUDER

Glass: Martini
Garnish: Raspberries on stick
Method: SHAKE all ingredients with ice and fine strain into chilled glass.

2	shot(s)	**Courvoisier V.S.O.P. cognac**
1½	shot(s)	**Ocean Spray cranberry juice**
½	shot(s)	**Crème de cassis or Chambord**
¼	shot(s)	**Freshly squeezed lime juice**

Origin: Originally created for Martell, long term sponsors of the Grand National, this is named after the horse that won in 2001.
Comment: Slightly sweet and fruity with a hint of raspberry and cognac's distinctive flavour.

RED
SNAPPER

Glass: Collins
Garnish: Rim the glass with black pepper and celery salt, add cherry tomato on a stick
Method: SHAKE all ingredients with ice and strain into ice-filled glass. Serve with straws.

2	shot(s)	Tanqueray London dry gin
4	shot(s)	Pressed tomato juice
½	shot(s)	Freshly squeezed lemon juice
7	drops	Tabasco pepper sauce
4	dashes	Lea & Perrins Worcestershire sauce
2	pinch	Celery salt
2	grinds	Black pepper

Variant: Bloody Mary
Today, the term Red Snapper means a Bloody Mary made with gin instead of vodka. But the first known recipes, from the 1940s, describe a 50-50 blend of vodka and tomato juice, with spices, just like an early Bloody Mary: one book even states that the Red Snapper is identical to the Bloody Mary. Cocktail lore states that the Bloody Mary was officially renamed the Red Snapper at the St. Regis Hotel, at some point after the fabulously wealthy Vincent Astor bought it in 1935. Fernand Petiot, who most likely created the original drink (see 'Bloody Mary'), was working there, but Astor apparently found the title too crude for his clientele and insisted the drink be renamed. Customers, of course, continued to order Bloody Marys, but the Red Snapper found a drink of its own in due course.
Comment: Looks like a Bloody Mary but features gin's aromatic botanicals.

RED SNAPPER

R

RICKEY

REMSEN COOLER

Glass: Collins
Garnish: Whole lemon peel
Method: POUR ingredients into ice-filled glass and serve with straws.

2½	shot(s)	**Johnnie Walker Scotch whisky**
Top up with		**Soda** (from siphon)

Origin: Adapted from a recipe purloined from David Embury's classic book, The Fine Art of Mixing Drinks, and so named because it was originally made with the now defunct Remsen Scotch whisky. Embury claims this is "the original cooler".
Comment: Scotch and soda for the sophisticate.

> 'HELL IS FULL OF MUSICAL AMATEURS: MUSIC IS THE BRANDY OF THE DAMNED.'
> GEORGE BERNARD SHAW

RESOLUTE

Glass: Martini
Garnish: Lemon zest twist
Method: SHAKE all ingredients with ice and fine strain into chilled glass.

2	shot(s)	**Tanqueray London dry gin**
1	shot(s)	**Bols apricot brandy liqueur**
½	shot(s)	**Freshly squeezed lemon juice**
¾	shot(s)	**Chilled mineral water** (omit if wet ice)

Origin: Adapted from a recipe purloined from a 1930 edition of The Savoy Cocktail Book by Harry Craddock.
Comment: Simple but tasty. All three flavours work in harmony.

RICKEY (GENERIC NAME)

Glass: Collins (small 8oz)
Garnish: Immerse length of lime peel in drink.
Method: SHAKE first three ingredients with ice and strain into ice-filled glass. TOP with soda.

2	shot(s)	**Liquor** (of your choice)
		Tanqueray London dry gin
		Ketel One vodka
		Bacardi Superior rum
½	shot(s)	**Freshly squeezed lime juice**
¼	shot(s)	**Sugar syrup** (2 sugar to 1 water)
Top up with		**Soda water**

Variant: Gin Rickey, Vodka Rickey, Apricot Rickey
Origin: Believed to have been created at the Shoemaker's restaurant in Washington, circa 1900, and named after Colonel Joe Rickey for whom it was invented. Coincidentally or not, Rickey went on to become a major importer of limes into the US.
   Many confuse the Rickey and the Collins. For the record a Rickey is made with lime juice and a Collins with lemon juice. A Rickey is also usually served in a shorter glass than a Collins but that difference is secondary.
Comment: Clean, sharp and refreshing.

ROB ROY

Glass: Martini
Garnish: Cherry & lemon zest twist (discard twist)
Method: STIR all ingredients with ice and strain into chilled glass.

2	shot(s)	**Johnnie Walker Scotch whisky**
1	shot(s)	**Martini Rosso sweet vermouth**
2	dashes	**Angostura aromatic bitters**
⅛	shot(s)	**Maraschino syrup** (optional)

Variant: 'Highland', made with orange bitters in place of Angostura.
Origin: Created in 1894 at New York's Waldorf-Astoria Hotel (the Empire State Building occupies the site today), and named after a Broadway show playing at the time.
Comment: A Sweet Manhattan made with Scotch in place of bourbon. The dry, peaty whisky and bitters ensure it's not too sweet

THE ROFFIGNAC

Glass: Collins
Garnish: Lime wedge
Method: SHAKE first two ingredients with ice and strain into ice-filled glass. TOP with soda, lightly stir and serve with straws.

2	shot(s)	**Courvoisier V.S.O.P. cognac**
1	shot(s)	**Crème de cassis or Chambord**
Top up with		**Soda water** (club soda)

Origin: This classic cocktail is named after Count Louis Philippe Joseph de Roffignac, Mayor of New Orleans 1820-1828. Roffignac is noted for introducing street lights to the city and laying cobblestones on the roads in the French Quarter.
Comment: This bright red, fruity drink is simple but moreish.

ROSELYN MARTINI

R

Glass: Martini
Garnish: Maraschino cherry
Method: SHAKE all ingredients with ice and fine strain into chilled glass.

2	shot(s)	**Tanqueray London dry gin**
1	shot(s)	**Noilly Prat dry vermouth**
¼	shot(s)	**Pomegranate (grenadine) syrup**

Origin: Adapted from a recipe in Harry Craddock's 1930 Savoy Cocktail Book.
Comment: Subtle and beautifully balanced. A wet Martini made 'easy' by a dash of pomegranate syrup.

DRINKS ARE GRADED AS FOLLOWS:

● DISGUSTING	●● PRETTY AWFUL	●● BEST AVOIDED
●●● DISAPPOINTING	●●● ACCEPTABLE	●●●● GOOD
●●●● RECOMMENDED	●●●●● HIGHLY RECOMMENDED	
●●●●● OUTSTANDING / EXCEPTIONAL		

ROSSINI

Glass: Flute
Garnish: Strawberry on rim
Method: MUDDLE strawberries in base of shaker. Add liqueur, **SHAKE** with ice and fine strain into chilled glass. **TOP** with champagne and gently stir.

4	fresh	**Strawberries**
¾	shot(s)	**Crème de cassis or Chambord**
Top up with		**Brut champagne**

Origin: Named for the 19th century opera composer, this is one of the most popular Bellini variants in Venice.
Comment: Strawberries seem to complement Champagne even better than white peaches.

ROY ROGERS (MOCKTAIL)

Glass: Collins
Garnish: Lime wedge
Method: POUR both ingredients into ice-filled glass and stir. Serve with straws.

¼	shot(s)	**Pomegranate (grenadine) syrup**
Top up with		**Cola**

Comment: I wouldn't bother.

ROYAL MOJITO

Glass: Collins
Garnish: Mint sprig
Method: Lightly **MUDDLE** (just to bruise) mint in base of glass. Add rum, lime juice and sugar. Half fill glass with crushed ice and **CHURN** (stir) with bar spoon. Fill glass with more crushed ice and **CHURN** some more. **TOP** with champagne, lightly stir and serve with straws.

12	fresh	**Mint leaves**
2	shot(s)	**Bacardi Superior rum**
¾	shot(s)	**Freshly squeezed lime juice**
¼	shot(s)	**Sugar syrup** (2 sugar to 1 water)
Top up with		**Brut champagne**

AKA: Luxury Mojito
Comment: A Mojito topped with champagne instead of soda water. There's posh!

RUBY MARTINI

Glass: Martini
Garnish: Raspberry & lemon twist
Method: SHAKE all ingredients with ice and fine strain into chilled glass.

1½	shot(s)	**Courvoisier V.S.O.P. cognac**
½	shot(s)	**Cointreau triple sec**
½	shot(s)	**Crème de cassis or Chambord**
½	shot(s)	**Martini Rosso sweet vermouth**

Origin: Created by Wayne Collins, London, England.
Comment: Fruity and slightly sweet.

RUSSIAN SPRING PUNCH

Glass: Sling
Garnish: Lemon slice & berries
Method: SHAKE first four ingredients with ice and strain into glass filled with crushed ice. **TOP** with champagne, lightly stir and serve with straws.

1	shot(s)	**Ketel One vodka**
¼	shot(s)	**Crème de cassis or Chambord**
1	shot(s)	**Freshly squeezed lemon juice**
¼	shot(s)	**Sugar syrup** (2 sugar to 1 water)
Top up with		**Champagne**

Origin: My version of a drink created in the 1990s by Dick Bradsell, London, England.
Comment: Well balanced, complex and refreshing.

SAIGON COOLER

Glass: Collins
Garnish: Three raspberries
Method: MUDDLE raspberries in base of shaker. Add other ingredients, **SHAKE** with ice and fine strain into ice-filled glass.

7	fresh	**Raspberries**
2	shot(s)	**Tanqueray London dry gin**
½	shot(s)	**Crème de cassis or Chambord**
3	shot(s)	**Ocean Spray cranberry juice**
¾	shot(s)	**Freshly squeezed lime juice**

Origin: Created at Bam-Bou, London, England.
Comment: Well balanced sweet 'n' sour with a rich fruity flavour.

> 'IT WAS MY UNCLE GEORGE WHO DISCOVERED THAT ALCOHOL WAS A FOOD WELL IN ADVANCE OF MEDICAL THOUGHT.'
> P. G. WODEHOUSE

ST. KITTS (MOCKTAIL)

Glass: Collins
Garnish: Lime wedge
Method: SHAKE first three ingredients with ice and strain into ice-filled glass. **TOP** with ginger ale, lightly stir and serve with straws.

3	shot(s)	**Pressed pineapple juice**
½	shot(s)	**Freshly squeezed lime juice**
¼	shot(s)	**Pomegranate (grenadine) syrup**
Top up with		**Ginger ale**

Variant: Add 3 dashes Angostura aromatic bitters. This adds a tiny amount of alcohol but greatly improves the drink.
Comment: Rust coloured and refreshing.

ROYAL MOJITO

SANGRITA

Glass: Shot
Method: SHAKE all ingredients with ice and fine strain into shot glass. Serve with a shot of tequila. The drinker can either down the tequila and chase it with sangrita or sip the two drinks alternately.

½	shot(s)	**Tomato juice**
½	shot(s)	**Pomegranate juice**
¼	shot(s)	**Freshly squeezed orange juice**
½	shot(s)	**Freshly squeezed lime juice**
⅛	shot(s)	**Pomegranate (grenadine) syrup**
2	drops	**Tabasco**
2	dashes	**Worcestershire sauce**
1	pinch	**Salt**
1	grind	**Black pepper**

Origin: The name means 'little blood' in Spanish and the drink is served with tequila in practically every bar in Mexico.
Comment: In Mexico the quality of the homemade Sangrita can make or break a bar. This recipe is spicy and slightly sweet and perfect for chasing tequila.

SANTIAGO DAIQUIRI

Glass: Martini
Garnish: Maraschino cherry
Method: SHAKE all ingredients with ice and fine strain into chilled glass.

2	shot(s)	**Bacardi Superior rum**
1	shot(s)	**Freshly squeezed lemon juice**
½	shot(s)	**Pomegranate (grenadine) syrup**
½	shot(s)	**Chilled mineral water** (omit if wet ice)

Origin: Adapted from a recipe in Harry Craddock's 1930 Savoy Cocktail Book.
Comment: This Daiquiri is particularly delicate in its balance between sweet and sour.

SATAN'S WHISKERS (STRAIGHT)

Glass: Martini
Garnish: Orange zest twist
Method: SHAKE all ingredients with ice and fine strain into chilled glass.

1	shot(s)	**Tanqueray London dry gin**
1	shot(s)	**Noilly Prat dry vermouth**
1	shot(s)	**Martini Rosso sweet vermouth**
½	shot(s)	**Grand Marnier liqueur**
1	shot(s)	**Freshly squeezed orange juice**
1	dash	**Fee Brothers orange bitters** (optional)

Variant: 'Curled' use triple sec in place of Grand Marnier.
Origin: Adapted from a recipe in Harry Craddock's 1930 Savoy Cocktail Book.
Comment: A variation on the Bronx. Perfectly balanced tangy orange.

SCOFFLAW

Glass: Martini
Garnish: Lemon zest twist
Method: SHAKE all ingredients with ice and fine strain into chilled glass.

1½	shot(s)	**Bulleit bourbon whiskey**
1½	shot(s)	**Noilly Prat dry vermouth**
½	shot(s)	**Freshly squeezed lemon juice**
¼	shot(s)	**Pomegranate (grenadine) syrup**
1	dash	**Fee Brothers orange bitters** (optional)

Origin: During the height of Prohibition, The Boston Herald ran a competition asking readers to coin a new word for "a lawless drinker of illegally made or illegally obtained liquor". Out of 25,000 entries, 'Scofflaw' was chosen and on 15th January 1924 the $200 prize was shared between the two people who had submitted the word. This cocktail was created by Jock at Harry's American Bar, Paris, to celebrate the new term.
Comment: This rust-coloured drink is made or broken by the quality of pomegranate syrup used.

> '...ALL MY LIFE I'VE BEEN TERRIBLE AT REMEMBERING PEOPLE'S NAMES. I ONCE INTRODUCED A FRIEND OF MINE AS MARTINI. HER NAME WAS ACTUALLY OLIVE.'
> TALLULAH BANKHEAD

SARATOGA COCKTAIL

Glass: Wine glass (small)
Garnish: Quarter slice of lemon
Method: Vigorously SHAKE all ingredients with just two cubes of ice and strain into glass.

1	shot(s)	**Courvoisier V.S.O.P. cognac**
1	shot(s)	**Bulleit bourbon whiskey**
1	shot(s)	**Martini Rosso sweet vermouth**
2	dashes	**Angostura aromatic bitters**

Origin: Recipe adapted from Jerry Thomas' 1862 'The Bartenders Guide'.
Comment: Frothy topped yet hardcore.

SCOTCH MILK PUNCH

Glass: Martini
Garnish: Grate nutmeg over drink
Method: SHAKE all ingredients with ice and fine strain into chilled glass.

2	shot(s)	**Johnnie Walker Scotch whisky**
½	shot(s)	**Sugar syrup** (2 sugar to 1 water)
¾	shot(s)	**Double (heavy) cream**
¾	shot(s)	**Milk**

Comment: A creamy, malty affair.

SCREWDRIVER

Glass: Collins
Garnish: Orange slice
Method: **POUR** vodka into ice-filled glass and top with orange juice. Lightly stir and serve with straws.

2	shot(s)	**Ketel One vodka**
Top up with		**Freshly squeezed orange juice**

Origin: This cocktail first appeared in the 1950s in the Middle East. Parched US engineers working in the desert supposedly added orange juice to their vodka and stirred it with the nearest thing to hand, usually a screwdriver.
Comment: The temperature at which this drink is served and the freshness of the orange juice makes or breaks it.

SHARK'S TOOTH

Glass: Sling (10oz Pilsner glass)
Garnish: Lime wedge
Method: **SHAKE** first three ingredients with ice and strain into ice-filled glass. **TOP** with soda and serve with straws.

2½	shot(s)	**Bacardi Superior rum**
1	shot(s)	**Freshly squeezed lemon juice**
½	shot(s)	**Pomegranate (grenadine) syrup**
Top up with		**Soda water** (club soda)

Origin: Adapted from Victor Bergeron's 'Trader Vic's Bartender's Guide' (1972 revised edition).
Comment: Sounds hard; looks pink. Tastes great!

SEABREEZE #1 (SIMPLE)

Glass: Collins
Garnish: Lime slice
Method: **SHAKE** all ingredients with ice and strain into ice-filled glass.

2	shot(s)	**Ketel One vodka**
3	shot(s)	**Ocean Spray cranberry juice**
1½	shot(s)	**Freshly squeezed grapefruit juice**

Origin: Thought to have originated in the early 1990s in New York City.
Comment: Few bartenders bother to shake this simple drink, instead simply pouring and stirring in the glass.

SHIRLEY TEMPLE (MOCKTAIL)

Glass: Collins
Garnish: Maraschino cherry & lemon slice
Method: **POUR** ingredients into ice-filled glass, lightly stir and serve with straws.

¼	shot(s)	**Pomegranate (grenadine) syrup**
¼	shot(s)	**Freshly squeezed lemon juice**
Top up with		**Ginger ale**

Comment: I've added a splash of lemon juice to the usual recipe. It's still not that exciting.

SEABREEZE #2 (LAYERED)

Glass: Collins
Garnish: Lime wedge
Method: **POUR** cranberry juice into ice-filled glass. **SHAKE** other ingredients with ice and carefully strain into glass to **LAYER** over the cranberry juice.

3	shot(s)	**Ocean Spray cranberry juice**
2	shot(s)	**Ketel One vodka**
1½	shot(s)	**Freshly squeezed grapefruit juice**
½	shot(s)	**Freshly squeezed lime juice**

Comment: This layered version requires mixing with straws prior to drinking.

SHOWBIZ

Glass: Martini
Garnish: Blackcurrants on stick
Method: **SHAKE** all ingredients with ice and fine strain into chilled glass.

1¾	shot(s)	**Ketel One vodka**
1	shot(s)	**Crème de cassis or Chambord**
1¾	shot(s)	**Freshly squeezed grapefruit juice**

Comment: Sweet cassis soured with grapefruit and fortified with vodka.

S

SHADY GROVE COOLER

Glass: Collins
Garnish: Lime wedge
Method: **SHAKE** first three ingredients with ice and strain into ice-filled glass. **TOP** with ginger ale, lightly stir and serve with straws.

2	shot(s)	**Tanqueray London dry gin**
1	shot(s)	**Freshly squeezed lime juice**
½	shot(s)	**Sugar syrup** (2 sugar to 1 water)
Top up with		**Ginger ale**

Comment: Long and refreshing with lime freshness and a hint of ginger.

SIDECAR #1 (EQUAL PARTS CLASSIC FORMULA)

Glass: Martini
Garnish: Lemon zest twist
Method: **SHAKE** all ingredients with ice and fine strain into chilled glass.

1¼	shot(s)	**Courvoisier V.S.O.P. cognac**
1¼	shot(s)	**Cointreau triple sec**
1¼	shot(s)	**Freshly squeezed lemon juice**

Variant: Apple Cart
Comment: Dry and tart but beautifully balanced and refined.

SIDECAR
(DIFFORDS FORMULA)

Glass: Martini
Garnish: Lemon zest twist
Method: SHAKE all ingredients with ice and fine strain into chilled glass.

1½	shot(s)	**Courvoisier V.S.O.P. cognac**
1	shot(s)	**Cointreau triple sec**
1	shot(s)	**Freshly squeezed lemon juice**
½	shot(s)	**Chilled mineral water** (omit if wet ice)

Variant: Apple Cart
Origin: In his 1948 'Fine Art of Mixing Drinks', David A. Embury writes of the Sidecar: "It was invented by a friend of mine at a bar in Paris during World War I and was named after the motorcycle sidecar in which the good captain customarily was driven to and from the little bistro where the drink was born and christened."

Embury doesn't name the bar but it's commonly assumed that he meant Harry's New York Bar and that the cocktail was created by its owner, Harry MacElhone. However, in Harry's own book he credits the drink to Pat MacGarry of Buck's Club, London.

The proportions of this drink are debated as much as its origin. Perhaps due to ease rather than balance, the equal parts formula (1 x brandy, 1 x triple sec and 1 x lemon juice) was the earliest published recipe (Robert Vermeire's 1922 'Cocktails: How to Mix Them' and Harry McElhone's 1922 'ABC of mixing cocktails') and still seems popular to this day.

Embury writes of the 'equal parts' Sidecar, "This is the most perfect example of a magnificent drink gone wrong". He argues that "Essentially the Sidecar is nothing but a Daiquiri with brandy in the place of rum and Cointreau in the place of sugar syrup" and so the Daiquiri formula should be followed (2 x brandy, 1/2 x triple sec and 1/4 lemon juice). This may work for a Daiquiri but makes for an overly dry Sidecar.

In his 1930 'The Savoy Cocktail Book', Harry Craddock calls for 2 x brandy; 1 x Cointreau and 1 x lemon juice. The formula I use here takes the middle ground between The Savoy and the 'equal parts' camp. I also find this drink benefits from a little extra dilution.
Comment: There have been periods when it has been fashionable to coat the rim of the glass in which this drink is to be served with sugar. Thankfully sugar rims are now out of vogue and, as Embury writes in his book, "A twist of lemon may be used if desired and the peel dropped into the glass. Otherwise no decoration."

SIDECAR

SIDECAR #3 (EMBURY'S FORMULA)

Glass: Martini
Garnish: Lemon zest twist
Method: SHAKE all ingredients with ice and fine strain into chilled glass.

2	shot(s)	**Courvoisier V.S.O.P. cognac**
½	shot(s)	**Freshly squeezed lemon juice**
½	shot(s)	**Cointreau triple sec**
½	shot(s)	**Chilled mineral water** (omit if wet ice)

Origin: In The Fine Art of Mixing Drinks, David Embury writes of the 'equal parts' Sidecar, "This is the most perfect example of a magnificent drink gone wrong". He argues that "Essentially the Sidecar is nothing but a Daiquiri with brandy in the place of rum and Cointreau in the place of sugar syrup" and so the Daiquiri formula should be followed as above.
Comment: A Sidecar for those with a dry palate.

SILENT THIRD

Glass: Martini
Garnish: Lemon zest twist
Method: SHAKE all ingredients with ice and fine strain into chilled glass.

1½	shot(s)	**Johnnie Walker Scotch whisky**
1	shot(s)	**Cointreau triple sec**
¾	shot(s)	**Freshly squeezed lemon juice**
½	shot(s)	**Chilled mineral water** (omit if wet ice)

Comment: Basically a Sidecar made with Scotch in place of Cognac.

SILVER FIZZ

Glass: Collins (8oz max)
Garnish: Lemon slice
Method: SHAKE first four ingredients with ice and strain into chilled glass (no ice). **TOP** with soda from siphon.

2	shot(s)	**Liquor** (of your choice)
		Tanqueray London dry gin
		Bulleit bourbon whiskey
		Johnnie Walker Scotch whisky
		Ketel One vodka
1	shot(s)	**Freshly squeezed lemon or lime juice**
½	shot(s)	**Sugar syrup** (2 sugar to 1 water)
½	fresh	**Egg white**
Top up with		**Soda water** (from siphon)

Origin: A mid-19th century classic.
Variant: Omit the egg white and this is a mere Fizz.
Comment: I prefer my Fizzes with the addition of egg white. Why not also try a Derby Fizz, which combines liqueur and spirits?

SIR WALTER COCKTAIL

Glass: Martini
Garnish: Lemon zest twist
Method: SHAKE all ingredients with ice and fine strain into chilled glass.

¾	shot(s)	**Bacardi Superior rum**
¾	shot(s)	**Courvoisier V.S.O.P. cognac**
¼	shot(s)	**Grand Marnier liqueur**
¾	shot(s)	**Freshly squeezed lemon juice**
¼	shot(s)	**Pomegranate (grenadine) syrup**
2	dashes	**Angostura aromatic bitters**

Origin: Adapted from Victor Bergeron's 'Trader Vic's Bartender's Guide' (1972 revised edition).
Comment: This blend of rum & cognac has more than a hint of Tiki fruitiness.

> YOU CAN'T BE A REAL COUNTRY UNLESS YOU HAVE A BEER AND AN AIRLINE - IT HELPS IF YOU HAVE SOME KIND OF A FOOTBALL TEAM, OR SOME NUCLEAR WEAPONS, BUT AT THE VERY LEAST YOU NEED A BEER.
> FRANK ZAPPA

SILVER BRONX

Glass: Martini
Garnish: Maraschino cherry
Method: SHAKE all ingredients with ice and fine strain into chilled glass.

2	shot(s)	**Tanqueray London dry gin**
¼	shot(s)	**Noilly Prat dry vermouth**
¼	shot(s)	**Martini Rosso sweet vermouth**
1	shot(s)	**Freshly squeezed orange juice**
½	fresh	**Egg white**

Origin: A vintage cocktail adapted from the classic Bronx Cocktail, created in 1906 by Johnny Solon, a bartender at New York's Waldorf-Astoria Hotel, and named after the newly opened Bronx Zoo.
Comment: A Bronx made 'silver' by the addition of egg white.

SLEEPY HOLLOW

Glass: Old-fashioned
Garnish: Lemon slice
Method: Lightly **MUDDLE** (just to bruise) mint in base of shaker. Add other ingredients, **SHAKE** with ice and fine strain into glass filled with crushed ice. Serve with straws.

10	fresh	**Mint leaves**
2	shot(s)	**Tanqueray London dry gin**
½	shot(s)	**Bols apricot brandy liqueur**
1	shot(s)	**Freshly squeezed lemon juice**
½	shot(s)	**Sugar syrup** (2 sugar to 1 water)

Origin: An adaption of a drink created in the early 1930s and named after Washington Irving's novel and its enchanted valley with ghosts, goblins and headless horseman.
Comment: Hints of lemon and mint with gin and apricot fruit. Very refreshing.

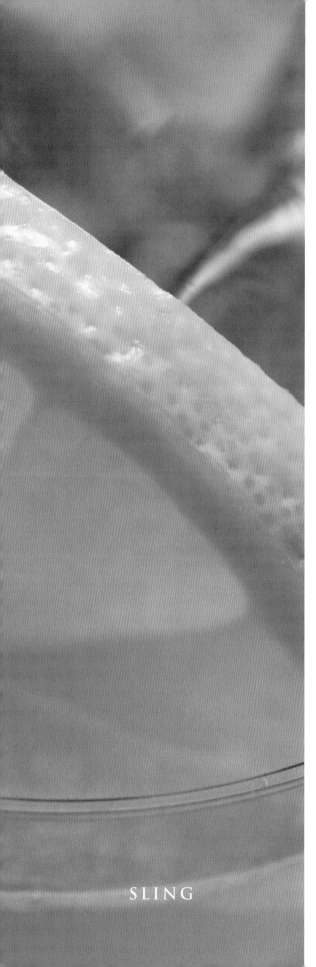

SLING

SLING
(GENERIC NAME)

Glass: Sling
Garnish: Lemon slice
Method: SHAKE first three ingredients with ice and strain into ice-filled glass. **TOP** with soda or ginger ale.

2	shot(s)	**Liquor** (of your choice)
		Bacardi Superior rum
		Tanqueray London dry gin
		Bulleit bourbon whiskey
		Johnnie Walker Scotch whisky
½	shot(s)	**Freshly squeezed lemon juice**
¼	shot(s)	**Sugar syrup** (2 sugar to 1 water)
Top up with		**Soda or ginger ale**

Origin: The word 'Sling' comes from the German 'schlingen', meaning 'to swallow', and Slings based on a spirit mixed with sugar and water were popularly drunk in the late 1800s.

Slings are similar to Toddies and like Toddies can be served hot. (Toddies, however, are never served cold.) The main difference between a Toddy and a Sling is that Slings are not flavoured by the addition of spices. Also, Toddies tend to be made with plain water, while Slings are charged with water, soda water or ginger ale.

The earliest known definition of 'cocktail' describes it as a bittered sling.
Comment: Sugar balances the citrus juice, the spirit fortifies and the carbonate lengthens.

SLOPPY JOE

Glass: Martini
Garnish: Lime wedge
Method: SHAKE all ingredients with ice and fine strain into chilled glass.

1	shot(s)	**Bacardi Superior rum**
1	shot(s)	**Noilly Prat dry vermouth**
¼	shot(s)	**Cointreau triple sec**
1	shot(s)	**Freshly squeezed lime juice**
½	shot(s)	**Sugar syrup** (2 sugar to 1 water)
¼	shot(s)	**Pomegranate (grenadine) syrup**

Comment: Nicely balanced sweet and sourness.

SMOKY MARTINI

Glass: Martini
Garnish: Lemon zest twist
Method: STIR all ingredients with ice and strain into chilled glass.

2½	shot(s)	**Tanqueray London dry gin**
½	shot(s)	**Noilly Prat dry vermouth**
¼	shot(s)	**Johnnie Walker Scotch whisky**

Variant: Substitute vodka for gin.
Comment: A pleasant variation on the classic Dry Martini.

SNOW WHITE DAIQUIRI

Glass: Martini
Garnish: Pineapple wedge on rim
Method: SHAKE all ingredients with ice and fine strain into chilled glass.

2	shot(s)	**Bacardi Superior rum**
½	shot(s)	**Pressed pineapple juice**
½	shot(s)	**Freshly squeezed lime juice**
¼	shot(s)	**Sugar syrup** (2 sugar to 1 water)
½	fresh	**Egg white**

Origin: My adaptation of a classic cocktail.
Comment: The pineapple and egg white ensure that this delightful Daiquiri has an appropriately white frothy head.

SNYDER MARTINI

Glass: Martini
Garnish: Orange zest twist
Method: SHAKE all ingredients with ice and fine strain into chilled glass.

2	shot(s)	**Tanqueray London dry gin**
1	shot(s)	**Noilly Prat dry vermouth**
¼	shot(s)	**Grand Marnier liqueur**

Origin: Adapted from a recipe in Harry Craddock's 1930 Savoy Cocktail Book.
Comment: Dry, hardcore and yet mellow.

SOUR
(GENERIC NAME)

Glass: Old-fashioned
Garnish: Lemon slice & cherry on stick (sail)
Method: SHAKE all ingredients with ice and strain into ice-filled glass

2	shot(s)	**Liquor** (of your choice)
		Bacardi Superior rum
		Courvoisier V.S.O.P cognac
		Tanqueray London dry gin
		Bulleit bourbon whiskey
		Johnnie Walker Scotch whisky
1	shot(s)	**Freshly squeezed lemon juice**
½	shot(s)	**Sugar syrup** (2 sugar to 1 water)
½	fresh	**Egg white**
3	dashes	**Angostura aromatic bitters**

Origin: Sours are aptly named drinks. Their flavour comes from either lemon or lime juice, which is balanced with sugar. Sours can be based on practically any spirit but the bourbon based Whiskey Sour is by far the most popular. Many (including myself) believe this drink is only properly made when smoothed with a little egg white. Sours are served either straight-up in a Sour glass (rather like a small flute) or on the rocks in an old-fashioned glass. They are traditionally garnished with a cherry and an orange slice, or sometimes a lemon slice.
Comment: This 4:2:8 formula is a tad sourer than the classic 3:4:8 which translates as: three quarter part of the sour ingredient (lemon juice), one part of the sweet ingredient (sugar syrup) and two parts of the strong ingredient (spirit). So if you find my formula to sour than best follow the classic proportions in future.

SOUR

SOUTHSIDE

Glass: Martini
Garnish: Mint leaf
Method: **SHAKE** all ingredients (including mint) with ice and fine strain into chilled glass.

7	fresh	**Mint leaves**
2	shot(s)	**Tanqueray London dry gin**
1	shot(s)	**Freshly squeezed lime juice**
½	shot(s)	**Sugar syrup** (2 sugar to 1 water)

Origin: This vintage cocktail is purported to have originated at New York's Twenty-One Club. A long version served over crushed ice is said to have come from the southside of Chicago during Prohibition where it was drunk by the Southside mobsters, while on the other side of town hoodlums enjoyed the Northside (gin and ginger ale).
Comment: Gin and mint with a splash of lime. Refreshingly balanced.

SOUTHSIDE ROYALE

Glass: Martini
Garnish: Mint leaf
Method: Lightly **MUDDLE** (just to bruise) mint in base of shaker. Add next three ingredients, **SHAKE** with ice and fine strain into chilled glass. **TOP** with a splash of champagne.

7	fresh	**Mint leaves**
2	shot(s)	**Tanqueray London dry gin**
1	shot(s)	**Freshly squeezed lemon juice**
½	shot(s)	**Sugar syrup** (2 sugar to 1 water)
Top up with		**Brut champagne**

Origin: Created during Prohibition, either at a New York City speakeasy called Jack & Charlie's, or at Manhattan's Stork Club, or by Chicago's Southside gang to make their bootleg liquor more palatable.
Comment: A White Lady with fresh mint and champagne.

SPENCER COCKTAIL

Glass: Martini
Garnish: Orange zest twist (discarded) & maraschino cherry
Method: **SHAKE** all ingredients with ice and fine strain into chilled glass.

2	shot(s)	**Tanqueray London dry gin**
1	shot(s)	**Bols apricot brandy liqueur**
¼	shot(s)	**Freshly squeezed orange juice**
1	dash	**Angostura aromatic bitters**

Origin: Adapted from a recipe in Harry Craddock's 1930 Savoy Cocktail Book.
Comment: To quote Craddock, "Very mellifluous: has a fine and rapid action: for morning work."

SPEYSIDE MARTINI

Glass: Martini
Garnish: Lemon zest twist
Method: **MUDDLE** grapes in base of shaker. Add other ingredients, **SHAKE** with ice and fine strain into chilled glass.

7	fresh	**Seedless white grapes**
2	shot(s)	**Johnnie Walker Scotch whisky**
¾	shot(s)	**Bols apricot brandy liqueur**
¾	shot(s)	**Freshly squeezed grapefruit juice**

Origin: Discovered in 2004 at Indigo Yard, Edinburgh, Scotland.
Comment: Scotch, grape juice, apricot liqueur and grapefruit get on well together.

SPUTNIK

Glass: Old-fashioned
Garnish: Orange slice
Method: **SHAKE** all ingredients with ice and strain into ice-filled glass.

1	shot(s)	**Bacardi Superior rum**
1	shot(s)	**Courvoisier V.S.O.P. cognac**
2	shot(s)	**Freshly squeezed orange juice**
½	shot(s)	**Sugar syrup** (2 sugar to 1 water)

Origin: A cocktail served in underground clubs all over the former Eastern Bloc where it was originally made with Cuban rum, Georgian brandy and tinned orange juice.
Comment: Orange, cognac and rum meld well.

STANLEY COCKTAIL

Glass: Martini
Garnish: Lemon zest twist
Method: **SHAKE** all ingredients with ice and fine strain into chilled glass.

1½	shot(s)	**Tanqueray London dry gin**
1½	shot(s)	**Bacardi Superior rum**
½	shot(s)	**Freshly squeezed lemon juice**
½	shot(s)	**Pomegranate (grenadine) syrup**

Origin: Adapted from a recipe in Harry Craddock's 1930 Savoy Cocktail Book.
Comment: Salmon pink with a splash of gin.

STRAWBERRY BLONDE

Glass: Collins
Garnish: Strawberry on rim
Method: **MUDDLE** strawberries in base of shaker. Add next three ingredients, **SHAKE** with ice and fine strain into ice-filled glass. **TOP** with soda and serve with straws.

2	fresh	**Hulled Strawberries (3 if small)**
2	shot(s)	**Ketel One vodka**
1½	shot(s)	**Freshly squeezed lemon juice**
¾	shot(s)	**Sugar syrup** (2 sugar to 1 water)
Top up with		**Soda water**

Origin: Created in 2008 by yours truly at The Cabinet Room, London, England.
Comment: Lurid orange-red in colour and basically alcoholic strawberry flavoured real lemonade.

STRAWBERRY DAIQUIRI

Glass: Martini
Garnish: Strawberry on rim
Method: MUDDLE strawberries in base of shaker. Add other ingredients, **SHAKE** with ice and fine strain into chilled glass.

7	fresh	**Hulled strawberries**
2	shot(s)	**Bacardi Superior rum**
½	shot(s)	**Freshly squeezed lime juice**
¼	shot(s)	**Sugar syrup** (2 sugar to 1 water)

Origin: A popular drink in Cuba where it is known as a Daiquiri de Fresa.
Comment: Makes strawberries and cream appear very dull.

STRAWBERRY FROZEN DAIQUIRI

Glass: Martini
Garnish: Split strawberry
Method: BLEND all ingredients with 6oz scoop of crushed ice.

2	shot(s)	**Bacardi Superior rum**
¾	shot(s)	**Freshly squeezed lime juice**
½	shot(s)	**Sugar syrup** (2 sugar to 1 water)
5	fresh	**Hulled strawberries (chopped)**

Comment: A delicious twist on a classic – Strawberry Mivvi for grown-ups.

STRAWBERRY MARGARITA

Glass: Martini
Garnish: Strawberry on rim
Method: MUDDLE strawberries in base of shaker. Add other ingredients, **SHAKE** with ice and fine strain into chilled glass.

5	fresh	**Hulled strawberries (chopped)**
2	shot(s)	**Don Julio 100% agave tequila**
1	shot(s)	**Freshly squeezed lime juice**
¾	shot(s)	**Sugar syrup** (2 sugar to 1 water)

Origin: Formula by yours truly in 2004.
Comment: Fresh strawberries combine well with tequila in this fruit margarita.

STRAWBERRY MARTINI

Glass: Martini
Garnish: Strawberry on rim
Method: MUDDLE strawberries in base of shaker. Add other ingredients, **SHAKE** with ice and fine strain into chilled glass.

5	fresh	**Hulled strawberries (chopped)**
2½	shot(s)	**Ketel One vodka**
½	shot(s)	**Sugar syrup** (2 sugar to 1 water)
2	grinds	**Black pepper**

Origin: Created by yours truly in 2004.
Comment: Rich strawberries fortified with vodka and a hint of pepper spice

SUMMER TIME MARTINI

Glass: Martini
Garnish: Kumquat
Method: SHAKE all ingredients with ice and fine strain into chilled glass.

1½	shot(s)	**Tanqueray London dry gin**
1	shot(s)	**Grand Marnier liqueur**
1½	shot(s)	**Freshly squeezed orange juice**
¼	shot(s)	**Pomegranate (grenadine) syrup**

Comment: Smooth, gin laced fruit for a summer's day.

SUNDOWNER #1

Glass: Martini
Garnish: Orange zest twist
Method: SHAKE all ingredients with ice and fine strain into chilled glass.

2	shot(s)	**Courvoisier V.S.O.P. cognac**
½	shot(s)	**Grand Marnier liqueur**
½	shot(s)	**Freshly squeezed orange juice**
¼	shot(s)	**Freshly squeezed lemon juice**
¾	shot(s)	**Chilled mineral water** (omit if wet ice)

Variant: Red Lion
Origin: This cocktail is popular in South Africa where it is made with locally produced brandy and a local orange liqueur called Van der Hum.
Comment: Cognac and orange served 'up'.

SUNSHINE COCKTAIL #1

Glass: Martini
Garnish: Pineapple wedge on rim
Method: SHAKE all ingredients with ice and fine strain into chilled glass.

1½	shot(s)	**Bacardi Superior rum**
1½	shot(s)	**Noilly Prat dry vermouth**
1½	shot(s)	**Pressed pineapple juice**
⅛	shot(s)	**Pomegranate (grenadine) syrup**

Origin: Adapted from a recipe in my 1949 copy of Esquire's Handbook For Hosts.
Comment: Light, fruity and a tad on the sweet side, but could well brighten your day.

SUNSHINE COCKTAIL #2

Glass: Martini
Garnish: Lemon zest twist
Method: SHAKE all ingredients with ice and fine strain into chilled glass.

1½	shot(s)	**Bacardi Superior rum**
1½	shot(s)	**Noilly Prat dry vermouth**
¼	shot(s)	**Crème de cassis or Chambord**
¼	shot(s)	**Freshly squeezed lemon juice**

Origin: Adapted from a recipe in Harry Craddock's 1930 Savoy Cocktail Book.
Comment: Fruity, flavoursome and well-balanced all the same.

SUNSTROKE

Glass: Martini
Garnish: Orange zest twist (round to make sun)
Method: SHAKE all ingredients with ice and fine strain into chilled glass.

1	shot(s)	**Ketel One vodka**
1	shot(s)	**Cointreau triple sec**
2	shot(s)	**Freshly squeezed grapefruit juice**

Comment: Fruity but balanced. One to sip in the shade.

THE SURFER

Glass: Collins
Garnish: Lemon slice
Method: POUR lemonade into ice-filled glass to two-thirds full. **FLOAT** cognac over lemonade. Serve with straws and instruct drinker to stir ingredients before drinking.

²/₃	fill	**Lemonade (artisanal style)**
¹/₃	fill	**Courvoisier V.S.O.P. cognac**

Origin: An adaption of a Cognac Surfer by yours truly. The original is made by floating cognac on mineral water.
Comment: Good quality lemonade adds lemon freshness and smoothes the cognac.

SWIZZLE (GENERIC NAME)

Glass: Old-fashioned
Garnish: Fruit or mint sprigs
Method: POUR ingredients into glass filled with crushed ice. **SWIZZLE** with a swizzle stick and serve with straws.

2	shot(s)	**Liquor**
		Bacardi Superior rum
		Tanqueray London dry gin
		Bulleit bourbon whiskey
		Johnnie Walker Scotch whisky
½	shot(s)	**Fresh lemon or lime juice**
¼	shot(s)	**Sugar syrup or liqueur**

Variants: With rum try orgeat syrup or Velvet Falernum in place of the sugar syrup. With whiskey try Chartreuse.
Origin: Swizzles originated in the Caribbean. They are sour style drinks that, distinctively, must be churned with a swizzle stick.

Originally a twig from a species of tree called Quararibea turbinata which grow in the southern islands of the Caribean. These trees have forked branches which make perfect swizzle sticks. Today swizzle sticks are usually made of metal or plastic and have several blades or fingers attached to the base at right angles to the shaft. To use one, simply immerse the blades in the drink, hold the shaft between the palms of both hands and rotate the stick rapidly by sliding your hands back and forth against it. If you do not have a bona fide swizzle stick, use a barspoon in the same manner.

Swizzles can be served as short drinks or lengthened with mineral water.
Comment: Match the appropriate citrus juice and sweetener to your spirit and you'll have a superb drink.

TABU

Glass: Coconut shell or Tiki mug
Garnish: Pineapple cubes & cherry on stick, mint sprig
Method: BLEND all ingredients with 12oz scoop crushed ice.

1	shot(s)	**Bacardi Superior rum**
1	shot(s)	**Ketel One vodka**
1½	shot(s)	**Pressed pineapple juice**
½	shot(s)	**Freshly squeezed lemon juice**
¼	shot(s)	**Sugar syrup (2 sugar to 1 water)**

Origin: Adapted from Victor Bergeron's 'Trader Vic's Bartender's Guide' (1972 revised edition) where Vic states the drink "originated in Seattle".
Comment: Ice cold fresh pineapple laced with rum and vodka with a splash of citrus.

TAHITIAN HONEY BEE

Glass: Martini
Garnish: Lemon zest twist
Method: STIR honey with rum in base of shaker s as to dissolve honey. Add lemon juice, **SHAKE** with ice and fine strain into chilled glass.

2	shot(s)	**Bacardi Superior rum**
2	spoons	**Runny honey**
½	shot(s)	**Freshly squeezed lemon juice**

Origin: Adapted from Victor Bergeron's 'Trader Vic's Bartender's Guide' (1972 revised edition).
Comment: Basically a honey Daiquiri – very tasty too.

TANGO MARTINI

Glass: Martini
Garnish: Orange zest twist
Method: SHAKE all ingredients with ice and fine strain into chilled glass.

1½	shot(s)	**Tanqueray London dry gin**
½	shot(s)	**Martini Rosso sweet vermouth**
½	shot(s)	**Noilly Prat dry vermouth**
½	shot(s)	**Cointreau triple sec**
1	shot(s)	**Freshly squeezed orange juice**

Origin: Adapted from a recipe in Harry Craddock's 1930 Savoy Cocktail Book.
Comment: Balanced and complex with hints of gin and orange.

TENNESSEE ICED TEA

Glass: Sling
Garnish: Lemon wedge on rim
Method: SHAKE first six ingredients with ice and strain into ice-filled glass. **TOP** with cola and serve with straws.

1	shot(s)	**Bulleit bourbon whiskey**
½	shot(s)	**Bacardi Superior rum**
½	shot(s)	**Ketel One vodka**
½	shot(s)	**Cointreau triple sec**
¾	shot(s)	**Freshly squeezed lemon juice**
¼	shot(s)	**Sugar syrup (2 sugar to 1 water)**
Top up with		**Cola**

Comment: Bourbon and cola with extra interest courtesy of several other spirits and lemon juice.

TEQUILA FIZZ

Glass: Sling
Garnish: Orange zest twist
Method: **SHAKE** first four ingredients with ice and strain into ice-filled glass. **TOP** with lemonade.

2	shot(s)	**Don Julio 100% agave tequila**
1	shot(s)	**Freshly squeezed orange juice**
1	shot(s)	**Freshly squeezed lime juice**
½	shot(s)	**Sugar syrup** (2 sugar to 1 water)
Top up with		**Sprite/lemonade/7-Up**

Comment: Refreshing with lingering lime.

TEQUILA SLAMMER

Glass: Shot
Method: **POUR** tequila into glass and then carefully **LAYER** with champagne. The drinker should hold and cover the top of the glass with the palm of their hand so as to grip it firmly and seal the contents inside. Then they should briskly pick the glass up and slam it down (not so hard as to break the glass), then quickly gulp the drink down in one while it is still fizzing.

1	shot(s)	**Don Julio 100% agave tequila**
1	shot(s)	**Brut champagne**

Variants: With cream soda or ginger ale.
Origin: Originally topped with ginger ale and not champagne, this infamous libation is thought to have started out as a Hell's Angel drink – it needs no ice and can be carried in a bike bag.

The simplest slammer is a lick of salt, a shot of tequila and then a bite of lemon (or lime). A Bermuda Slammer involves straight tequila, salt, a slice of lemon and a partner: one has to lick the salt off the other one's neck and bite the lemon (held between their partner's teeth) before downing a shot of tequila.

To quote Victor Bergeron (Trader Vic), "You know, this rigmarole with a pinch of salt and lemon juice and tequila - in whatever order - was originally for a purpose: It's hot in Mexico. People dehydrate themselves. And they need more salt. Here, it's not so hot, and we don't need salt in the same way. So you can drink tequila straight right out of the bottle, if you want to."
Comment: Seems a waste of good tequila and champagne but there's a time and a place.

TEQUILA SOUR

Glass: Old-fashioned
Garnish: Lime zest twist
Method: **SHAKE** all ingredients with ice and fine strain into ice-filled glass.

2	shot(s)	**Don Julio 100% agave tequila**
1	shot(s)	**Freshly squeezed lime juice**
½	shot(s)	**Sugar syrup** (2 sugar to 1 water)
½	fresh	**Egg white**

Comment: A standard sour but with tequila zing.

TEQUILA SUNRISE

Glass: Collins
Garnish: Orange slice & cherry
Method: **SHAKE** first two ingredients with ice and strain into ice-filled glass. **POUR** grenadine in a circle around the top of the drink. (It will sink to create a sunrise effect.)

2	shot(s)	**Don Julio 100% agave tequila**
3	shot(s)	**Freshly squeezed orange juice**
¾	shot(s)	**Pomegranate (grenadine) syrup**

Comment: Everyone has heard of this drink, but those who have tried it will wonder why it's so famous.

TEQUILA SUNSET

Glass: Sling
Garnish: Lemon slice
Method: **STIR** honey with tequila in base of shaker until honey dissolves. Add lemon, **SHAKE** with ice and strain into ice-filled glass. **TOP** with soda.

7	spoons	**Runny honey**
2	shot(s)	**Don Julio 100% agave tequila**
2	shot(s)	**Freshly squeezed lemon juice**
Top up with		**Soda Water**

Comment: A good sweet and sour balance with subtle honey hints.

TEQUILA'TINI

Glass: Martini
Garnish: Lime zest twist
Method: **SHAKE** all ingredients with ice and fine strain into chilled glass.

2	shot(s)	**Don Julio 100% agave tequila**
1	shot(s)	**Noilly Prat dry vermouth**
3	dashes	**Angostura aromatic bitters**
½	shot(s)	**Sugar syrup** (2 sugar to 1 water)

Comment: If you like tequila and strong drinks – this is for you.

TEX COLLINS

Glass: Collins
Garnish: Lemon slice
Method: **STIR** honey with gin in base of shaker to dissolve honey. Add grapefruit juice, **SHAKE** with ice and strain into ice-filled glass. **TOP** with soda water.

2	shot(s)	**Tanqueray London dry gin**
2	spoons	**Runny honey**
2	shot(s)	**Freshly squeezed grapefruit juice**
Top up with		**Soda water** (club soda)

Origin: Adapted from a recipe in the 1949 edition of Esquire's Handbook For Hosts.
Comment: A dry, tart blend of grapefruit and gin.

TEXAS ICED TEA

Glass: Sling
Garnish: Lemon wedge on rim
Method: SHAKE first six ingredients with ice and strain into ice-filled glass. TOP with cola.

1	shot(s)	**Don Julio 100% agave tequila**
½	shot(s)	**Bacardi Superior rum**
½	shot(s)	**Ketel One vodka**
½	shot(s)	**Cointreau triple sec**
¾	shot(s)	**Freshly squeezed lemon juice**
¼	shot(s)	**Sugar syrup** (2 sugar to 1 water)
Top up with		**Cola**

Comment: My favourite of the Iced Tea family of drinks. The tequila shines through.

TEXSUN

Glass: Martini
Garnish: Lemon zest twist
Method: SHAKE all ingredients with ice and fine strain into chilled glass.

1½	shot(s)	**Bulleit bourbon whiskey**
1½	shot(s)	**Noilly Prat dry vermouth**
1½	shot(s)	**Freshly squeezed grapefruit juice**

Origin: Adapted from a recipe in the 1949 edition of Esquire's Handbook for Hosts.
Comment: Bone dry with fruity herbal hints.

THREE MILER

Glass: Martini
Garnish: Lemon zest twist
Method: SHAKE all ingredients with ice and fine strain into chilled glass.

1½	shot(s)	**Courvoisier V.S.O.P. cognac**
1½	shot(s)	**Bacardi Superior rum**
½	shot(s)	**Freshly squeezed lemon juice**
½	shot(s)	**Pomegranate (grenadine) syrup**

Origin: Adapted from the Three Miller Cocktail in the 1930 Savoy Cocktail Book. Most other cocktail books spell it with one 'l' as I have here.
Comment: A seriously strong drink, in flavour and in alcohol.

TIPPERARY

Glass: Martini
Garnish: Mint leaf
Method: Lightly MUDDLE (just to bruise) mint in base of shaker. Add other ingredients, SHAKE with ice and fine strain into chilled glass.

7	fresh	**Mint leaves**
2	shot(s)	**Tanqueray London dry gin**
1	shot(s)	**Noilly Prat dry vermouth**
¼	shot(s)	**Freshly squeezed orange juice**
¼	shot(s)	**Pomegranate (grenadine) syrup**

Origin: Adapted from a drink purloined from David Embury's classic book, The Fine Art of Mixing Drinks.
Comment: Delicate with subtle hints of mint, orange and gin.

TNT (TEQUILA 'N' TONIC')

Glass: Collins
Garnish: Lime wedge
Method: POUR all ingredients into ice filled glass and STIR.

1½	shot(s)	**Don Julio 100% agave tequila**
½	shot(s)	**Freshly squeezed lime juice**
Top up with		**Tonic water**

Origin: Adapted from Victor Bergeron's 'Trader Vic's Bartender's Guide' (1972 revised edition).
Comment: A simple but very tasty way to enjoy tequila.

TOM ARNOLD

Glass: Collins
Garnish: Lemon slice
Method: SHAKE all ingredients with ice and strain into ice-filled glass.

1½	shot(s)	**Ketel One vodka**
1½	shot(s)	**Freshly squeezed lemon juice**
¾	shot(s)	**Sugar syrup** (2 sugar to 1 water)
2	shot(s)	**Cold breakfast tea**

Variants: Arnold Palmer, John Daly
Origin: This is one of a series of tea-based drinks that were originally named after golfers. It takes its name from the actor and comedian who starred in 'National Lampoon's Golf Punk'.
Comment: Traditional lemonade laced with vodka and lengthened with tea makes a light and refreshing drink.

TOM COLLINS

Glass: Collins
Garnish: Orange slice & cherry on stick (sail)
Method: SHAKE first three ingredients with ice and strain into ice-filled glass. TOP with soda, lightly stir and serve with straws.

2	shot(s)	**Tanqueray London dry gin**
1	shot(s)	**Freshly squeezed lemon juice**
¾	shot(s)	**Sugar syrup** (2 sugar to 1 water)
Top up with		**Soda water** (club soda)

Origin: This drink is traditionally credited to John Collins, a bartender who worked at Limmer's Hotel, Conduit Street, London, during the early 19th century. However, others say it was created in New York and named after the Great Tom Collins Hoax of 1874.
Comment: A medium-sweet gin Collins.

TOMAHAWK

Glass: Collins
Garnish: Pineapple wedge
Method: SHAKE all ingredients with ice and strain into ice-filled glass.

1	shot(s)	**Don Julio 100% agave tequila**
1	shot(s)	**Cointreau triple sec**
2	shot(s)	**Ocean Spray cranberry juice**
2	shot(s)	**Pressed pineapple juice**

Comment: A simple recipe, and an effective drink.

TOREADOR

Glass: Martini
Garnish: Lime zest twist
Method: SHAKE all ingredients with ice and fine strain into chilled glass.

2	shot(s)	**Don Julio 100% agave tequila**
1	shot(s)	**Bols apricot brandy liqueur**
1	shot(s)	**Freshly squeezed lime juice**

Origin: This drink was published in W. J. Tarling's 1937 'Café Royal Cocktail Book', 16 years before the first known written reference to a Margarita. He also lists a Picador, which is identical to the later Margarita.
Comment: Apricot brandy replaces triple sec, giving a fruity twist to the classic Margarita.

AN INTELLIGENT MAN IS SOMETIMES FORCED TO BE DRUNK TO SPEND TIME WITH HIS FOOLS.
FOR WHOM THE BELL TOLLS, ERNEST HEMMINGWAY

TRE MARTINI

Glass: Martini
Garnish: Lemon zest twist
Method: SHAKE all ingredients with ice and fine strain into chilled glass.

2	shot(s)	**Bacardi Superior rum**
½	shot(s)	**Crème de cassis or Chambord**
1½	shot(s)	**Freshly pressed apple juice**

Origin: Created in 2002 by Åsa Nevestveit at Sosho, London, England.
Comment: A simple, well balanced, fruity drink laced with rum.

UNCLE VANYA

Glass: Martini
Garnish: Lime wedge on rim
Method: SHAKE all ingredients with ice and fine strain into chilled glass.

1¾	shot(s)	**Ketel One vodka**
1	shot(s)	**Crème de cassis or Chambord**
1	shot(s)	**Freshly squeezed lime juice**
½	shot(s)	**Sugar syrup** (2 sugar to 1 water)
½	fresh	**Egg white**

Origin: Named after Anton Chekhov's greatest play – a cheery tale of envy and despair. A popular drink in Britain's TGI Friday's bars, its origins are unknown.
Comment: Simple but great – smooth, sweet 'n' sour blackberry, although possibly a tad on the sweet side for some.

VALENCIA

Glass: Flute
Garnish: Orange zest twist
Method: POUR first three ingredients into chilled glass. **TOP** with champagne.

½	shot(s)	**Bols apricot brandy liqueur**
¼	shot(s)	**Freshly squeezed orange juice**
4	dashes	**Fee Brothers orange bitters** (optional)
Top up with		**Brut champagne**

Variant: Also served as a Martini with gin in place of champagne.
Origin: Adapted from the Valencia Cocktail No. 2 in The Savoy Cocktail Book.
Comment: Floral and fruity – makes Bucks Fizz look a tad sad.

VAMPIRO

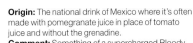

Glass: Old-fashioned
Garnish: Lime wedge
Method: SHAKE all ingredients with ice and strain into ice-filled glass.

2	shot(s)	**Don Julio 100% agave tequila**
1	shot(s)	**Pressed tomato juice**
1	shot(s)	**Freshly squeezed orange juice**
½	shot(s)	**Freshly squeezed lime juice**
½	shot(s)	**Pomegranate (grenadine) syrup**
7	drops	**Hot pepper sauce**
1	pinch	**Celery salt**
1	pinch	**Freshly ground black pepper**

Origin: The national drink of Mexico where it's often made with pomegranate juice in place of tomato juice and without the grenadine.
Comment: Something of a supercharged Bloody Mary with tequila and a hint of sweet grenadine.

'I HAVE TAKEN MORE OUT OF ALCOHOL THAN ALCOHOL HAS TAKEN OUT OF ME.'
WINSTON CHURCHILL

VAVAVOOM

Glass: Flute
Method: POUR ingredients into chilled glass and lightly stir.

½	shot(s)	**Freshly squeezed lemon juice**
½	shot(s)	**Cointreau triple sec**
¼	shot(s)	**Sugar syrup** (2 sugar to 1 water)
Top up with		**Brut champagne**

Origin: Adapted from a drink created in 2002 by Yannick Miseriaux at The Fifth Floor Bar, London, England, and named after the Renault television advertisements.
Comment: The ingredients do indeed give champagne vavavoom.

THE VESPER MARTINI

Glass: Martini
Garnish: Lemon zest twist
Method: SHAKE all ingredients with ice and fine strain into chilled glass.

3	shot(s)	**Tanqueray London dry gin**
1	shot(s)	**Ketel One vodka**
½	shot(s)	**Noilly Prat dry vermouth**

Origin: This variation on the Dry Martini is said to have been created by Gilberto Preti at Duke's Hotel, London, for the author Ian Fleming. He liked it so much that he included it in his first James Bond novel, Casino Royale, published in 1951.
In chapter seven Bond explains to a Casino bartender exactly how to make and serve the drink: "In a deep champagne goblet. Three measures of Gordon's, one of vodka, half a measure of Kina Lillet [now called Lillet Blanc]. Shake it very well until it's ice-cold, then add a large slice of lemon peel." When made, 007 compliments the bartender, but tells him it would be better made with a grain-based vodka. He also explains his Martini to Felix Leiter, the CIA man, saying, "This drink's my own invention. I'm going to patent it when I can think of a good name."

In chapter eight, Bond meets the beautiful agent Vesper Lynd. She explains why her parents named her Vesper and Bond asks if she'd mind if he called his favourite Martini after her. Like so many of Bond's love interests Vesper turns out to be a double agent and the book closes with his words, "The bitch is dead now."
Comment: Many bartenders advocate that a Martini should be stirred and not shaken, some citing the ridiculous argument that shaking will "bruise the gin". If you like your Martinis shaken (as I do) then avoid the possible look of distaste from your server and order a Vesper. This Martini is always shaken, an action that aerates the drink, and makes it colder and more dilute than simply stirring. It also gives the drink a slightly clouded appearance and can leave small shards of ice on the surface of the drink. This is easily prevented by the use of a fine strainer when pouring.

VESPER MARTINI

VICTORIAN LEMONADE

Glass: Collins
Garnish: Lemon slice
Method: Lightly **MUDDLE** (just to bruise) mint in base of shaker. Add other ingredients, **SHAKE** with ice and fine strain into ice-filled glass.

12	fresh	**Mint leaves**
1½	shot(s)	**Tanqueray London dry gin**
1	shot(s)	**Freshly squeezed lemon juice**
¾	shot(s)	**Sugar syrup** (2 sugar to 1 water)
2½	shot(s)	**Chilled mineral water**

Comment: Gin laced, mint flavoured, traditional lemonade.

VODKA COLLINS

Glass: Collins
Garnish: Orange slice & cherry on stick (sail)
Method: SHAKE first three ingredients with ice and strain into ice-filled glass. **TOP** with soda, lightly stir and serve with straws.

2	shot(s)	**Ketel One vodka**
1	shot(s)	**Freshly squeezed lemon juice**
½	shot(s)	**Sugar syrup** (2 sugar to 1 water)
Top up with		**Soda water** (club soda)

AKA: Joe Collins
Comment: A Tom Collins with vodka – a refreshing balance of sweet and sour.

VODKA RICKEY

Glass: Collins (small 8oz)
Garnish: Immerse length of lime peel in drink.
Method: SHAKE first three ingredients with ice and strain into ice-filled glass. **TOP** with soda.

2	shot(s)	**Ketel One vodka**
½	shot(s)	**Freshly squeezed lime juice**
¼	shot(s)	**Sugar syrup** (2 sugar to 1 water)
Top up with		**Soda water**

Comment: Lacks interest but balanced and hard to fault as a simple refreshing drink.

VODKA SOUR

V

Glass: Old-fashioned
Garnish: Lemon slice & cherry on stick (sail)
Method: SHAKE all ingredients with ice and strain into ice-filled glass.

2	shot(s)	**Ketel One vodka**
1	shot(s)	**Freshly squeezed lemon juice**
½	shot(s)	**Sugar syrup** (2 sugar to 1 water)
3	dashes	**Angostura aromatic bitters**
½	fresh	**Egg white**

Comment: A great vodka based drink balancing sweet and sour.

VODKATINI

Glass: Martini
Garnish: Lemon zest twistor olives
Method: SHAKE all ingredients with ice and fine strain into chilled glass.

2½	shot(s)	**Ketel One vodka**
¼	shot(s)	**Noilly Prat dry vermouth**

AKA: Kangaroo
Variant: Stir rather than shake.
Comment: Temperature is key to the enjoyment of this modern classic. Consume while icy cold.

WANTON ABANDON

Glass: Martini
Garnish: Strawberry on rim
Method: MUDDLE strawberries in base of shaker. Add next three ingredients, **SHAKE** with ice and fine strain into chilled glass. **TOP** with champagne.

5	fresh	**Strawberries**
2	shot(s)	**Ketel One vodka**
¾	shot(s)	**Freshly squeezed lemon juice**
½	shot(s)	**Sugar syrup** (2 sugar to 1 water)
Top up with		**Brut champagne**

Comment: A crowd pleaser – looks great and its fruity, balanced flavour will offend few.

WARD EIGHT

Glass: Martini
Garnish: Orange slice & cherry
Method: SHAKE all ingredients with ice and fine strain into chilled glass.

2¼	shot(s)	**Bulleit bourbon whiskey**
¾	shot(s)	**Freshly squeezed lemon juice**
¾	shot(s)	**Freshly squeezed orange juice**
¼	shot(s)	**Pomegranate (grenadine) syrup**
½	shot(s)	**Chilled mineral water** (omit if wet ice)

Origin: Ward Eight was a voting district of Boston and famed for its political corruption. This drink was first served by Tom Hussion in November 1898 at Boston's Locke-Ober Café, in honour of Martin Lomasney, who owned the café and was running for election in Ward Eight.
Comment: This is a spirited, sweet and sour

WEBSTER MARTINI

Glass: Martini
Garnish: Lime zest twist
Method: SHAKE all ingredients with ice and fine strain into chilled glass.

2	shot(s)	**Tanqueray London dry gin**
1	shot(s)	**Noilly Prat dry vermouth**
½	shot(s)	**Bols apricot brandy liqueur**
½	shot(s)	**Freshly squeezed lime juice**

Origin: Adapted from a recipe in Harry Craddock's 1930 Savoy Cocktail Book. Craddock writes of this drink, "A favourite cocktail at the bar of the S.S. Mauretania."
Comment: Balanced rather than sweet. The old-school Dry Martini meets the contemporary fruit driven Martini.

WET MARTINI

Glass: Martini
Garnish: Olive or twist
Method: STIR all ingredients with ice and strain into chilled glass.

3	shot(s)	**Tanqueray London dry gin**
1½	shot(s)	**Noilly Prat dry vermouth**

Origin: A generous measure of vermouth to two of gin, hence the name 'Wet' Martini.
Comment: Reputed to be a favourite of HRH Prince Charles.

WHAT THE HELL

Glass: Martini
Garnish: Lime wedge on rim
Method: SHAKE all ingredients with ice and fine strain into chilled glass.

2	shot(s)	**Tanqueray London dry gin**
1	shot(s)	**Bols apricot brandy liqueur**
¾	shot(s)	**Noilly Prat dry vermouth**
¼	shot(s)	**Freshly squeezed lime juice**
⅛	shot(s)	**Sugar syrup** (2 sugar to 1 water)

Comment: Gin and dry apricots.

WHISKEY COLLINS

Glass: Collins
Garnish: Orange slice & cherry on stick (sail)
Method: SHAKE first four ingredients with ice and strain into ice-filled glass. **TOP** with soda water, lightly stir and serve with straws.

2	shot(s)	**Bulleit bourbon whiskey**
¾	shot(s)	**Freshly squeezed lemon juice**
½	shot(s)	**Sugar syrup** (2 sugar to 1 water)
3	dashes	**Angostura aromatic bitters**
Top up with		**Soda water** (club soda)

Comment: A whiskey based twist on the classic Tom Collins.

WHISKEY DAISY

Glass: Martini
Garnish: Lemon zest twist
Method: SHAKE all ingredients with ice and fine strain into chilled glass.

1¾	shot(s)	**Bulleit bourbon whiskey**
¾	shot(s)	**Freshly squeezed lemon juice**
½	shot(s)	**Cointreau triple sec**
¼	shot(s)	**Pomegranate (grenadine) syrup**

Comment: This venerable, bourbon led classic has a strong citrus flavour.

WHISKEY SOUR #1 (CLASSIC FORMULA)

Glass: Old-fashioned
Garnish: Lemon slice & cherry on stick (sail)
Method: SHAKE all ingredients with ice and strain into ice-filled glass.

2	shot(s)	**Bulleit bourbon whiskey**
¾	shot(s)	**Freshly squeezed lemon juice**
1	shot(s)	**Sugar syrup** (2 sugar to 1 water)
3	dashes	**Angostura aromatic bitters**
½	fresh	**Egg white**

Origin: This recipe follows the classic sour proportions (3:4:8): three quarter part of the sour ingredient (lemon juice), one part of the sweet ingredient (sugar syrup) and two parts of the strong ingredient (whiskey).
Comment: I find the classic formulation more sweet than sour and prefer the 4:2:8 ratio below.

WHISKEY SOUR #2 (DIFFORD'S FORMULA)

Glass: Old-fashioned
Garnish: Lemon slice & cherry on stick (sail)
Method: SHAKE all ingredients with ice and strain into ice-filled glass.

2	shot(s)	**Bulleit bourbon whiskey**
1	shot(s)	**Freshly squeezed lemon juice**
½	shot(s)	**Sugar syrup** (2 sugar to 1 water)
3	dashes	**Angostura aromatic bitters**
½	fresh	**Egg white**

Origin: My 4:2:8 sour formula.
Comment: Smooth with a hint of citrus sourness and an invigorating blast of whiskey.

WHISKY COBBLER

Glass: Goblet
Garnish: Lemon slice & mint sprig
Method: SHAKE all ingredients with ice and strain into glass filled with crushed ice.

2	shot(s)	**Johnnie Walker Scotch whisky**
½	shot(s)	**Courvoisier V.S.O.P. cognac**
½	shot(s)	**Grand Marnier liqueur**

Comment: A hardcore yet sophisticated drink.

WHISKY FIZZ

Glass: Collins
Garnish: Lemon slice
Method: SHAKE first three ingredients with ice and strain into ice-filled glass. **TOP** with soda, lightly stir and serve with straws.

2	shot(s)	**Johnnie Walker Scotch whisky**
1	shot(s)	**Freshly squeezed lemon juice**
½	shot(s)	**Sugar syrup** (2 sugar to 1 water)
Top up with		**Soda** (from siphon)

Comment: The character of the whisky shines through this refreshing, balanced, sweet and sour drink.

WHITE LADY

Glass: Martini
Garnish: Lemon zest twist
Method: SHAKE all ingredients with ice and fine strain into chilled glass.

2	shot(s)	**Tanqueray London dry gin**
¾	shot(s)	**Cointreau triple sec**
¾	shot(s)	**Freshly squeezed lemon juice**
1	fresh	**Egg white**

Origin: In 1919 Harry MacElhone, while working at Ciro's Club, London, England, created his first White Lady with 2 shots triple sec, 1 shot white crème de menthe and 1 shot lemon juice. In 1923, he created the White Lady above at his own Harry's New York Bar in Paris, France.
Comment: A simple but lovely classic drink with a sour finish.

WHITE LION

Glass: Martini
Garnish: Lime wedge on rim
Method: SHAKE all ingredients with ice and fine strain into chilled glass.

2	shot(s)	**Bacardi Superior rum**
¼	shot(s)	**Cointreau triple sec**
½	shot(s)	**Freshly squeezed lime juice**
¼	shot(s)	**Pomegranate (grenadine) syrup**

Origin: Adapted from a recipe purloined from David Embury's classic book, The Fine Art of Mixing Drinks.
Comment: This fruity Daiquiri is superb when made with quality pomegranate syrup and rum.

THE ZAMBOANGA 'ZEINIE' COCKTAIL

Glass: Martini
Garnish: Lime zest twist (discarded) & cherry
Method: SHAKE all ingredients with ice and fine strain into chilled glass.

2	shot(s)	**Courvoisier V.S.O.P. cognac**
1	shot(s)	**Pressed pineapple juice**
½	shot(s)	**Freshly squeezed lime juice**
¼	shot(s)	**Maraschino syrup (from cherries)**
2	dashes	**Angostura aromatic bitters**

Origin: Adapted from a recipe in Charles H. Baker Jr's classic book, The Gentleman's Companion. He describes this as "another palate twister from the land where the Monkeys Have No Tails. This drink found its way down through the islands to Mindanao from Manila…".
Comment: Reminiscent of a tropical Sidecar.

ZOOM

Glass: Martini
Garnish: Dust with cocoa powder
Method: SHAKE all ingredients with ice and fine strain into chilled glass.

2½	shot(s)	**Courvoisier V.S.O.P. cognac**
3	spoons	**Runny honey**
½	shot(s)	**Double (heavy) cream**
½	shot(s)	**Milk**

Variant: Base on other spirits or add a dash of cacao.
Comment: Cognac is smoothed with honey and softened with milk and cream in this classic cocktail.

Z